VOL. III. The Temple at Philae. West Quay Wall. (From Colonel Lyons' *Report*, plate 31.) [*Frontispiece.*

Books on Egypt and Chaldaea

THE DECREES OF MEMPHIS AND CANOPUS

IN THREE VOLUMES

THE DECREE OF CANOPUS

VOLUME III.

BY

E. A. WALLIS BUDGE, M.A., LITT.D., D.LITT., D.LIT.

KEEPER OF THE EGYPTIAN AND ASSYRIAN ANTIQUITIES
IN THE BRITISH MUSEUM

ILLUSTRATED

ISBN: 978-1-63923-973-3

Printed: March 2023

Published and Distributed By:
Lushena Books
607 Country Club Drive, Unit E
Bensenville, IL 60106
www.lushenabks.com

ISBN: 978-1-63923-973-3

CONTENTS.

CHAPTER I.

PAGE

THE DECREE OF CANOPUS 1

CHAPTER II.

TRANSLATION OF THE HIEROGLYPHIC TEXT OF THE DECREE OF CANOPUS 17

HIEROGLYPHIC TEXT WITH INTERLINEAR TRANSLITERATION AND TRANSLATION 35

CHAPTER III.

GERMAN AND FRENCH TRANSLATIONS OF THE HIEROGLYPHIC TEXT OF THE DECREE OF CANOPUS:

I. LEPSIUS' TRANSLATION 85

II. ROESLER AND REINISCH'S TRANSLATION . . 94

III. PIERRET'S TRANSLATION 105

CHAPTER IV.

ENGLISH RENDERING OF THE DEMOTIC TEXT OF THE DECREE OF CANOPUS 114

THE

DECREE OF CANOPUS

CHAPTER I.

THE DECREE OF CANOPUS.

THE famous stele in the Egyptian National Museum at Cairo, which is now universally known as the "Stele of Canopus," was discovered on April 15th, 1866, at Ṣân, in the Eastern Delta, by a party of German savants, which included Professor R. Lepsius, Herr Weidenbach, Professor S. L. Reinisch and Professor E. R. Roesler. The place which the Arabs now call "Ṣân," or "Ṣân al-Hagar," صان الحجر, i.e. "Ṣân of the Stones," is covered with remains of several ancient Egyptian temples, and marks the site of the city of TCHARU 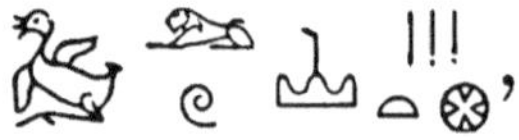, or TCHART , the old strongly fortified city on the east of Egypt, which was built by Rameses II., about B.C. 1350, and which was commonly known as "Tanis" and "Zoan." The "field of Zoan" mentioned in Psalm lxxviii. 43 is no other than the SEKHET-TCHĀNET or "FIELD OF TCHĀNET (Zoan)" , of the hieroglyphic texts. Tcharu, or Tanis, or Ṣân, was the metropolis of the XIVth Nome of Lower Egypt, called KHENT-ÀBT 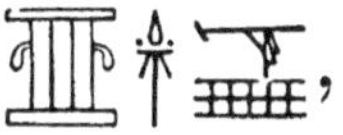, and played a prominent part in the great wars which were waged by Rameses II. against the Syrians and other Eastern peoples who rebelled against him. The ruins lie near the modern village of Ṣân, on the Mu'izz Canal, and are about one day's journey (twenty-eight or thirty miles) nearly due north of the modern Fâḳûs, a small town about half way between Abû Kebir and Es-Ṣâliḥiyeh, the last railway station on the old caravan road that runs to Al-Ḳanṭara on the Suez Canal. That the ruins near Ṣân marked the site of the ancient Tanis was known long before the above mentioned travellers visited it in 1866, and believing in the possibility of making important finds there Mariette carried out extensive excavations at this place in 1864; it was to see the results of Mariette's works that Lepsius and his friends visited Ṣân. It is somewhat difficult in reading the different accounts [1] of the finding of the Stele of Canopus to describe with justice to all concerned what part each gentleman took in the discovery. According to Reinisch and Roesler, whilst Lepsius was going to the

[1] See *Entdeckung eines bilinguen Dekretes durch Lepsius*, in *Aeg. Zeit.*, 1866, p. 29; *Das Dekret von Kanopus-Erklärung*, *ibid.*, p. 49; Reinisch and Roesler, *Die Zweisprachige Inschrift von Tanis*, p. 7 ff.

village to obtain workmen from the *shêkh* of the place, they and Weidenbach marched on to the ruins, where Reinisch saw the corner of a stone with a Greek inscription projecting from a heap of dirt. As soon as Lepsius appeared he declared that it must be the stone of which an engineer in the employ of the Suez Canal Company had told him. The removal of the earth above and about the stele was carried out at the common expense of the four *savants*, and as the work was going on Weidenbach noticed the hieroglyphic text upon it. Lepsius and Weidenbach made a paper "squeeze" of the inscriptions, and Reinisch and Roesler made copies of them. The last named gentlemen, finding that their copies were imperfect, made a second journey to Ṣân on April 20th; they stayed there for two days, and made a paper "squeeze," and copied the inscriptions, i.e., the hieroglyphic and Greek texts, from one end to the other, and took three photographs of the stele. With these materials Messrs. Reinisch and Roesler succeeded in making excellent reproductions of the hieroglyphic and Greek texts, which they printed, with a German translation of each, in their work entitled, *Die Zweisprachige Inschrift von Tanis, zum ersten Male herausgegeben und uebersetzt*, Vienna, 1866.

The Stele of Canopus is a fine limestone slab, measuring 7 ft. 4 in. in height, 2 ft. 8 in. in width, 13½ in. in thickness. The top is rounded, after the manner of most of the large memorial stelae of the

Ptolemaïc period, and on the flat surface above the inscriptions is sculptured a large pair of wings, which are intended to be those of Ḥeru-Beḥuṭet, the great god of Edfû. From the middle of the wings hang two uraei; that on the left of the beholder wears on its head the crown of the South, and that on the right the crown of the North. Within the curve of each uraeus, lying horizontally, is a fly-flapper 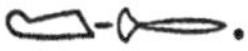. Between the uraei are the signs , *ṭā ānkh,* i.e., "Giver of life," the allusion, of course, being to the Sun-God. On the upper half of the Stele are cut thirty-seven lines of hieroglyphics, of the characteristic Ptolemaïc forms, and below these are seventy-six lines of Greek uncials; on the right hand edge of the stele are inscribed seventy-five lines of Demotic text, which the discoverers either did not notice, or regarded as mere scratches! This is a remarkable fact, for the value of the monument from an Egyptological point of view was recognized as soon as it was found, and each of its discoverers knew that they had lighted upon a stele of the same class as that to which the Rosetta Stone belonged. On the other hand, it is possible that as none of the *savants* who found the Stele had any knowledge of the Demotic character, they determined to issue their editions of the texts with translations, as soon as possible, and to leave the Demotic text for future study.

The inscription on the Stele of Canopus is *bilingual,* that is to say, is written in two languages, viz., in

Egyptian and in Greek; the Egyptian portion is written in the HIEROGLYPHIC character and in the DEMOTIC character, and the GREEK portion is in uncials. The value of both the Egyptian and Greek inscriptions is very great, for both are complete, and both are, comparatively speaking, easily to be understood. It is, however, somewhat difficult to account for the order in which the three texts, Hieroglyphic, Greek, and Demotic stand on the Stele of Canopus. The HIEROGLYPHIC text would naturally come first, because it had been employed for thousands of years in making copies of all the state and ceremonial documents which were intended to be seen by the public, and the Egyptians were always accustomed to see monuments of the kind inscribed in hieroglyphics. For all practical purposes, however, the hieroglyphic inscription was quite useless, for the majority of the people could not read it. After the hieroglyphic comes the GREEK text, instead of the Demotic, as in the case of the Rosetta Stone, and, in my opinion, it was intended to occupy the place of honour on the Stele, because Greek was the language in which the decree inscribed on it was originally written. Using exactly the same arguments which were used in the case of the Rosetta Stone, it is clear that when the Stele was mounted upon a plinth of suitable height and thickness, the beginning of the Greek text would be on the level of the eye of the beholder, and this would be the result naturally aimed at by those who planned the setting up of the Stele, especially if they were

Greeks, or if they wished to gain favour in the sight of the reigning Ptolemy. The Demotic inscription on the Stele is on the edge nearest the ends of the lines of the Greek text, with which it seems to have been intended to correspond, line for line; to me its position makes it certain that it is a translation from the Greek, and that it was added more or less as the result of an afterthought. That it was hurriedly done is clear, for the last sentence of the Decree of the priests at Canopus, which ordered that a stele, inscribed with a copy of the Decree in Hieroglyphics, Demotic, and Greek, was to be set up in each temple of the first, second, and third class, throughout Egypt, is omitted in the Demotic text. Apart from this consideration a study of the hieroglyphic text leads one irresistibly to the conclusion that it is a translation,[1] and not a document which was originally drawn up in the ancient language of the country, and when a Demotologist of M. Révillout's authority declares that the Demotic text is also a translation from the Greek, there is little more to be said on the subject.

The Decree inscribed on the Stele of Canopus was passed at a general Council of Egyptian priests, who assembled at Canopus on the seventh day of the

[1] The original language in which the Decree was drawn up was Greek, and the Hieroglyphic and Demotic versions are paraphrastic translations. Birch, *Records of the Past*, viii. p. 82. Reinisch and Roesler (op. cit., p. 9), on the other hand, regarded the Greek as a "compressed" translation of the minute and copious Egyptian text.

The temple of Edfû, founded by Ptolemy III. View from the pylon. (From a photograph by A. Beato of Luxor.)

Macedonian month Apellaios, which corresponded to the seventeenth day of the Egyptian month Tybi, in the ninth year of the reign of Ptolemy III, i.e., B.C. 238. The decree, then, was passed at least forty years before the decree of the priests of Memphis which is inscribed on the Rosetta Stone. When the Decree of Canopus was promulgated Apollonides, the son of Moschion, was the priest of Alexander, and of the Brother-gods, and of the Good-doing gods; and Menekrateia, the daughter of Philammon, was the bearer of the basket (Canephoros) before Queen Arsinoë. The decree sets forth the good deeds of Ptolemy III., and enumerates the benefits which he and his wife Berenice had conferred upon Egypt thus:—

1 Rich gifts and endowments to the temples.
2 Endowments for Apis and Mnevis and other sacred animals in Egypt.
3 War against Persia, made for the purpose of bringing back the statues of the gods which had been carried off to that country, and the restoration of the said statues to the temples to which they belonged.
4 The maintenance of peace in Egypt and her dependencies.
5 Remission of taxes during a period of famine caused by a low Nile.
6 The purchase of corn out of the private property of the crown, at high prices, from Syria, Phoenicia, and Cyprus, and the free distribution of the same,

whereby the lives of large numbers of the inhabitants of Egypt were saved.

As marks of their great appreciation of these acts of goodness the priests decreed that the following things should be done:—

1 Additional honours to be paid to Ptolemy III. and his wife Berenice, and to their parents, and to their grand-parents, i.e., all their ancestors in Egypt, in the temples of Egypt.

2 A new order of priests to be established, with the title of "Priests of the Good-doing Gods."

3 The title of this order of priests to be inserted in all the official documents of the temples.

4 Each priest of the order to have the title of his order engraved on the ring which he wore on his hand.

5 All the priests who had been appointed by the king between the first and ninth years of his reign, and all their children, were to be enrolled in the new order of priests of the Good-doing Gods.

6 Five additional Councillor Priests to be appointed,

7 The new order of priests shall share equally with the other four orders.

8 A governor of the new order shall be appointed.

9 In addition to the festivals whch are celebrated on the 5th, 9th, and 25th days of each month, and the yearly festivals, another festival shall be celebrated on the day of the rising of the star Sothis (Sirius, or the Dog-Star), which, in the 9th year of

the king's reign, shall be celebrated on the 1st day of Payni, in which month the festival of the New Moon, and the festivals of the goddess Bast, and of the harvest, and of the Inundation are celebrated.

10 This festival shall always be celebrated on the first day of Payni, for if it were allowed to be celebrated according to the day of the rising of the Dog-Star, it would advance one day in every four years, and eventually it would happen that a festival which ought to be kept in the summer would be held in winter. This festival shall last for five days, and the people shall wear crowns and make offerings in the temples.

11 That the festivals of the temples may correspond to the seasons of the year, national summer festivals shall be observed in the summer, and winter festivals in the winter. The year shall no longer consist of 360 days and five epagomenal days only, but every fourth year one day shall be added, after the five epagomenal days and before the New Year, and this day shall be kept as a festival in honour of the Good-doing Gods.

12 Everlasting honours to be paid in the temples to Queen Berenice, the daughter of the Good-doing Gods, who died suddenly in the month of Tybi.

13 A festival of four days to be kept in the month of Tybi, beginning on the 17th day, in her honour.

14 A gold statue, inlaid with precious stones, to be set up in the sanctuary of each temple of the first and second class.

15 The statue to be carried in the arms of a priest in all processions.

16 A specially shaped crown, made up of a sceptre, uraeus, and two ears of corn, to be made for the statue.

17 The daughters of the priests to prepare another statue of Berenice, "Queen of Virgins," and offer sacrifices to it during the month of Choiakh.

18 Other virgins, who are not daughters of priests, may do the same.

19 Sacred virgins, wearing the crowns of their gods, shall sing hymns to her.

20 At harvest time ears of corn shall be laid before the image.

21 Men and women shall sing to the statues day by day songs composed by the priests.

22 The daughters of the priests shall be maintained out of the temple revenues.

23 The wives of the priests shall be provided with a special kind of bread called the "Bread of Berenice."

24 A copy of this Decree, cut in stone or bronze, in hieroglyphics, in the writing of the books, and in Greek, to be set up in the most prominent place in each temple of the first, second, and third class throughout Egypt, so that all men may know how

great is the honour which the priests and their children show to the Good-doing Gods.

The above summary of the contents of the Stele of Canopus exhibits the extent of the power which the priests were beginning to obtain over the king, and the only matter which may be truly said to be of general interest mentioned in the inscriptions, is that which refers to the reform of the calendar which Ptolemy, or his priests, tried to introduce into Egypt. Inasmuch as the year is nearly a quarter of a day longer than the 360 days of the vague Egyptian year, and the five epagomenal days which were added at the end of it, Ptolemy ordered that one day, which was to be kept as a feast, was to be added to the 365 days of which the year then consisted. How long the reform was carried out at Canopus cannot be said, but it certainly does not appear to have been adopted generally throughout Egypt.

The following are the most important editions of the texts on the Stele of Canopus, and the translations and papers. The hieroglyphic and Greek texts were published for the first time by Professors Reinisch and Roesler (*Die Zweisprachige Inschrift von Tanis*, Vienna, 8vo.) in 1866. In the same year Dr. Lepsius published facsimiles of the hieroglyphic and Greek texts, the former with a transliteration and a German translation, and the latter with a transcript into ordinary Greek letters, and a German translation (*Das bilingue Dekret von Kanopus*, Berlin, folio). On the inscriptions generally may be noted Dr. Birch, *On the trilingual inscription of San*, and his English translation of the hieroglyphic text printed in *Records of the Past*, vol. viii., p. 83 ff. On the Demotic version must be specially noted, Révillout, *Chrestomathie Démotique*, p. lxxxvi. ff. and pp. 125-176, Paris, 1880 (Greek and Demotic texts, with French translations); Révillout, *ibid.*, pp. 435-472; Révillout, *Étude hist. et philol. sur les décrets de Rosette et de Canope* (*Revue Archéol.*, Nov., 1877); Révillout, *Les deux versions démotiques du décret de Canope* (in the *Album* of Leemans); P. Pierret, *Le Décret de Canope*, with a synoptical translation of the three texts, Paris, 1881; Pierret, *Glossaire Égyptien-grec du Décret de Canope*, Paris, 1873 (*Études Égyptol.*, p. 113 ff.); Brugsch, *Thesaurus*, Abth. vi, p. xiv., Leipzig, 1891 (German translation of the Demotic text, and the hieroglyphic and Demotic texts published interlinearly, p. 1554 ff.); W. N. Groff, *Le Décret de Canope* (*Rev. Égyptologique*, tom. vi., 1891, p. 13 ff.); Krall, *Demotische Lesestücke*, pt. 2, Vienna, 1903. For editions of the Greek text and English translations see Miller, *Découverte d'un nouvel exemplaire du décret de Canope* (*Journal des Savants*, April, 1883, pp. 294-229); Mahaffy, *Empire of the Ptolemies*, p. 229 ff., London, 1895; *The Ptolemaic Dynasty*, p. 112 ff., London, 1899; Strack, *Die Dynastie der Ptolemäer*, Berlin, 1897, p. 227 ff. On the chronology of the Stele of Canopus see Mahler, *Transactions of the Ninth Oriental Congress*, ii. 319-330, London, 1893.

Pylon of the temple of Edfû. (From a photograph by A. Beato of Luxor.)

CHAPTER II.

THE DECREE OF CANOPUS.

TRANSLATION OF THE HIEROGLYPHIC TEXT.

1 On the seventh day of the month APELLAIOS, which [correspondeth] to the seventeenth day of the first month of the season PERT, of the inhabitants of the Land of the Inundation, [in] the ninth year of the reign of [His] Majesty, the King of the South and North (Ptolemy, the everliving, the beloved of Ptaḥ), the son of (Ptolemy) and (Arsinoë), the two Brother-Gods; [when] APOLLONIDES, the son of MOSCHION, was libationer of (Alexander), whose word is law, and of the two Brother-Gods, and of the two Good-doing Gods;

2 and when MENEKRATEIA, the daughter of PHILAMMON, was the bearer of the basket before (Arsinoë) PHILADELPHOS: [on] this day [was passed the following] Decree. The chiefs of the temples, and the servants of the gods, and those

who are over the secret things of the gods, and the priests [who]
3 array the gods in their ornamental apparel, and the scribes of the divine books, and the learned men, and the divine fathers, and the libationers, according to their various classes and grades, who were wont to come from both groups of sanctuaries of the South and the North on the fifth day of the month DIOS, whereon is celebrated the new year (i.e., the birthday) of His Majesty, and also on the twenty-fifth day of the same month, whereon His Majesty received his
4 exalted rank from his father, gathered themselves together in the temple of the two Good-doing Gods which is in CANOPUS, and they spake thus:—
Inasmuch as (Ptolemy, the everliving, the beloved of Ptaḥ), the King of the South and North, the son of (Ptolemy) and (Arsinoë), the two Brother Gods, and the Queen (Berenice), his sister and wife, the two Good-doing Gods, are performing many great and
5 benevolent deeds for the temples of the Land of the Inundation, and are on every occasion sanctifying the words of the renown of the gods exceedingly; and behold, at all seasons they provide for the temporal wants of ḤĀPI, and MERUR (i.e., APIS and MNEVIS), and for all the

other animals who live in holy houses and are venerated in EGYPT, and they supply the things [they need] in large quantities, and provisions in overflowing abundance

6 in order to ensure their performance of the proper service; and in the matter of the divine images which the vile men of PERSIA carried off to [a country] outside EGYPT, His Majesty set out on an expedition to the lands of Asia, and he recaptured the images and brought them back to the Land of the Inundation and set them upon their thrones in the temples wherein they had stood originally; and he hath made EGYPT safe and secure

7 exceedingly by fighting outside it, in the valley, and on the plain, and in many foreign desert and mountain lands, and [he hath vanquished] the debased chiefs who were their overlords; and they (i.e., the King and Queen) have made safe and secure all living people of the Land of the Inundation, and the inhabitants of all the lands which are subject unto their Majesties; and behold, when during their reign there came a year with a very low Nile,

8 and the hearts of all men and women in EGYPT were smitten with grief, because there came into their minds the memory of the misery and want which had come upon the inhabitants of the Land of the Inundation during their own time when a low Nile came in the reign of former kings, His

Majesty himself and his sister were exceedingly careful in their minds

9 for every one of those who dwelt in the houses of the gods, and for the [ordinary] inhabitants of Egypt, and they took great and exceeding forethought on their behalf, and turned their backs upon much revenue [due to them] in their desire to keep men and women alive, and they caused corn to be brought to EGYPT from EASTERN SYRIA, and from the Land of KEFTET (PHOENICIA), and from the ISLAND OF INTHÀNAI[1] (CYPRUS) which is in the middle

10 of the GREAT GREEN SEA (i.e., the Mediterranean), and from vast foreign lands, and they expended much gold in purchasing the grain at a high price, being anxious only to keep safe the men and women who were living in the DIVINE LAND: [hereby] making to know their beneficence, which is everlasting, and their virtues (*or*, good qualities), [which are] many, both those who live at the present time, and those who shall come after them, and in return for these [deeds] the gods have given stability to their exalted dignity of the sovereignty of the lands of the South and North,

1 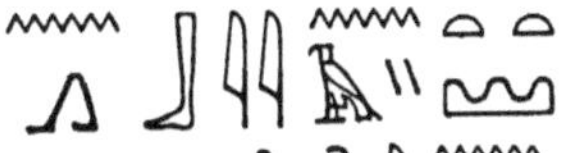 is an impossible form; and is a mistake for , or some such form; see H. R. Hall, *Keftiu and the Peoples of the Sea* (Annual of the British School of Athens, No. viii., p. 167).

11 and they shall reward them with good things of each and every kind for ever and ever. Strength and health!

And the priests of the Land of the Inundation have set it in their hearts to multiply in many respects the honour [which is paid to] the King of the South and North, (Ptolemy, the everliving, the beloved of Ptaḥ), and to Queen (Berenice), the two Good-doing Gods, in the temples, and that which is paid to the two Brother-Gods who begot them, and

12 that which is paid to the two Saviour-Gods who begot them; and the priests who are in all the temples of Egypt of each and every kind shall be magnified, and, in addition to the honourable priestly titles which they now bear, they shall be called "Priests of the two Good-doing Gods"; and their title of priests of the two Good-doing Gods shall be inscribed upon all documents, and cut upon the rings which they wear upon their hands; and there shall be formed another

13 tribe among the priests who are now living in each and every temple, in addition to the four tribes of priests which exist at the present day, and it shall be called the "Fifth tribe of the two Good-doing Gods," since there happened the most auspicious event, with strength and health, that

the King of the South and North, (Ptolemy, the everliving, the beloved of Ptaḥ), the son of the two Brother-Gods, was born on the fifth day of the month Dios, and this day was, in consequence, the beginning

14 of great prosperity and happiness of all living men and women; and the priests whom the King made to enter into the temples in the first year of His Majesty's reign, and also those who have entered [them] until the fourth month of the season Shemu (i.e., Mesore), and also their children, shall be in this tribe for ever; and the priests who existed before these up to the first year [of His Majesty's reign] shall remain in the tribes

15 wherein they were formerly, and their children likewise, from this day forward and for ever, shall be written down in the tribes wherein are their fathers; and instead of the twenty Priests Councillors who are elected at a certain period each year from the four tribes, five from each tribe, the Priests Councillors shall be twenty-five [in number],

16 and the five additional priests shall be brought from the fifth tribe of the two Good-doing Gods, and the priests of the fifth tribe of the two Good-doing Gods shall be permitted to have a share in all the appointed ceremonies, and they shall go into the temple to assist in the services of

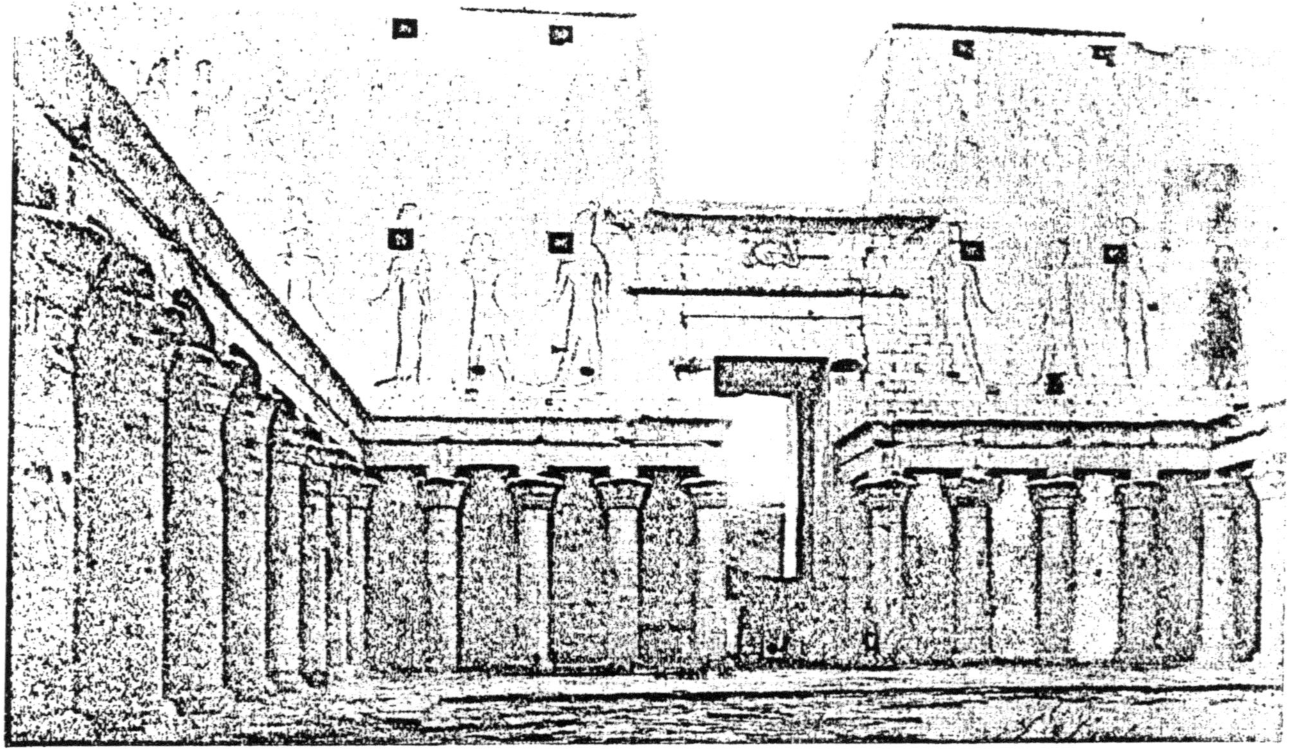

The Entrance and Colonnade of the Temple of Edfû, founded by Ptolemy III. (From a photograph by A. Beato of Luxor).

libations and in all the other duties which they [i.e., the priests of the four tribes] have to perform in them; and a prophet in the fifth tribe shall be Chief of the tribe (Phylarch) as in the other four tribes. And moreover, because
17 a festival is celebrated in honour of the Good-doing Gods in all the temples in the course of every month, on the fifth day, and on the ninth day, and on the twenty-fifth day, according to the decree which hath been set down in writing in times past, and because the festival which is made in honour of the great gods is observed universally as a very great festival throughout the Land of the Inundation at the proper season of the year, in like manner there shall be celebrated a great festival at the proper season of the year in honour of the King of the South and North, (Ptolemy, the ever-living, the beloved of Ptaḥ)
18 and (Queen Berenice), the two Good-doing Gods, in the sanctuaries of the South and North, and throughout all EGYPT, on the day when the divine star SOTHIS maketh its [first] appearance, which is called in the Books of the House of Life "the opening of the year" (i.e., New Year), which correspondeth to the first day of the second month of the season SHEMU (PAYNI) in the ninth year, on which shall be celebrated the festival of the

New Year, and the festival of BAST, and the great festival of BAST in this month, because it is the season of

19 the ingathering of fruits of all kinds, and the increase of the NILE. Now behold, when it happeneth that the festival of the divine star SOTHIS changeth to another day every four years, the day on which the festival of Ptolemy shall be celebrated shall not change also because of it, but the festival shall be celebrated on the first day of the second month of the season SHEMU (PAYNI) even as it was celebrated on that day in the ninth year;

20 and this festival shall be kept for five days, and [the people] shall wear garlands of flowers upon their heads and ornaments, and they shall lay offerings upon the altars, and they shall make drink offerings, and shall perform all things whatsoever it is right and proper to do. And thus it shall happen that they shall do whatsoever it is their duty to do, and their seasons of the year shall at all times be in accordance with ordinances (*or*, plans) whereon the heavens are founded to this very day; and it shall

21 never once happen that the general festivals which are celebrated throughout EGYPT in the season PERT (i.e., the Winter), shall be observed in the season SHEMU (i.e., the Summer) because of the change of the festival of the divine star SOTHIS one day every four years; for, behold, the

Philae : The Colonnades from the South. (From Col. Lyons' *Report*, plate 45.)

other festivals which at the present time it is customary to celebrate in the season ṢHEMU (i.e., the Summer) would be observed in the season PERT (i.e., the Winter) in the times to come, even as it hath already happened in the times of
22 our ancestors, and it would happen again if the year consisted [only] of 360 days and the five days which it is customary to add to them at the end [of them]. And moreover, from this day onward, one day, a festival of the Good-doing Gods, shall be added every four years, in addition to the five additional days, at the beginning of the New Year, so that it may be known unto all men that the arrangement of the seasons of the year was somewhat defective (*or*, short a little),
23 and that the year [itself], and the rules which exist as to the laws of the science of the ways of heaven have now been set right, and [what was lacking] hath been supplied by the two Good-doing Gods. And in respect of the daughter who was born to the King of the South and North, (Ptolemy, everliving, of Ptaḥ beloved) and the lady of the two lands (Berenice), the two Good-doing Gods, whose name was called (Berenice) and who was straightway appointed Queen, since
24 it hath happened that this goddess, being a virgin, entered heaven suddenly whilst the priests who

other festivals which at the present time it is customary to celebrate in the season ṢHEMU (i.e., the Summer) would be observed in the season PERT (i.e., the Winter) in the times to come, even as it hath already happened in the times of
22 our ancestors, and it would happen again if the year consisted [only] of 360 days and the five days which it is customary to add to them at the end [of them]. And moreover, from this day onward, one day, a festival of the Good-doing Gods, shall be added every four years, in addition to the five additional days, at the beginning of the New Year, so that it may be known unto all men that the arrangement of the seasons of the year was somewhat defective (*or,* short a little),
23 and that the year [itself], and the rules which exist as to the laws of the science of the ways of heaven have now been set right, and [what was lacking] hath been supplied by the two Good-doing Gods. And in respect of the daughter who was born to the King of the South and North, (Ptolemy, everliving, of Ptaḥ beloved) and the lady of the two lands (Berenice), the two Good-doing Gods, whose name was called (Berenice) and who was straightway appointed Queen, since
24 it hath happened that this goddess, being a virgin, entered heaven suddenly whilst the priests who

came from Egypt every year to the King of the South and North were in the house with His Majesty, they made a great lamentation immediately because of that which had happened. And they made supplication before the King and Queen, and put it in their hearts to allow

25 this goddess to rest with the god Osiris in the temple of Canopus, because it is among the temples of the first rank, and because it is held in very great honour, both by the King and by all the men and women who live in the Land of the Inundation—behold, now the god Osiris maketh his entry into this temple in the Sektet Boat at the stated time each year from the temple of

26 Aḳerbemret (i.e., Herakleion), on the twenty-ninth day of the fourth month of the season Shat (i.e., Choiakh), when all those who are in the temples of the first class make offerings by fire upon the altars of the temples of the first rank on the right and left hand sides of the courtyard of this temple—and after these things they performed everything which it was right and proper to do in respect of making her a deity, and in concluding the mourning [which was made] for her, and they did it with the

27 same readiness of heart and warmth which it is customary to show to Apis and Mnevis. And moreover, they passed a resolution to make the word[s] of everlasting renown of Queen

(Berenice), the daughter of the two Good-doing Gods, to be [known] in all the temples of the Land of the Inundation. And since it came to pass that she entered among the gods in the first month of the season PER (i.e., TYBI), which is the month
28 wherein the daughter of Rā entered into heaven, and he called her name the "Eye of Rā," and the "Meḥen Crown on his brow," because he loved her, and [since] festivals of procession in the great temples of the first class in this month wherein her majesty was made a goddess originally are celebrated in her [honour], there shall likewise be celebrated a festival and a procession for Queen (Berenice),
29 daughter of the two Good-doing Gods, in each and all the temples of the South and North, in the first month of the season PER (i.e., TYBI), and this festival and procession shall begin on the seventeenth day of the month, wherein her procession and the purification (*or*, conclusion) of the mourning for her were made originally, and shall last for four days; and moreover, a divine image of this goddess, made of gold and inlaid with precious stones of all kinds shall be set up in each and every temple of the first and second class, and the statue shall be placed
30 upon its pedestal in the temple, and a servant of the god (prophet), or one of the libationers who

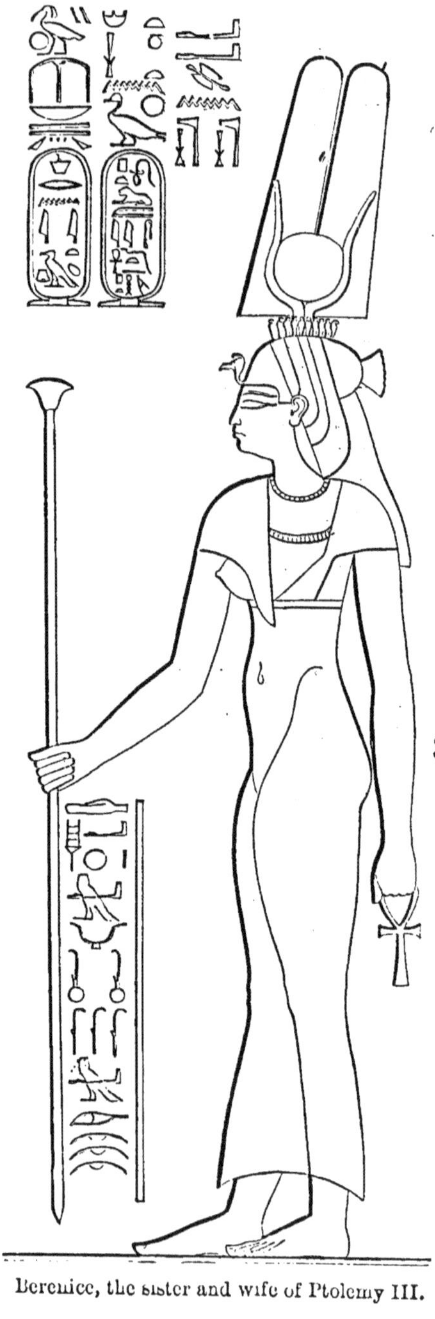

Berenice, the sister and wife of Ptolemy III.

hath been chosen to make the great libation and to array the gods in their festal apparel, shall carry it in his arms on the day of the great, general festival, on each and every one of the festivals of the god, so that all people may see that it is adored according to its sanctity, and the statue shall be called "Berenice
31 mistress of virgins."
And behold, the crown which shall be on the head of the divine image shall not be [like unto those] which are on the images of her mother, the goddess Berenice; for there shall be made [for it] two

ears of corn, between which shall be an uraeus, and behind this uraeus there shall be placed, in an upright position, a sceptre of papyrus plants, similar to that which is in the hands of the goddesses, and the tail of the uraeus shall be twined round

32 this sceptre, so that the construction (*or*, fashion) of this crown shall proclaim the name of (Berenice) according to its symbols in the writing (*or*, letters) of the House of Life (i.e., the hieroglyphics). And moreover, at the festival [which taketh place] in the days of Ḳaaubekh, in the fourth month of the season SHAT (i.e., KHOIAK), preceding the procession of Osiris, the virgin daughters and wives of the priests shall give (i.e., provide) another statue of (Berenice), the "mistress of virgins," and burnt offerings shall be made to it,

33 and there shall be performed for it every other thing which it is right and proper to do on the days of this festival, and the other virgins shall be at liberty to perform for this goddess in this respect whatsoever is right (*or*, customary) according to their desire. And behold, hymns of praise shall be sung to this goddess by the *qemāt* priestesses [and by those who are] chosen to minister to the gods and [to place] the crowns of the gods [on their heads], and who are therefore

their priestesses; and behold, when there are firstfruits of the crops ears of corn shall be carried by the *qemāt* priestesses into the sanctuary,

34 and presented to the divine image of this goddess, and the companies of the singing women [of the temple], and men and women [in general] shall sing to her image at the festivals, and [during] the processions of the gods, the hymns of praise which shall be composed by the learned men of the House of Life, and shall be given to the choirs of singing men, and copies [of the said hymns] shall be inscribed in the books of the House of Life; and when they (i.e., the priests) are made to enter into the temple by the King when the divine offerings of the priests are made in the temples,

35 provision (*or*, food) shall be given unto the female children of the priests, from the holy offerings which are made to the gods from the day whereon they are born, and the amount of the same shall be determined by the priests who are the Councillors in the temples, each and all of them, in proportion to the [amount of] the holy offerings. And the bread which shall be given

36 to the wives of the priests shall be distinguished by being made in the form of the *qefen* loaf, and shall be called by name the "Bread of (Berenice)." And the Councillors in the

temples, and the governors of the temples, and the temple-scribes shall set this DECREE in writing, and it shall be cut upon a stele

37 of stone or bronze in the writing of the House of Life, and in the writing of the books, and in the writing of the Greeks, and it shall be set up in the hall of the congregation in the temples of the first, and second, and third orders, to inform every person of the honour which hath been done by the priests of the temples of EGYPT to the two Good-doing Gods, and to their children, according to what is right and proper to do to them.

HIEROGLYPHIC TEXT WITH INTERLINEAR TRANSLITERATION AND TRANSLATION.

(1) 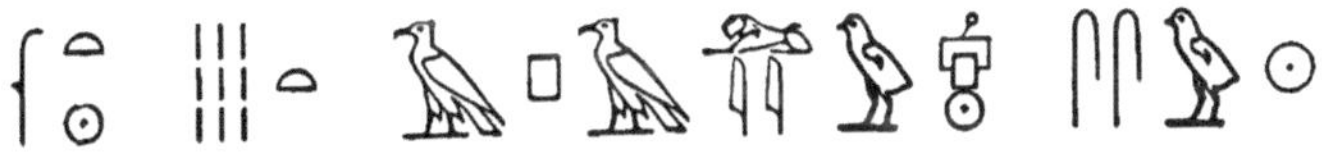

Renpit *pest* *Apaliusa* *sesu*

Year nine, [month of] Apellaios, day

sekhef *ṭep per* *sesu* *met-sekhef* *en*

seven, first [month] of PERT, day seventeen of

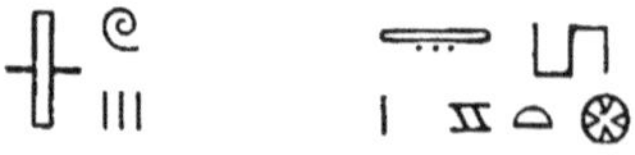

ȧmmu | *Ta-mert* | *kher* | *ḥen*

those who are in | Ta-mert, | under | the Majesty of

suten bȧt | *Ptulmis ānkh tchetta Ptaḥ meri*

the King of the South and North | Ptolemy, ever-living, of Ptaḥ beloved,

sa | *en* | *Ptulmis* | *Ȧrsenat*

son | of | Ptolemy [and] | Arsinoë,

neterui senui | *āb* | *en* | *Ȧrḳsanṭres*

the two brother gods, | priest | of | Alexander,

maāt-kheru | *ḥā* | *neterui senui* | *ḥā*

whose word is Law, | and [of] | the two brother gods, | and [of]

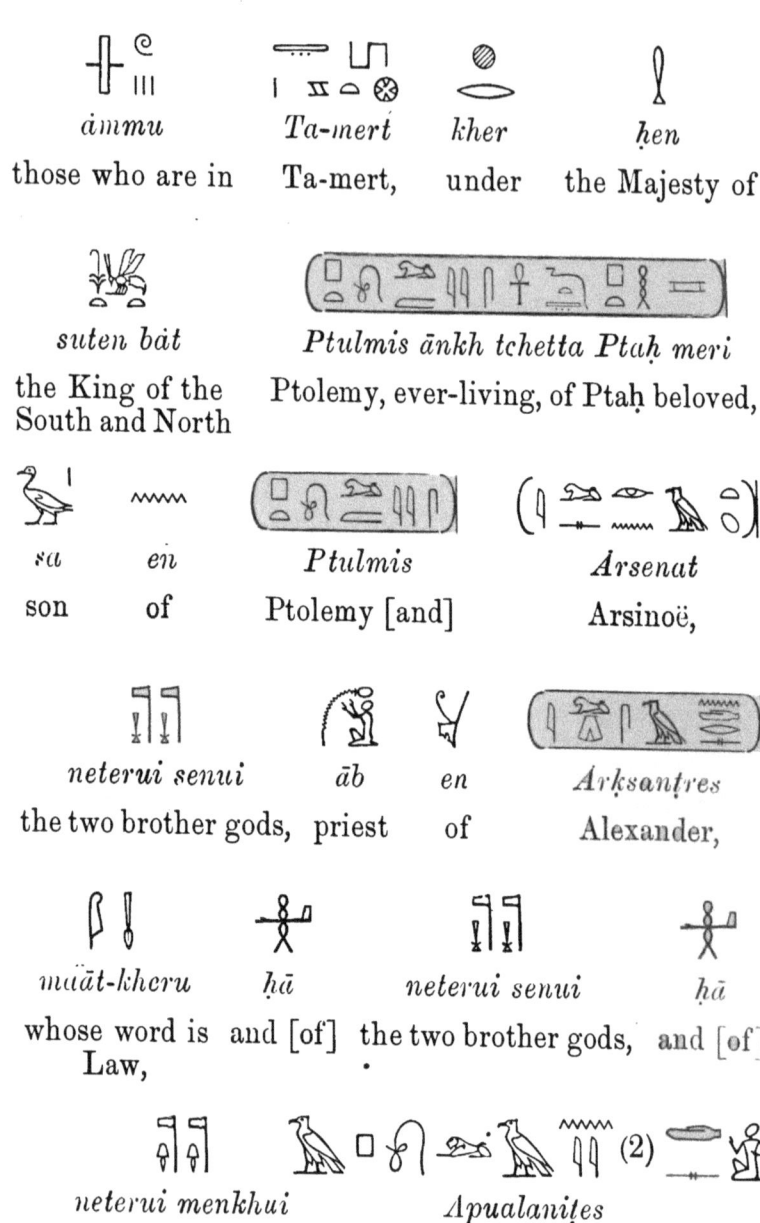

neterui menkhui | *Apualaniṭes*

the two good-doing gods | [being] Apollonides,

sa	*en*	*Māuskian*	*ȧu*
son	of	Moschion;	was

Māanaqeraṭa	*sat*
Menekrateia,	the daughter of

Pailamna	*fa*	*ṭenȧ*
Philammon,	bearer of	the basket

en embaḥ	*Ȧrsenat*	*sen mer*	*hru*
before	Arsinoë	Philadelphus,	[on] day

pen	*sekhau*	*ȧu*	*meru*	*maāu*
this.	DECREE.	Were	the chiefs of	temples,

neteru ḥenu	*heru seshetа neter*	*ābu*
servants of the gods,	those over the secrets of the gods,	the libationers,

semār	*neteru*	*em*	*satet-sen*
[who] array	the gods	in	their ornaments,

ānu	*neteru shāt*	*rekhu-khet*
the scribes of	the divine books,	the men who know things,

neteru tefu	*ābu*	*mȧ*	*qeṭ-sen*
the divine fathers,	libationers,	according to	their grades

i	*em*	*ȧterti*	*taui*
[who] came	from	the two sanctuaries	of the South and North

ȧu	*Ṭiauasa*	*hru*	*ṭua*	*ȧritu*
on	Dios	day	five	is celebrated

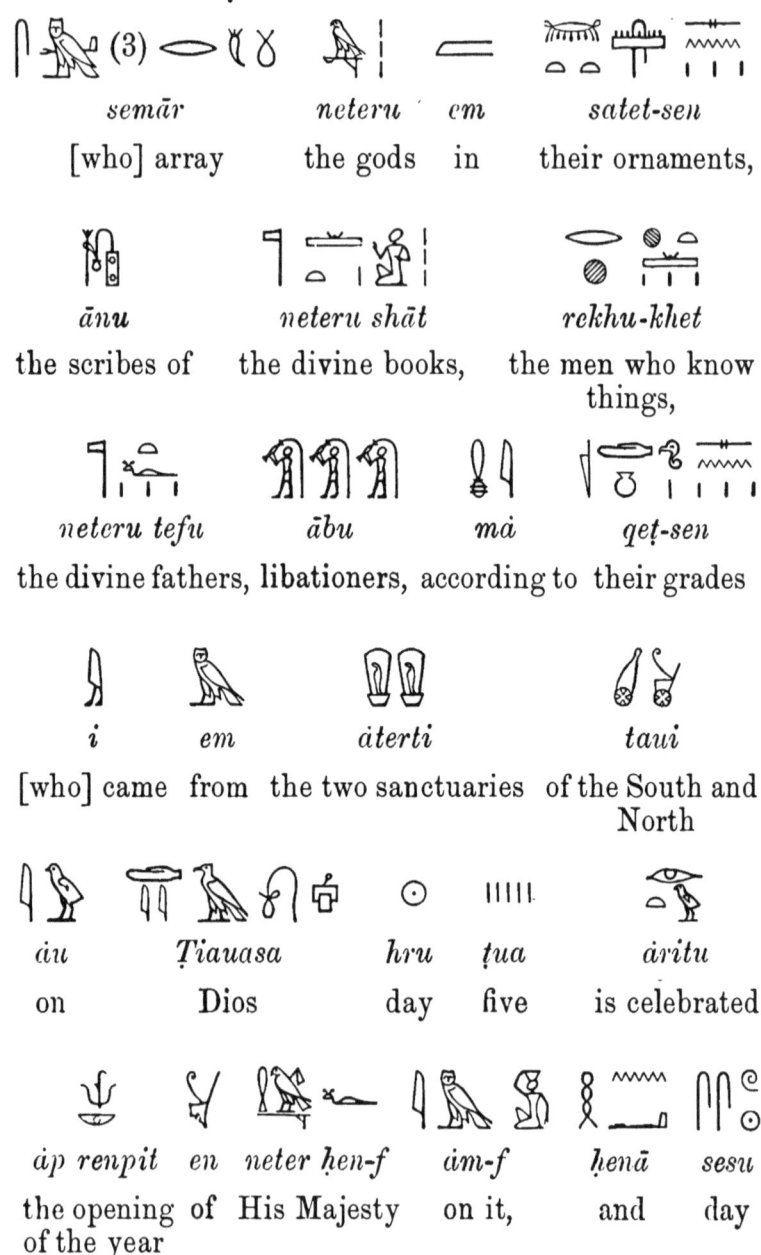

ȧp renpit	*en*	*neter ḥen-f*	*ȧm-f*	*ḥenā*	*sesu*
the opening of the year	of	His Majesty	on it,	and	day

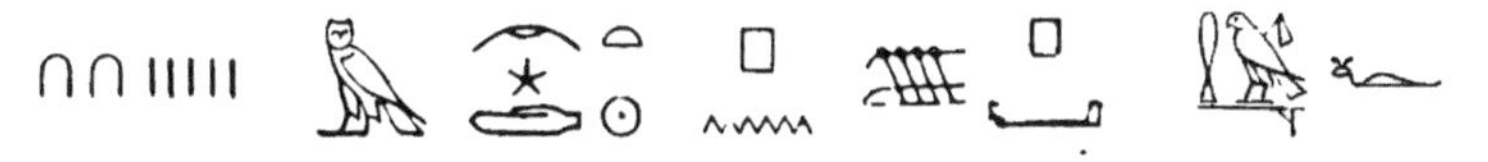

tchaut-ṭua em ȧbeṭet pen shep ḥen - f

twenty-five in month this received His Majesty

ȧaut - f urt mā tef - f ȧm-f

his rank great from his father on it,

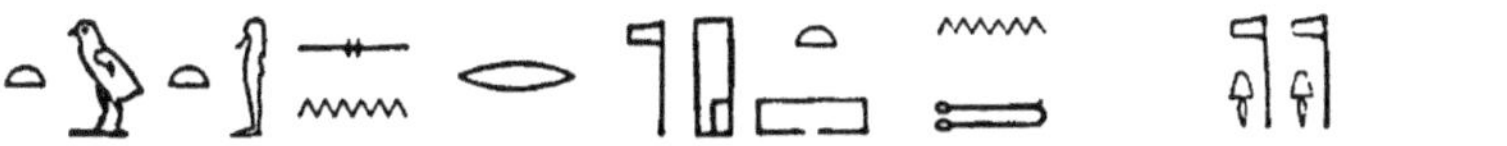

tut-sen er neter ḥet enth neterui menkhui

they assembled in the temple of the two good-doing gods

enti em Pekuathet ȧr tchet

which [is] in Canopus making speech [thus]:

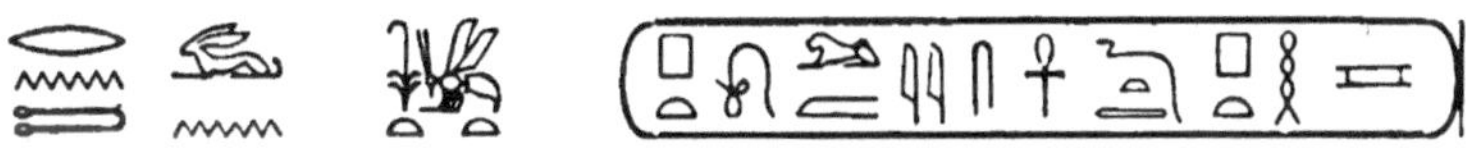

er-enth un suten bȧt Ptulmis ānkh tchetta Ptaḥ meri

Since are the king of the South and North, Ptolemy, ever-living, of Ptaḥ beloved,

sa en Ptulmis ḥā Ȧrsenat

the son of Ptolemy and Arsinoë,

neterui senui *ḥenā* *ḥeqt* *Berenikat*

the two brother gods, and the queen Berenice,

sent ḥemt f *neterui menkhui* *ḥer ári* *menkhiu*

his sister-wife, the two good-doing gods, doing acts of benevolence

(5) 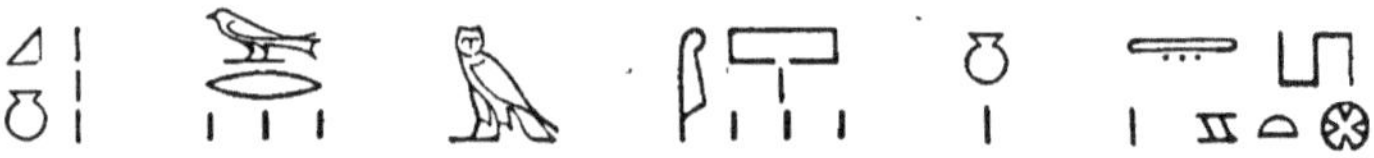

qennu *uru* *em* *maāu* *nu* *Ta-mert*

many great in the temples of Egypt,

áu . . . . *nebt* *ḥer tcheser* *meṭu* *peḥpeḥ*

[and] at time every exalting the words of the renown

en *neteru* *er* *āa* *ur* *un-sen* *ásk*

of the gods exceedingly, [and] they are, behold,

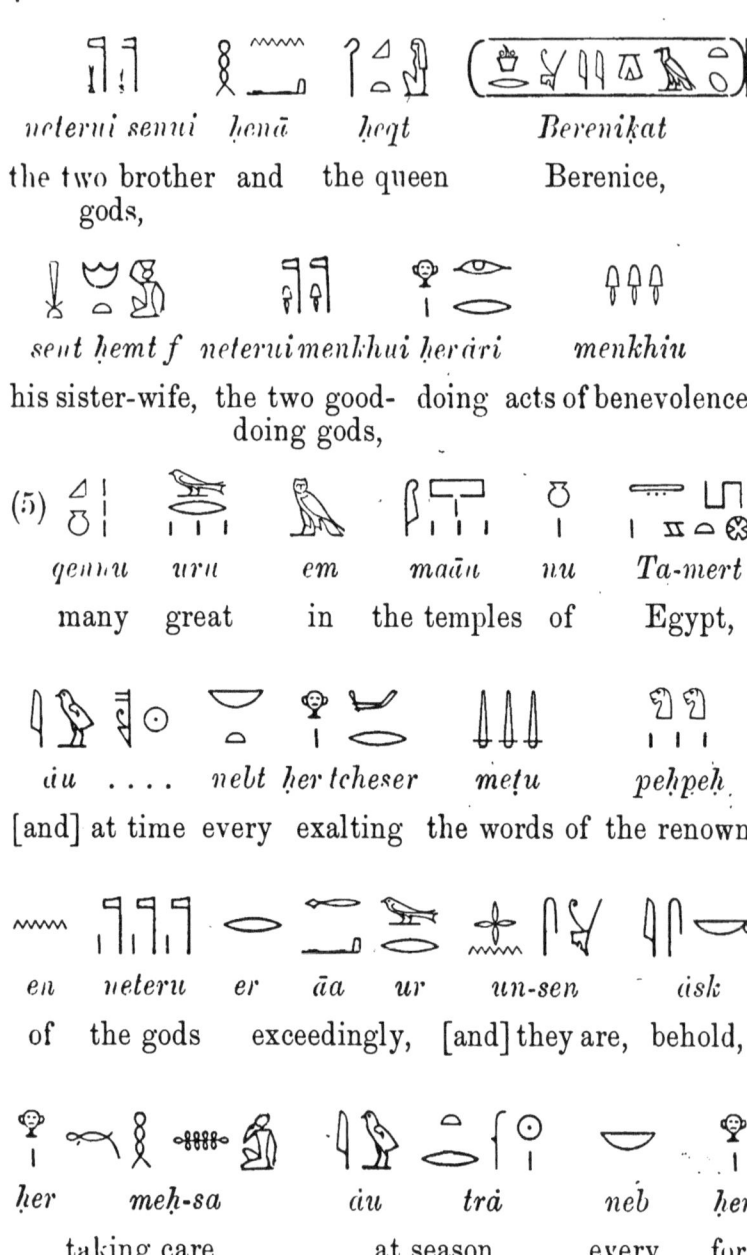

ḥer *meḥ-sa* *áu* *trá* *neb* *ḥer*

taking care at season every for

khet Ḥāp Mer-ur ḥā āutu

the matters of Ḥāpi [and] Mnevis and the animals

neter ḥet neb khu em Baqet

in the divine houses all honoured in Egypt,

ṭā-sen khet uru sept

[and] they give goods in great quantities [and] provisions

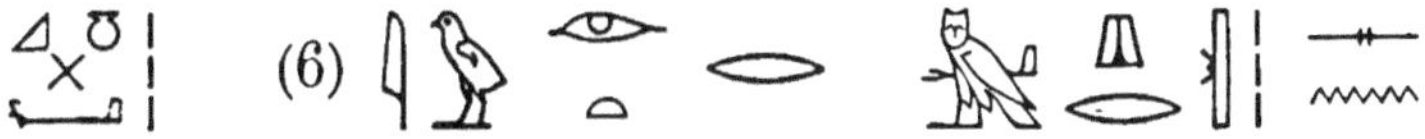

(6)

qennu àu àrit er mākher-sen

abundantly to perform their service

neter sesheshet thet en khasu en

for the divine images [which] carried off the vile men of

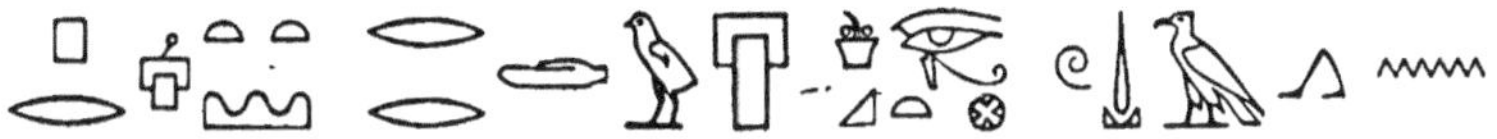

Persatet ererṭu Baqet utcha en

Persia outside Egypt, set out

ḥen - f er taui Satet neḥem-f-su

his Majesty for the lands of Asia, seized he them,

ȧn-f-su ȧu Ta-mert er ṭāt - nef - su

brought he them back to Egypt, placed he them

er ȧst-sen em maāu menmen-sen

on their thrones in the temples stood they

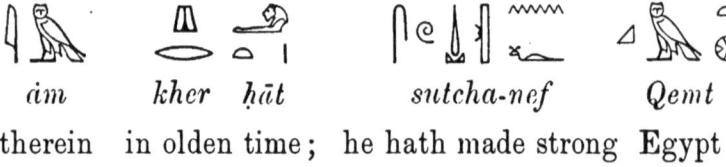

ȧm kher ḥāt sutcha-nef Qemt

therein in olden time; he hath made strong Egypt

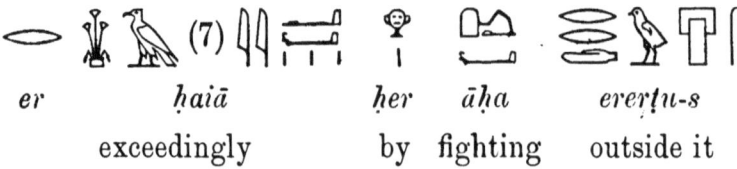

(7)

er ḥaiā ḥer āḥa erertu-s

exceedingly by fighting outside it

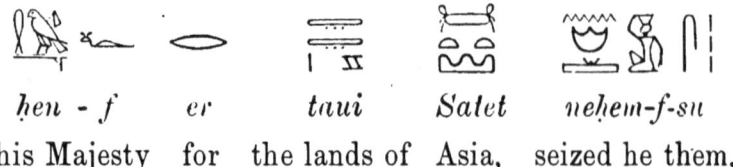

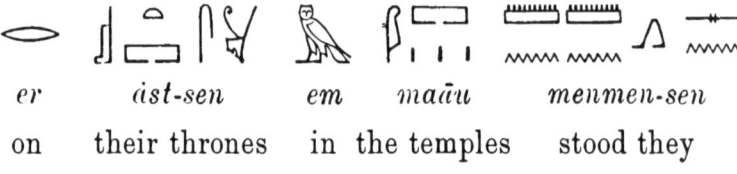

em ȧntet ḥer ḥā semtu

in the valley, [on] the plain, and in foreign lands

āsht	*ḥer*	*ṭepu-sen*	*kherp-sen*
very many	and	their chiefs	[who] ruled them;

un-sen	*ḥer*	*sutchā*	*ānkhiu*
were they		making strong	living people

nebt	*en*	*Ta-mert*	*ḥā*	*taiu*	*nebt*
all	of	Ta-mert	and	the men and women of lands	all

em	*netchi*	*en*	*ḥen-sen*	*ásk*
who are in	subjection	to	their Majesties;	behold

er - f	*kheper*	*renpit*	*en*	*Ḥāp*
moreover,	there happened	a year	of	the Nile

(8)

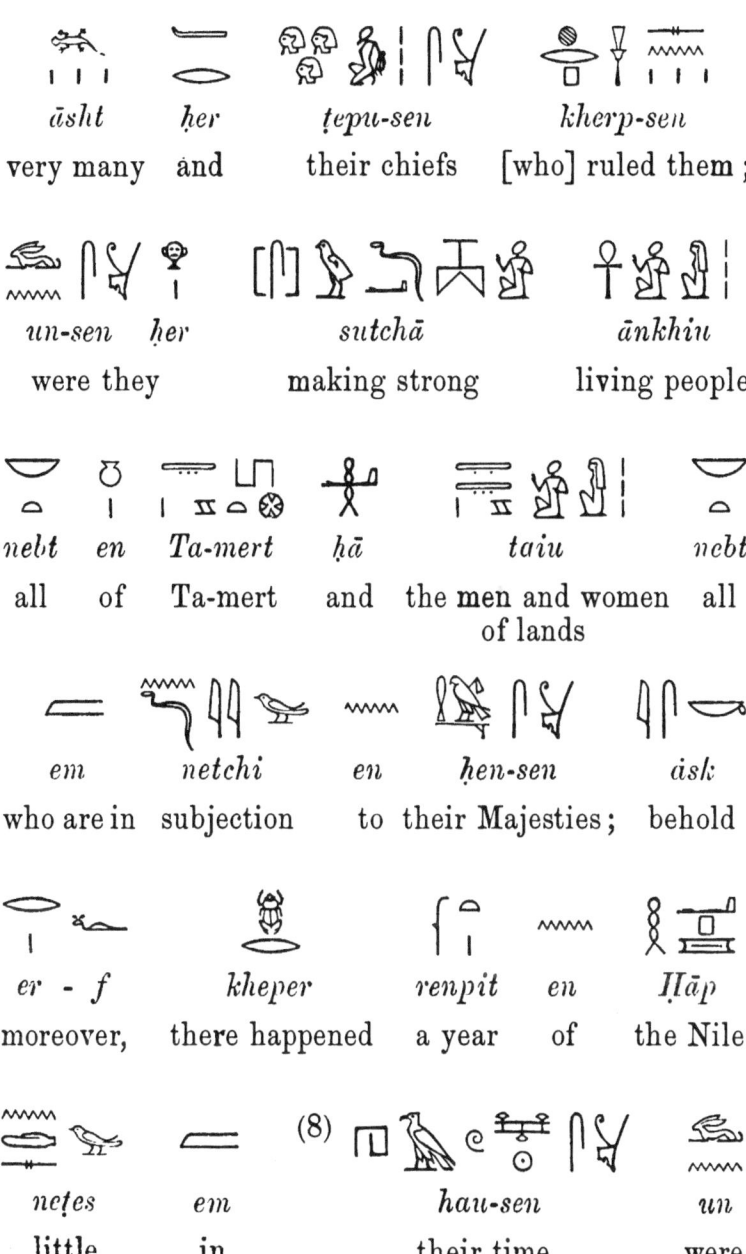

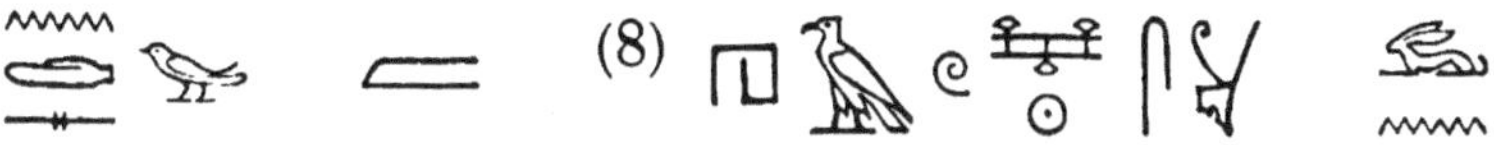

neṭes	*em*	*hau-sen*	*un*
little	in	their time,	were

ānkhiu nebt en Beq ȧb-sen ḳesen

living people all of Egypt heart their [in] grief

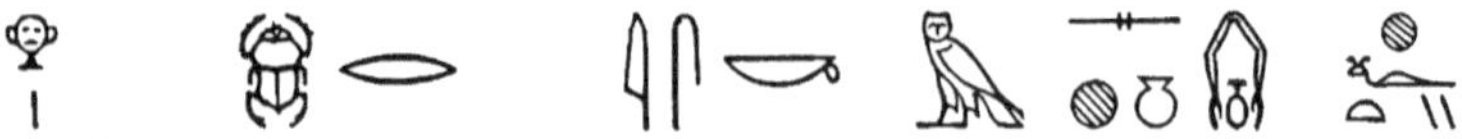

ḥer kheper ȧsk em sekhen khefti

at what had happened, behold, rose up in

sekhau-sen kherit khep khentet

their memory the disasters which had happened

em rek- suteniu ṭepāu er

in the time of the kings preceding when

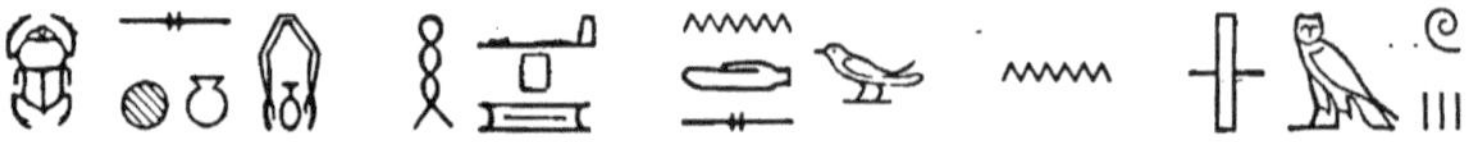

kheper sekhen Ḥāp neṭes en ȧmmu

happened a Nile little to those in

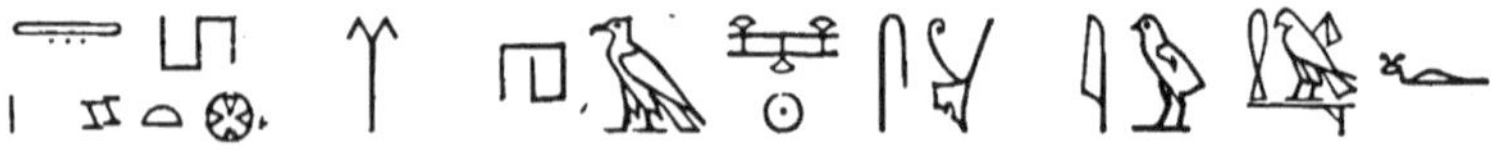

Ta-mert em ḥa-sen ȧu ḥen - f

Ta-mert in their time; His Majesty

tchesef	*ḥā*	*sent-f*	*ḥer*	*meḥsau*	*er*
himself	and	his sister		took care	in

ȧb-sen	*emkha*	*ḥer*	*ȧmmu*
their heart(s)	[which] burned	for	those who were in

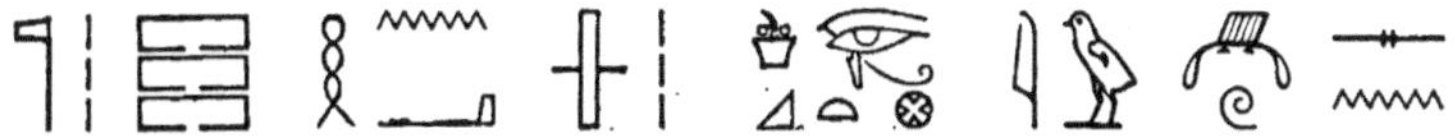

neteru pau	*ḥenā*	*ȧmmu*	*Baqet*	*ȧu*	*āu-sen*
the houses of the gods	and	those in	Egypt,	the whole of them,	

un-sen	*ḥer*	*mau*	*āsht*	*sep sen*
were they	caring anxiously		much	twice

ḥer erṭāt	*sa-sen*	*ȧu*	*ḥetrȧt*	*qennu*	*en*
and turning	their back	from	revenues	many	with

ȧb	*en*	*sānkh*	*rekhit*
the desire	of	keeping alive	men and women ;

áu-sen ḥer erṭāt àntu peru áu Qemt

were they making to be brought corn to Egypt

em Retennutet àbt em ta en Keftet

from Syria Eastern, from the land of Phoenicia,

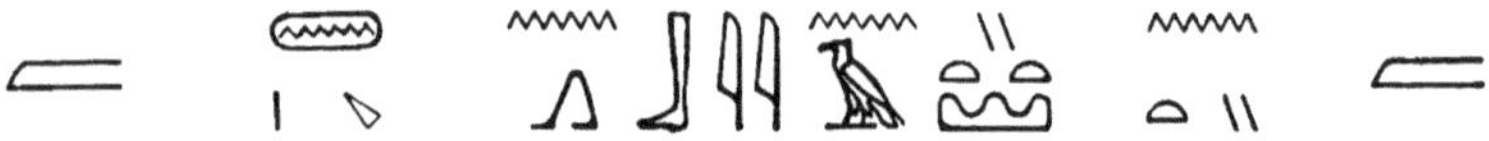

em ài Nebinaitet enti em

from the Island of Cyprus, which is in

ḥer àb Uatch-ur ḥenā semtu

the middle of (10) the Great Green, and foreign lands

uru ḥer erṭāt ḥetch āsht àu

great giving silver very much, was

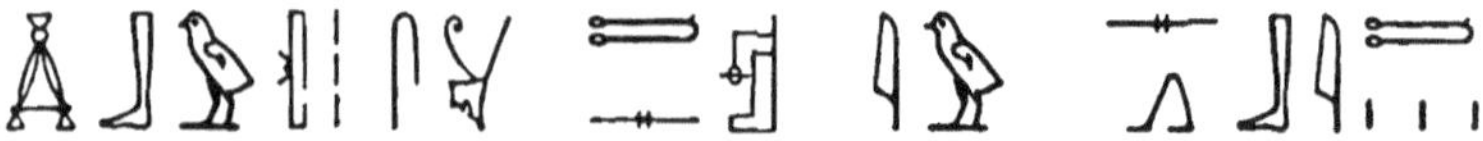

ṭebu-sen thes àu sebàth

their price high, were they anxious (?)

ḥer sutcha	*ānkhiu*	*un*	*em*
to make strong	the living people	who were	in

ta Netert	*ḥer*	*erṭāt*	*rekh-sen*
the Land Divine,	to make		them to know

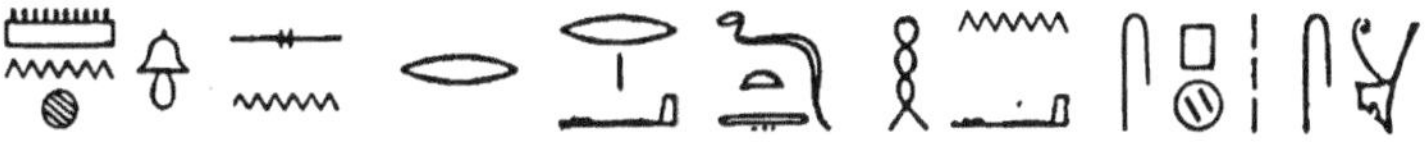

menkh-sen	*er*	*rā tchetta*	*ḥenā*	*sepu-sen*
their beneficence	[which is] ever-lasting,		and	their virtues

qennu	*em*	*ḥrà*	*en*	*kheperu*	[*ḥā*
many	in	the face	of	those who exist now	and

i	*ḥer-sa-sen*	*àu*	*erṭāt*	*en*	*neteru*
the comers after them;		have given			the gods

smen	*àaut-sen*	*en*	*ḥeq*
stability	to their dignity	of	sovereignty of

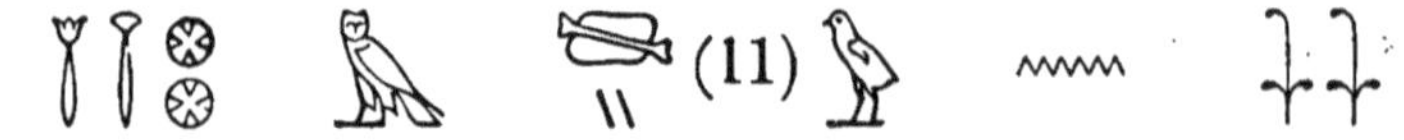

tawi *em* *àsiu,* *en* *enen*

the South and North in return for these things,

ḥā *feqau-sen* *em* *khu*

and they shall reward [them] with good things

er *āu-sen* *er* *rā tchetta* *utcha* *ḥā*

of all kinds for ever, strength and

snib *ertā* *em* *àb-sen* *àn* *ābu*

health. Gave in their heart[s] the priests

en *Ta-mert* *àu* *sur* *tcheser* *khet*

of Ta-mert to magnify the honour [in] things

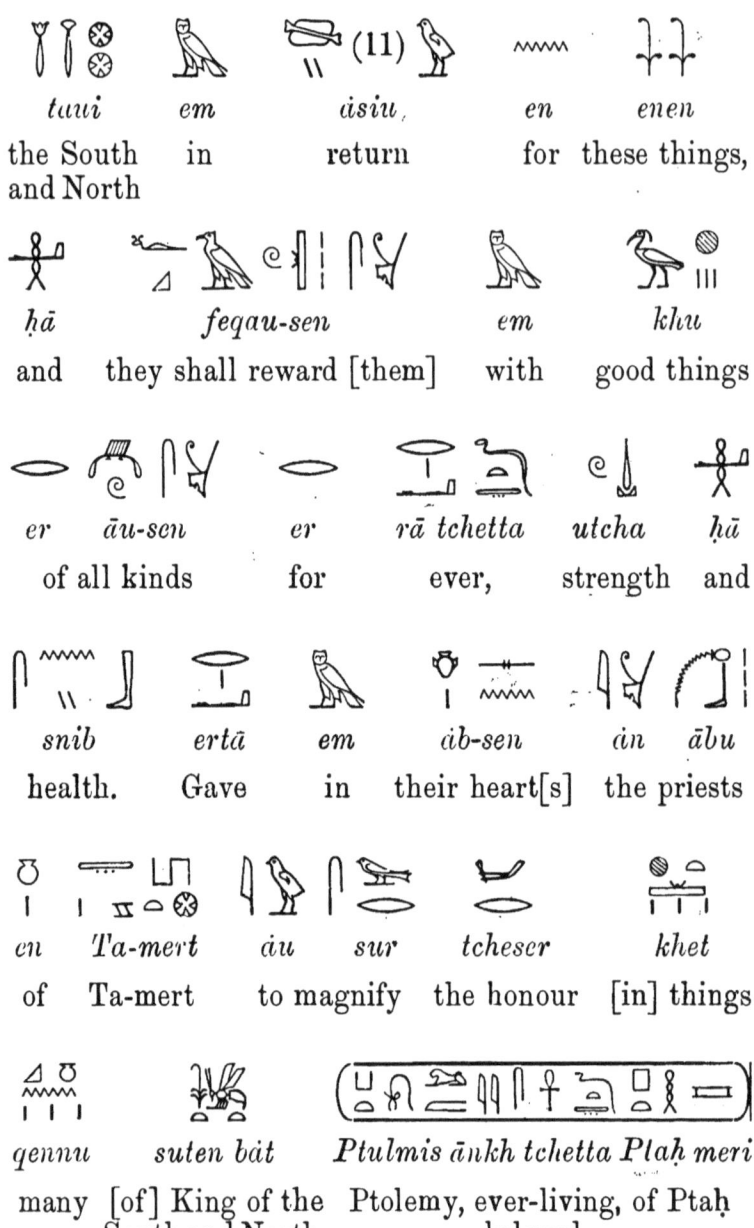

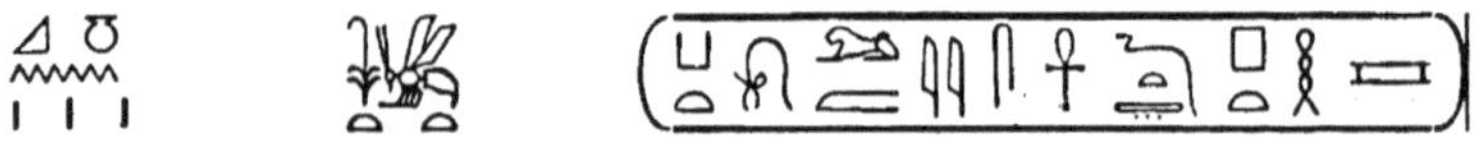

qennu *suten bàt* *Ptulmis ānkh tchetta Ptaḥ meri*

many [of] King of the South and North, Ptolemy, ever-living, of Ptaḥ beloved,

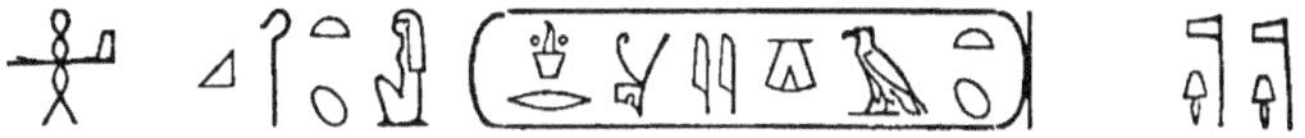

ḥā *ḥeqt* *Berenikat* *neterui menkhui*

and [of] the Queen Berenice, the two Good-doing Gods

em khent *maāu* *ḥā* *kheper* *en*

in the temples, and what happeneth for

 (12) 

neterui senui *qema-sen* *ḥenā* *kheper*

the two brother gods [who] begot them, and what happeneth

en *neterui netchui* *sekh* *āri-sen*

for the two saviour gods who begot their ancestor,

ḥer *sur-sen* *ābu* *pu* *āmmu* *neteru-pau*

and to magnify them the priests who are in the temples

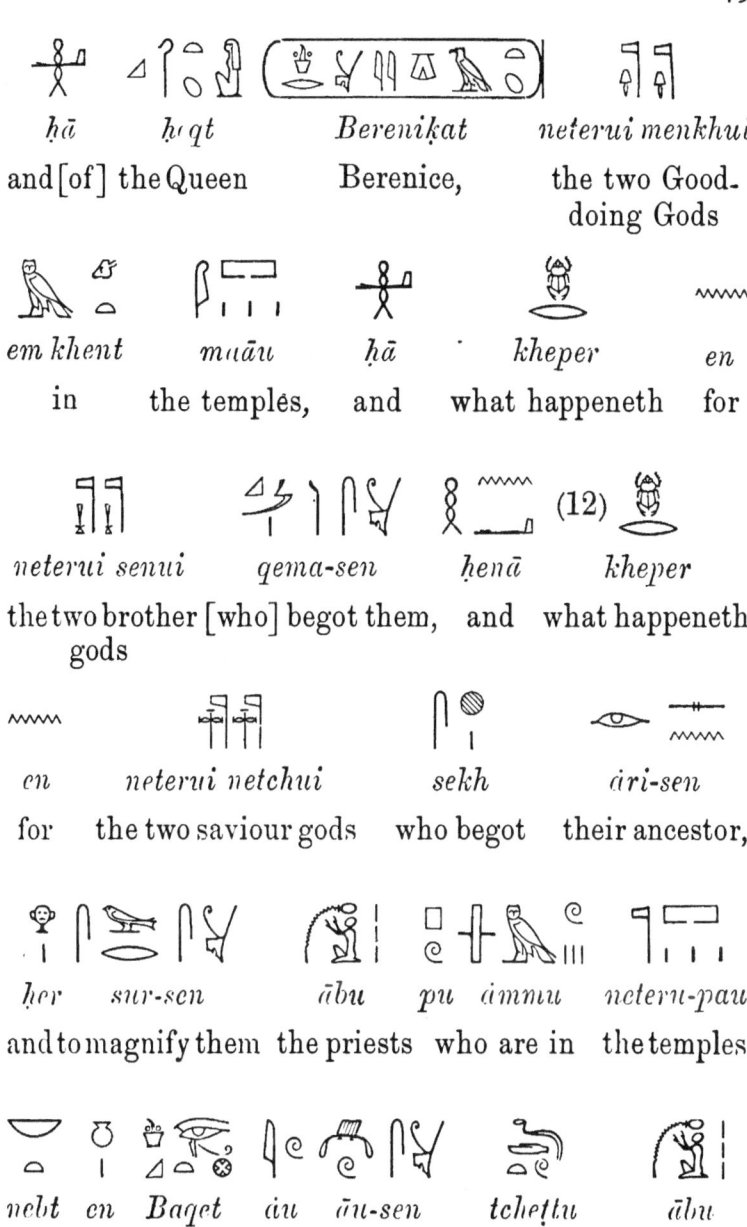

nebt *en* *Baqet* *āu* *āu-sen* *tchetṭu* *ābu*

all of Egypt all of them, shall be called "priests

en *neterui menkhui* *ḥer* *ren-sen* *uaḥtu*

of the two Good-doing Gods" on their names in addition

ḥer *ren* *en* *ȧaut* *neter-ḥen-sen*

to the name of the dignities of their priesthood,

ān *ren-sen* *ḥer* *sekheru* *nebu*

shall be written their name upon documents all,

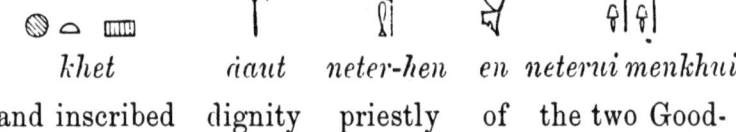

khet *ȧaut* *neter-ḥen* *en* *neterui menkhui*

and inscribed dignity priestly of the two Good-doing Gods

ḥer *khetem* *ȧri* *ṭet-sen* *sekheper-sen*

on the ring which is on their hand; they shall form

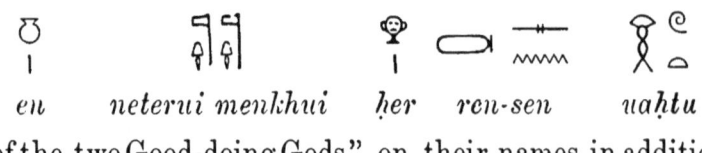

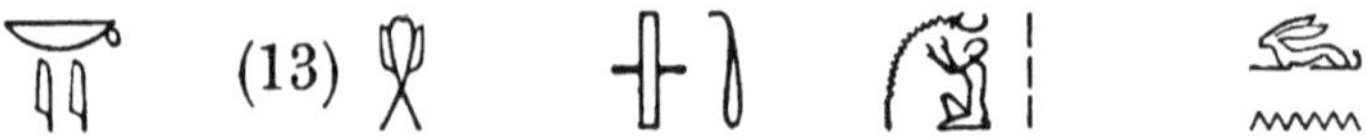

ki *sa* *ȧmth* *ābu* *un*

another (13) tribe among the priests now living

em *maāu* *ȧu* *āu-sen* *em uaḥ ḥer*

in the temples all of them in addition to

sa *fṭu* *khep* *ȧu* *hru* *pan*

the tribes four existing on day this,

tcheṭtu-nef *sa* *ṭua* *en* *neterui menkhui*

and it shall be called tribe fifth of the two Good-doing gods,

erenti *kheper* *sekhen* *nefer* *ḥā* *utcha*

since happened the event happy with strength

snib *mestu* *suten bȧt*

[and] health, was born the King of the South and North

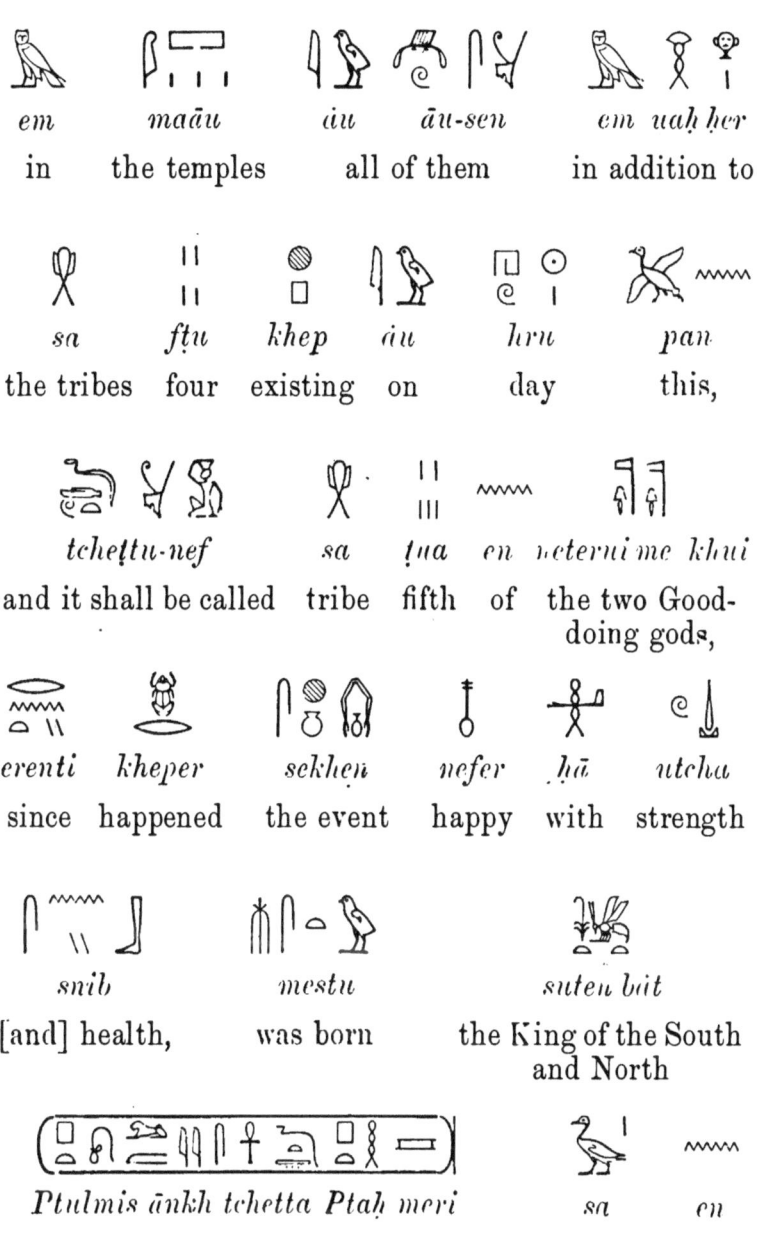

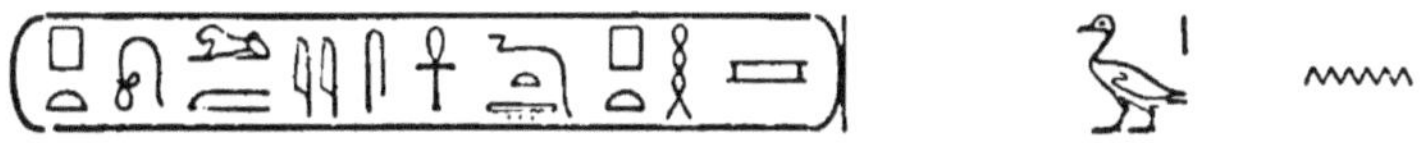

Ptulmis ānkh tchetta Ptaḥ meri *sa* *en*

Ptolemy, ever-living, of Ptaḥ beloved, son of

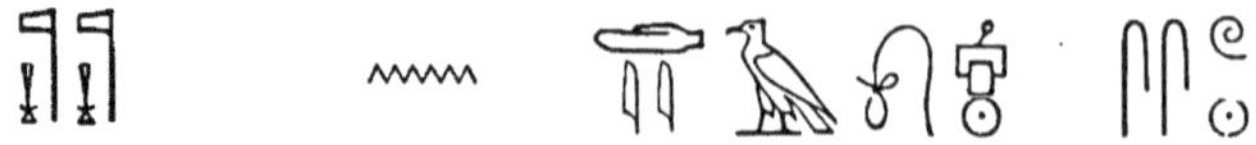

neterui senui | *en* | *Ṭiauasa* | *sesu*

the two Brother Gods | on | Dios | day

ṭua | *ȧu* | *ȧref* | *ḥru* | *pan* | *khentet pu* | *en*

five, | was | therefore | day | this | the beginning | of

(14) 

ȧri | *bu nefer* | *uru* | *en* | *ānkhiu*

the making of | happiness | great | of | living men and women

nebu | *ṭātu* | *ābu* | *bes* | *ȧn* | *suten*

all; | had made | the priests | to enter | the King

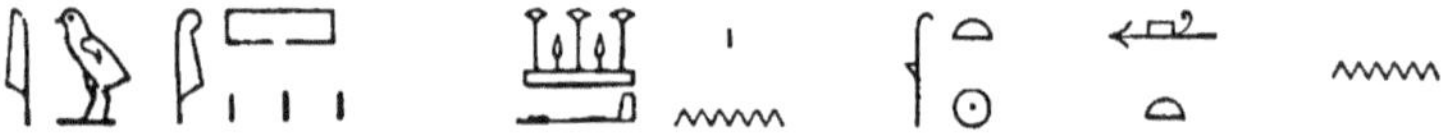

ȧu | *maāu* | *shaā* | *en* | *renpit* | *uāt* | *en*

into the temples | beginning with | year | one | of

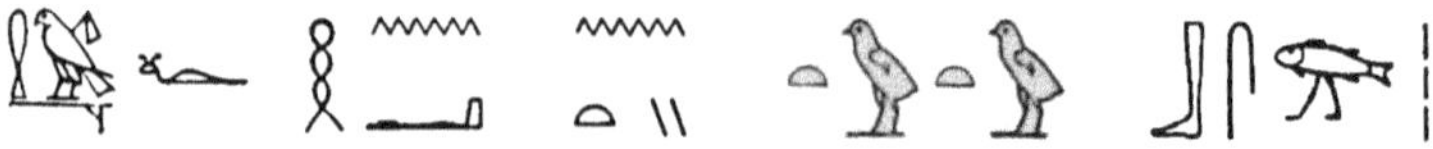

ḥen-f | *ḥenā* | *enti* | *tutu* | *besu*

his Majesty | and [those] who | likewise | have entered

āu-men renpit pest abeṭ ftu shemu

until year nine, month four of the season Shemu

kher sa pan ḥenā mesu-sen er rā tchetta

into tribe this and their children for ever;

ābu pu un kher ḥāt-sen ermen renpit

the priests who were before them up to year

 (15) 

uāt khep em sau un-sen am-sen

one shall be in the tribes were they in them

kher ḥāt matet āru en mesu-sen tcher hru pen

formerly, similarly their children from day this

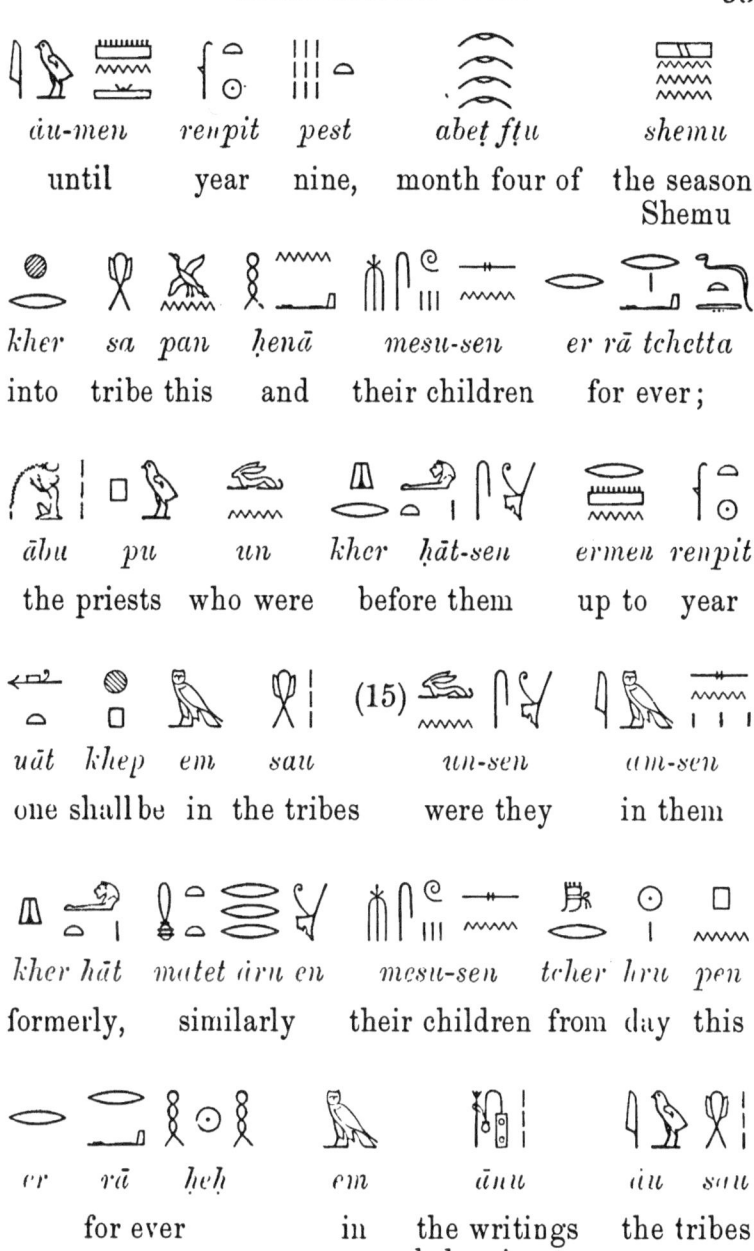

er rā ḥeḥ em ānu āu sau

for ever in the writings belonging to the tribes

enti er tef-sen em khent-sen āiri

which are their father[s] in them; shall be made

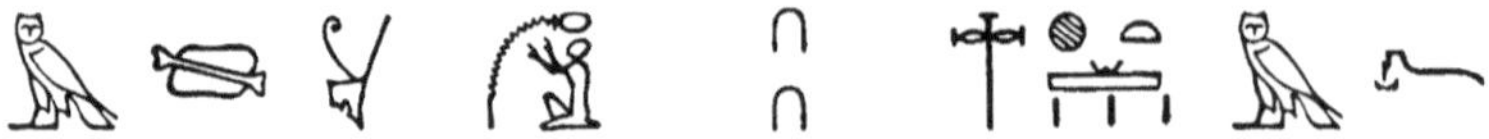

em-āsiu en ābu tchaut netch-khet em setep

instead of the priests twenty councillors chosen

er trā en renpit em sa

at a stated season of the year from the tribes

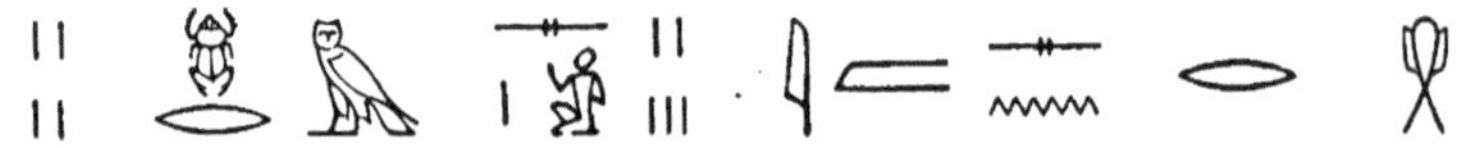

ftu kheper em sa ṭua ām-sen er sa

four being persons five among them from tribe

uā sekheper ābu tchaut ṭua (16) *ḥer*

one, shall be the priests twenty-five for

netchu khet au sa ṭua āntu em uaḥ

councillors, being persons five brought in addition

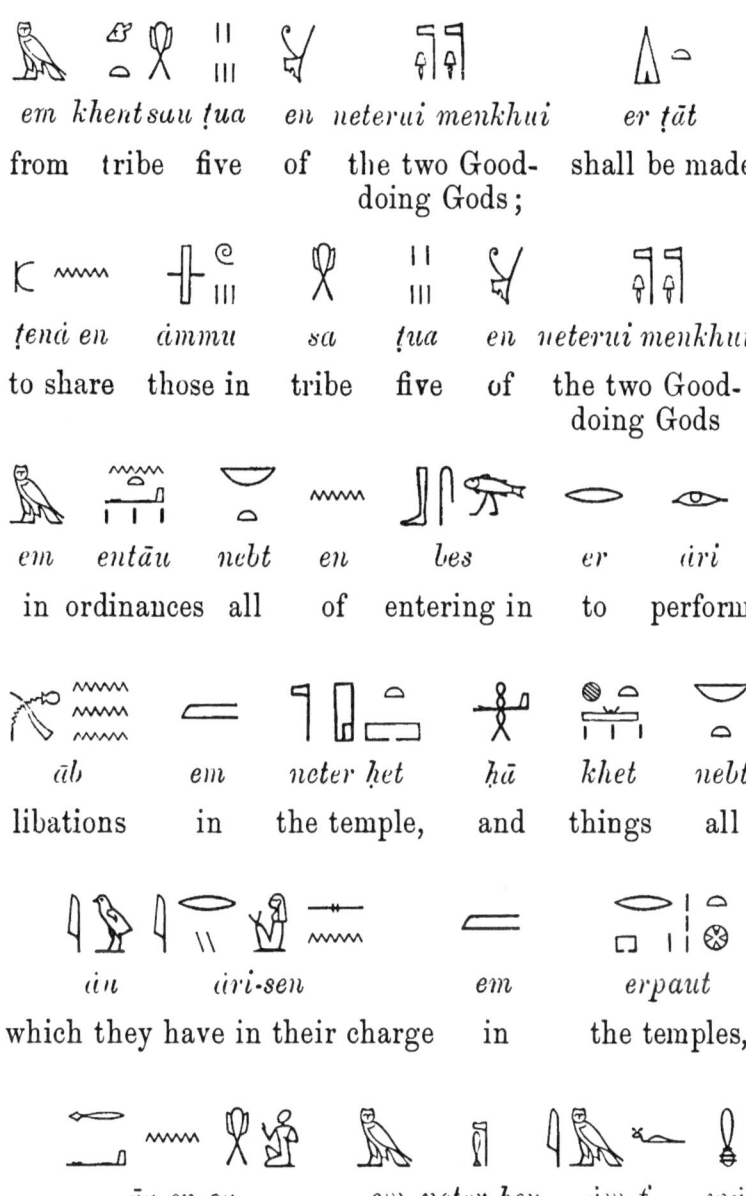

em khentsuu ṭua en neterui menkhui er ṭāt

from tribe five of the two Good-doing Gods; shall be made

ṭenā en āmmu sa ṭua en neterui menkhui

to share those in tribe five of the two Good-doing Gods

em entāu nebt en bes er āri

in ordinances all of entering in to perform

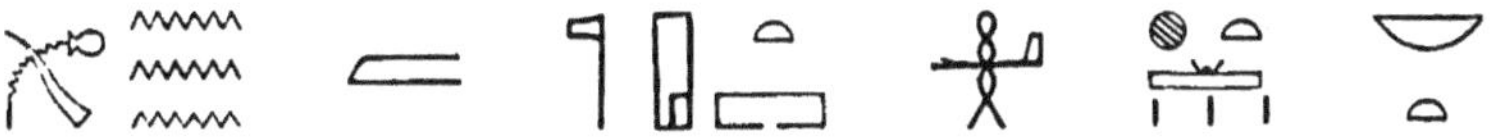

āb em neter ḥet ḥā khet nebt

libations in the temple, and things all

ān āri-sen em erpaut

which they have in their charge in the temples,

āa en-sa em neter ḥen ām-f mā

[shall be] a chief of the tribe as a prophet in it as

khep	*em*	*ki*	*sa*	*fṭu*	*erenti*
there is	in	the other	tribes	four.	And because

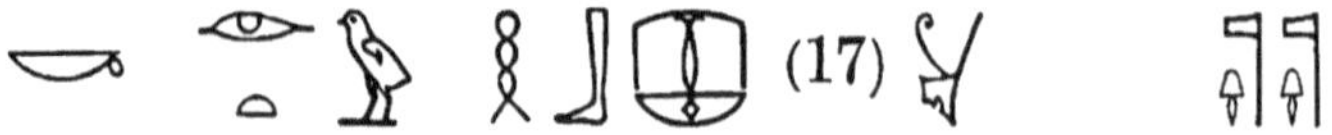

(17)

ki	*ȧri-tu*	*ḥeb*	*en*	*neterui menkhui*
also	is made	a festival	of	the Good-doing Gods

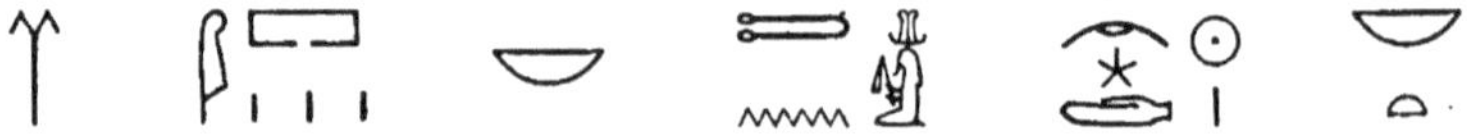

em	*maāu*	*neb*	*then*	*ȧbeṭ*	*nebt*
in	the temples	all	throughout	month	every

em	*sesu*	*ṭua*	*sesu*	*pest*	*sesu*	*tchaut-ṭua*
on	day	five,	day	nine,	day	twenty-five,

em	*ȧri*	*sekhau*	*serer*
according to	the making of	the decree	[which was] inscribed

kher ḥāt	*ȧu kher*	*ȧritu*	*ḥeb*
at an earlier period,	and besides	is made	a festival

en	*neteru*	*uru*	*khāā*	*en*	*āa*
of	the gods	great,	a festival	of	greatness,

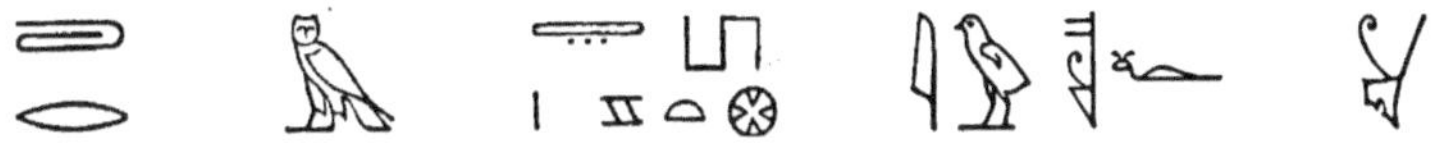

rer	*em*	*Ta-mert*	*àu . . . .-f*	*en*
universal,	in	Ta-mert	at its season	of

renpit	*emtutu*	*àri*	*khāā*	*āa*
the year,	likewise	shall be made	a festival	great

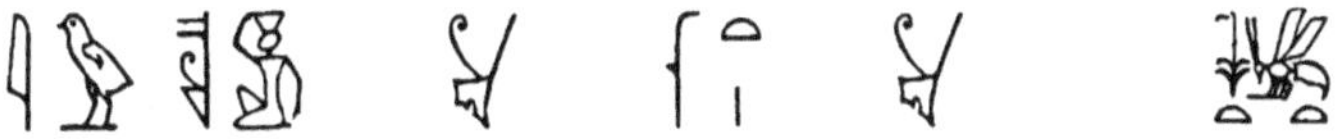

àu . . . .-f	*en*	*renpit*	*en*	*suten bat*
at its season	of	the year	of	the King of the South and North,

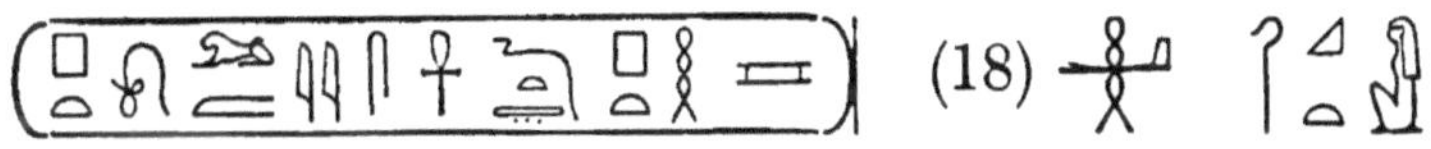

Ptulmis ānkh tchetta Ptaḥ meri	*ḥā*	*ḥeqt*
Ptolemy, ever-living, of Ptaḥ beloved,	and	Queen

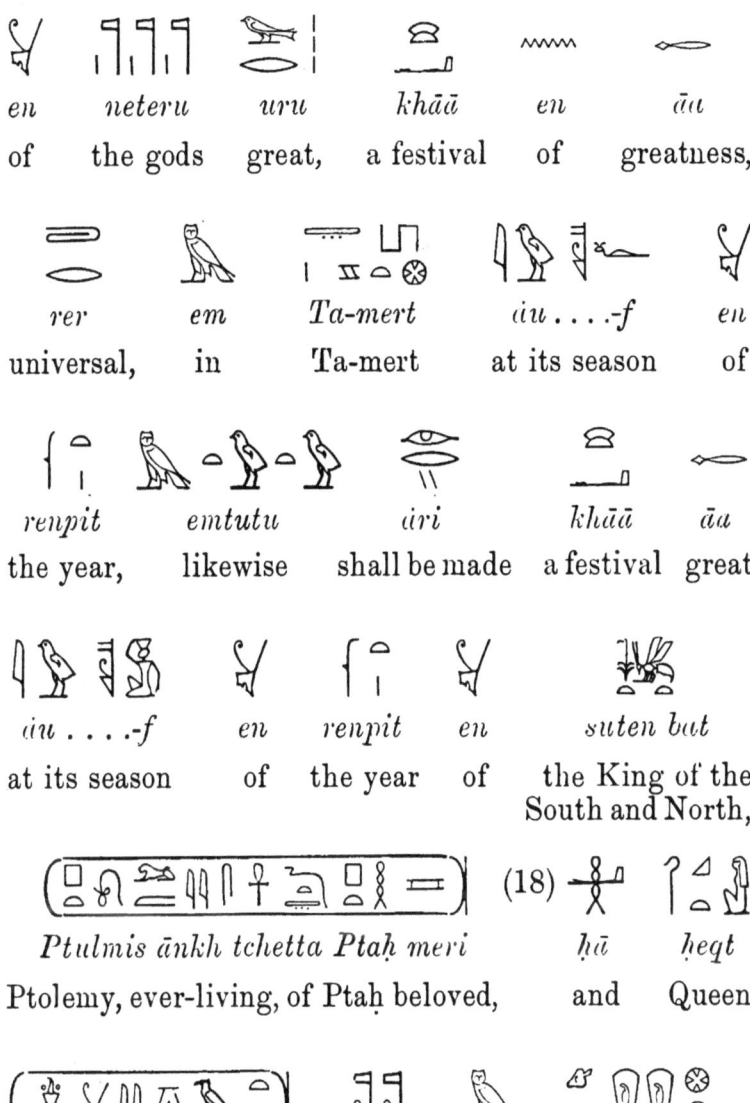

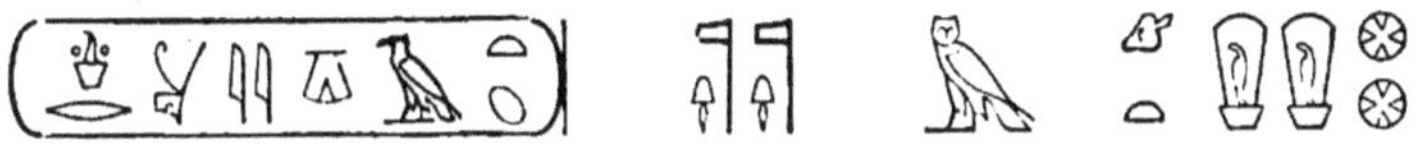

Berenikat	*neterui menkhui*	*em*	*khent àterti taui*
Berenice,	the two Good-doing Gods	in	the sanctuaries of the Two Lands

ḥer Baqet er āu-s em hru per

and Egypt throughout it on the day of the rise of

neter Sepṭ tchetut up renpit em

the divine Sothis, called opening of the year in

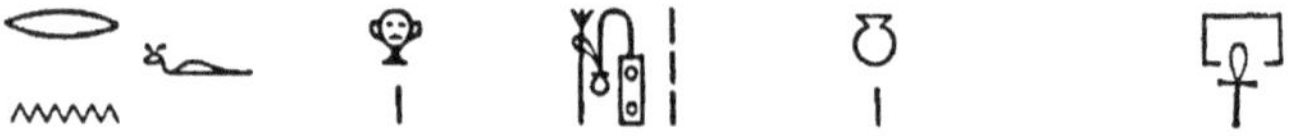

ren-f ḥer ānu nu pa-ānkh

its name in the books of the House of Life,

emtutu āri-f em renpit pest

which correspondeth to year nine,

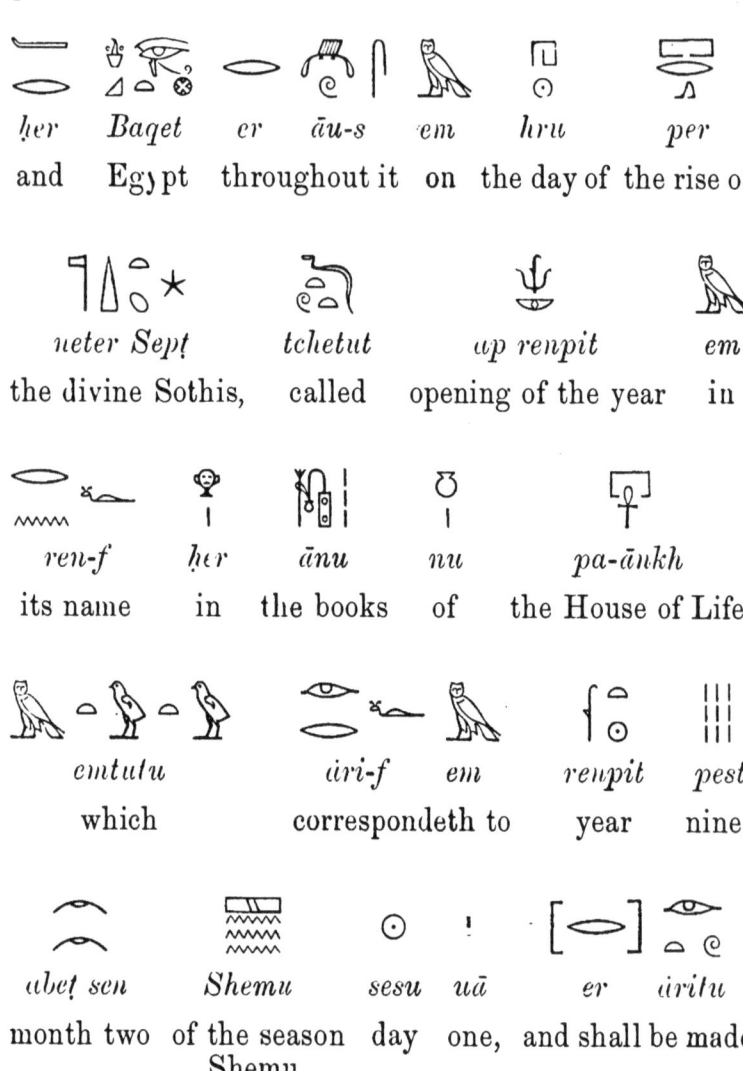

ubeṭ sen Shemu sesu uā er āritu

month two of the season Shemu, day one, and shall be made

ḥeb en āp-renpit ḥeb en Bast

the festival of the New Year, the festival of Bast,

ḥer khāā āa en Bast em ābeṭ

and the festival great of Bast in month

(19)

pan tcherenti . . . . en setut

this, because the season of the ingathering of

reṭu neb ḥai Ḥāp ām-f

fruit all [and] the increase of the Nile [are] in it.

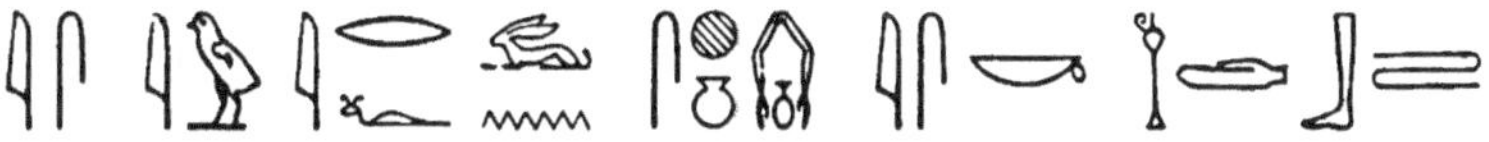

ās āu āref un sekhen āsk uṭeb

But if should happen the event, behold, a change of

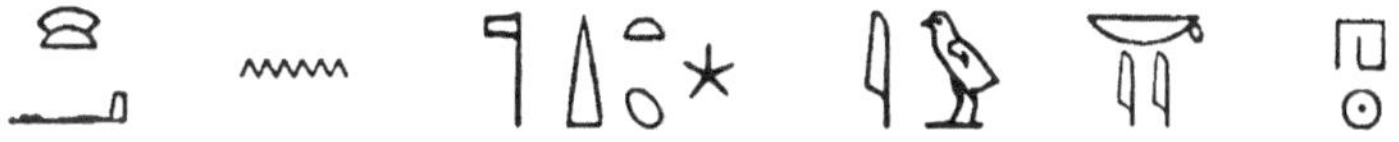

khāā en neter Sepṭ āu ki hru

the festival of the divine Sothis to another day

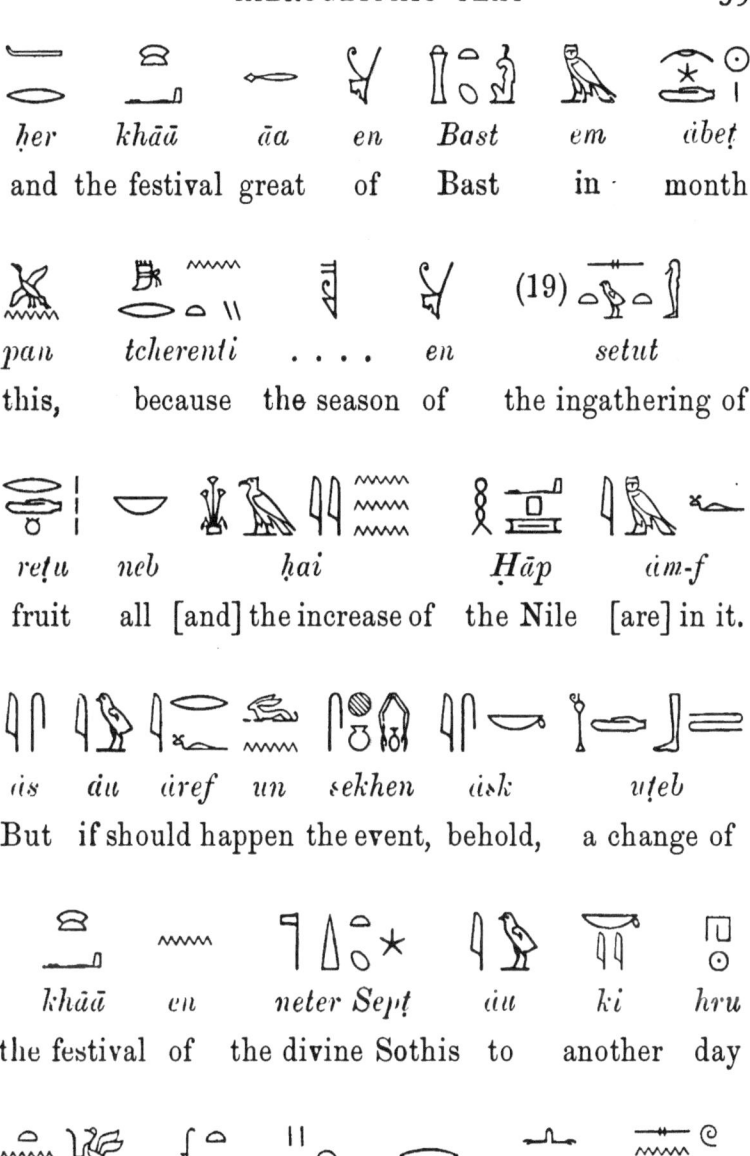

tennu renpit fṭut er ān sentu

every years four, then not shall pass

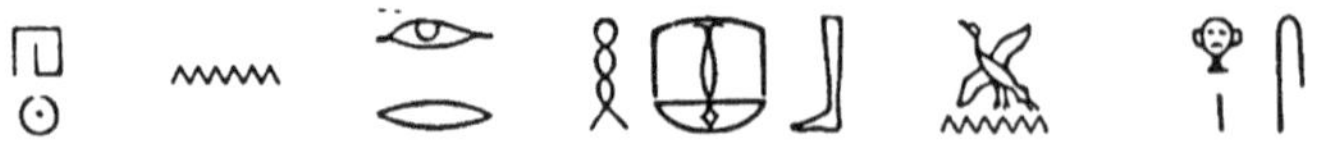

hru en àri ḥeb pan ḥer-s

the day of making festival this because of it,

er àritu-f àu màtet-f em àbeṭ sen

but it shall be made just the same on month two

shemu hru uā àritu ḥeb

of Shemu day one, and shall be made the festival

àm-f tut em renpit pest àritu

in it even as in year (20) nine; shall be made

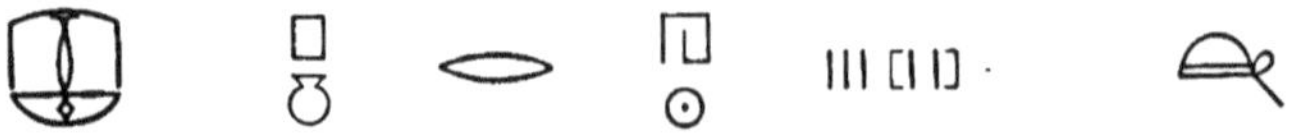

ḥeb pen er hru ṭua meḥ

festival this for days five, shall be crowned

ṭep-sen em ḥāu em thes khet ḥer

their heads with flowers, arranging offerings on

khaui *ḥer ȧri* *uṭen* *ḥā* *khet*

the altars, and making libations and things

nebt *setut* *en* *ȧri* *er erṭā* *kheper-f*

all which it is proper to do. So that it may be made to happen,

ȧsk *er* *trā-sen* *ḥer ȧri* *ȧri-sen*

behold, at their seasons that they do what it is their duty [to do]

er *reri* *nebt* *mā* *sekheru*

at times all according to the ordinances

un *petet* *smen* *ḥer-s* *em* *hru* *pen*

is heaven founded upon them at day this,

(21) 

er *ben* *ses* *sekhen* *khep* *er*

that not once the event may happen that

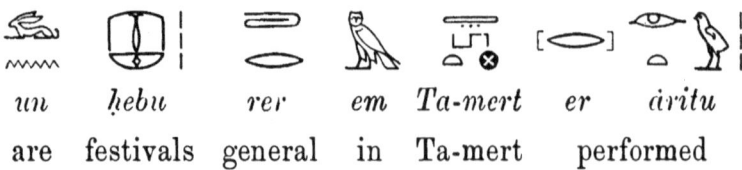

un ḥebu rer em Ta-mert er àritu

are festivals general in Ta-mert performed

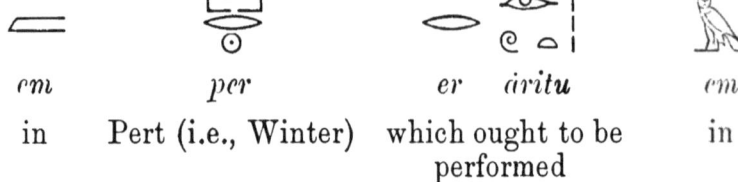

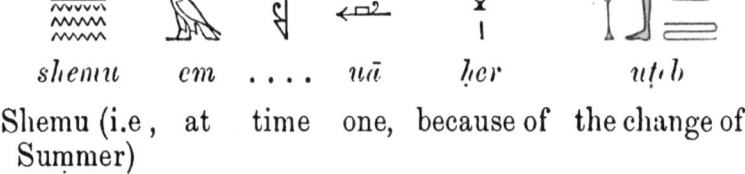

em per er àritu em

in Pert (i.e., Winter) which ought to be performed in

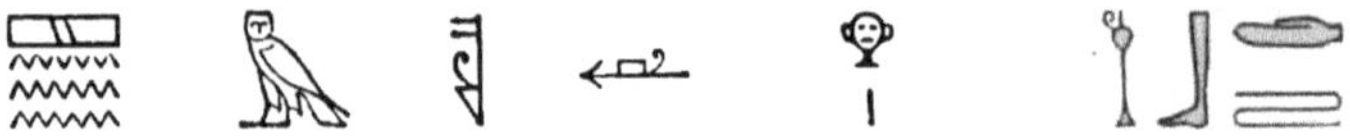

shemu em . . . . uā ḥer uṭeb

Shemu (i.e , Summer) at time one, because of the change of

khāā en neter Sepṭ em hru uā

the festival of the divine Sothis by day one

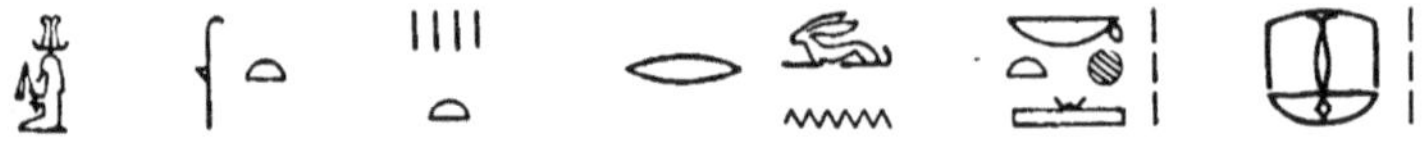

ten renpit fṭut er un ketekhu ḥebu

every years four; and would be other festivals,

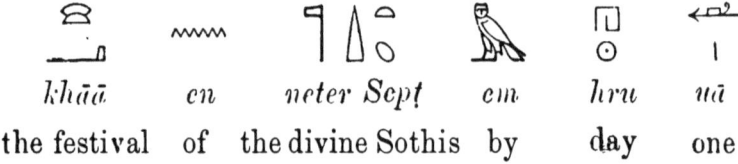

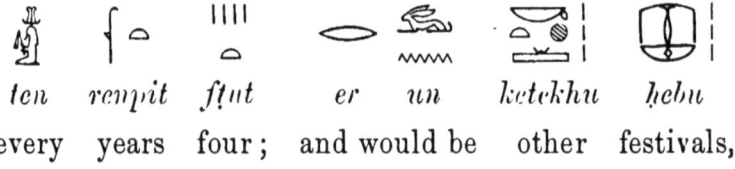

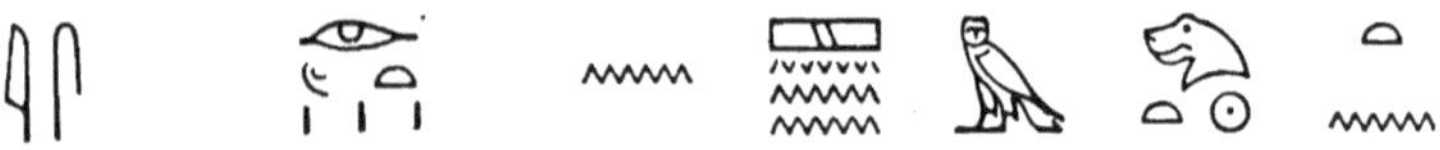

às àritu en shemu em at ten

behold, which are made in Shemu at time this

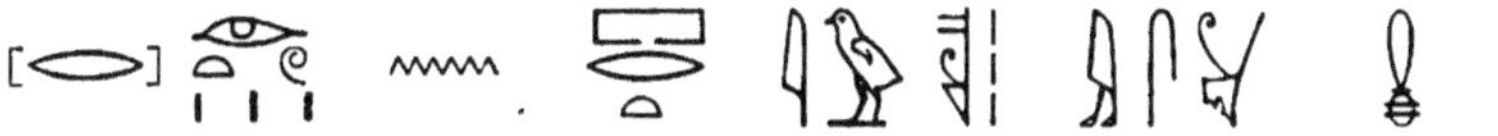

[er] áritu en pert áu . . . . i-sen má

made in Pert in times to come, even as

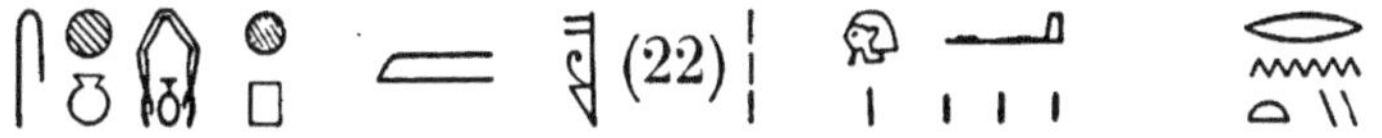

sekhen khep em . . . . ṭep-āu erenti

has happened in times of the ancestors because this

kheper ásk ár ás un renpit

would now happen, behold, if consisted the year

ḥer hru 300 + 60 ḥā hru ṭua áptu

of days 360 and the days five which it is customary

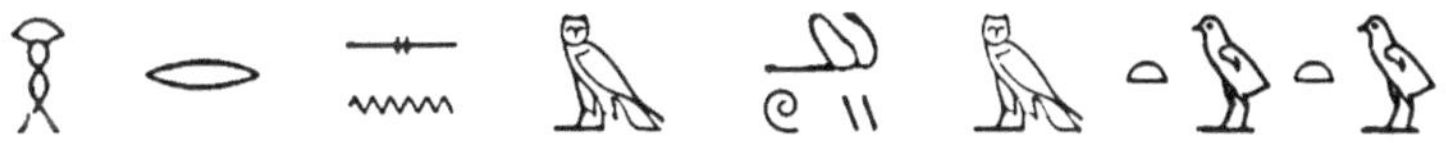

uaḥ er sen em peḥui em-tutu

to add to them at the end. Likewise

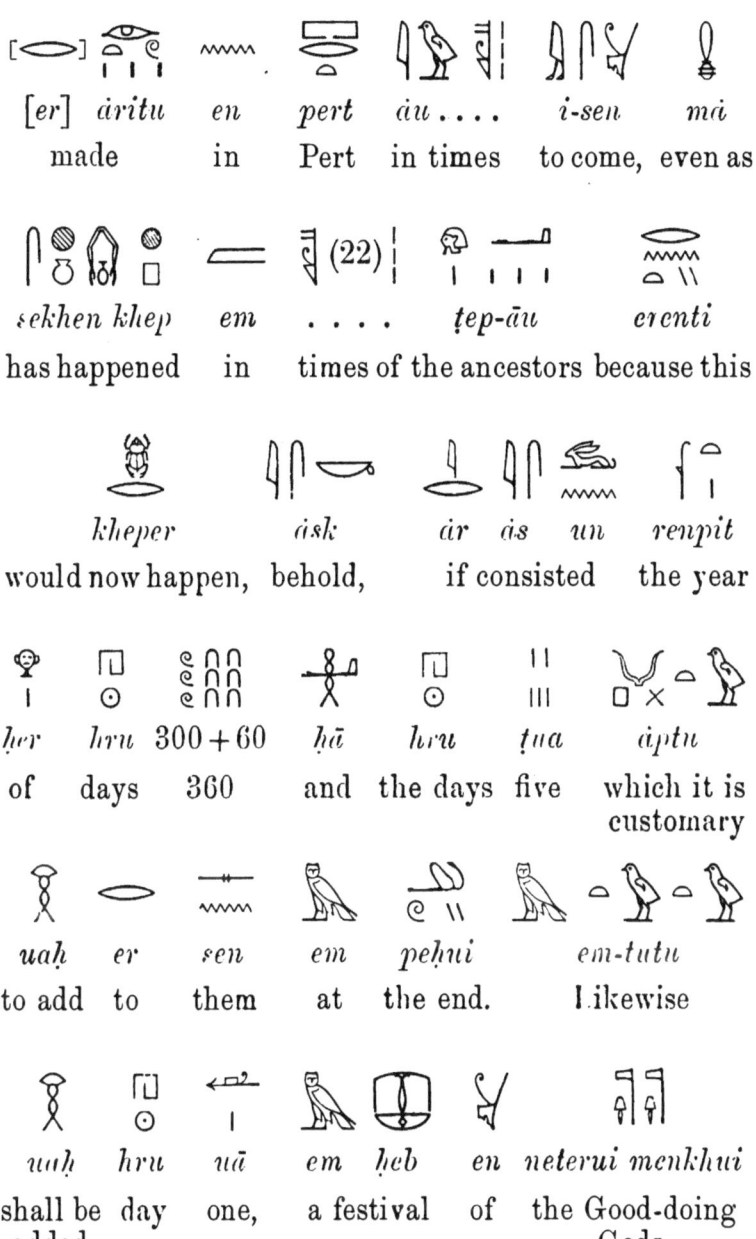

uaḥ hru uā em ḥeb en neterui menkhui

shall be added day one, a festival of the Good-doing Gods,

shuā en ḥru pen ten renpit fṭut

beginning from day this every years four,

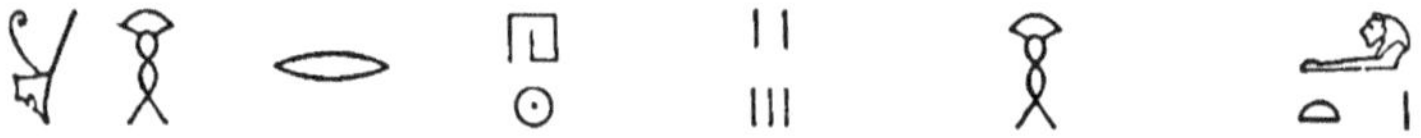

en uaḥ er hru ṭua uaḥ ḥāt

adding to the days five additional at the beginning of

āp renpit kheper-f rekh en bu-nebt

the New Year, that it may be known to all men

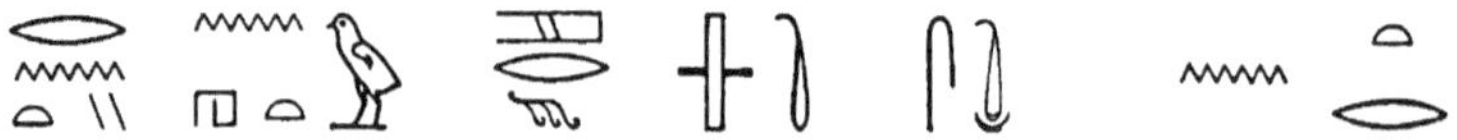

erenti nehetu sher āmth smen en trāiu

that were short a little in arrangement the seasons

(23) 

ḥā renpit ḥā meṭu

of the year, and the year, and the decisions

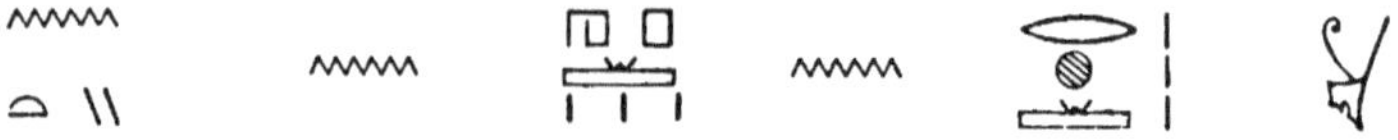

enti en hepu en rekh en

which exist as to the laws of the science of

màtenu petet sekhen às

the ways of heaven, it hath happened that [they are] now

ṭā metu àu meḥ ḥer neterui menkhui

made right [and] filled up by the Good-doing Gods.

enti sek satet kheper en suten bàt

And since now the daughter who was to King of the South and North,

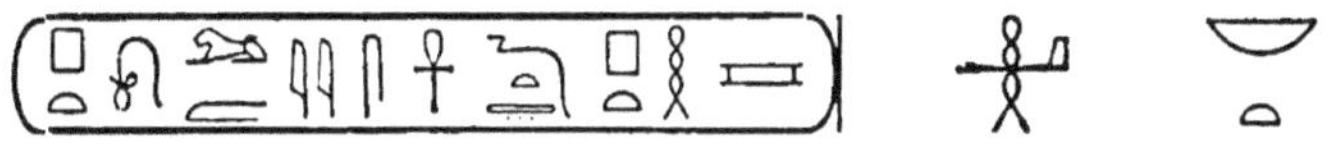

Ptulmis ānkh tchetta Ptaḥ meri ḥā nebt

Ptolemy, ever-living, of Ptaḥ beloved, and the lady of

taui Bereniḳat neterui menkhui

the two lands Berenice, the two Good-doing Gods,

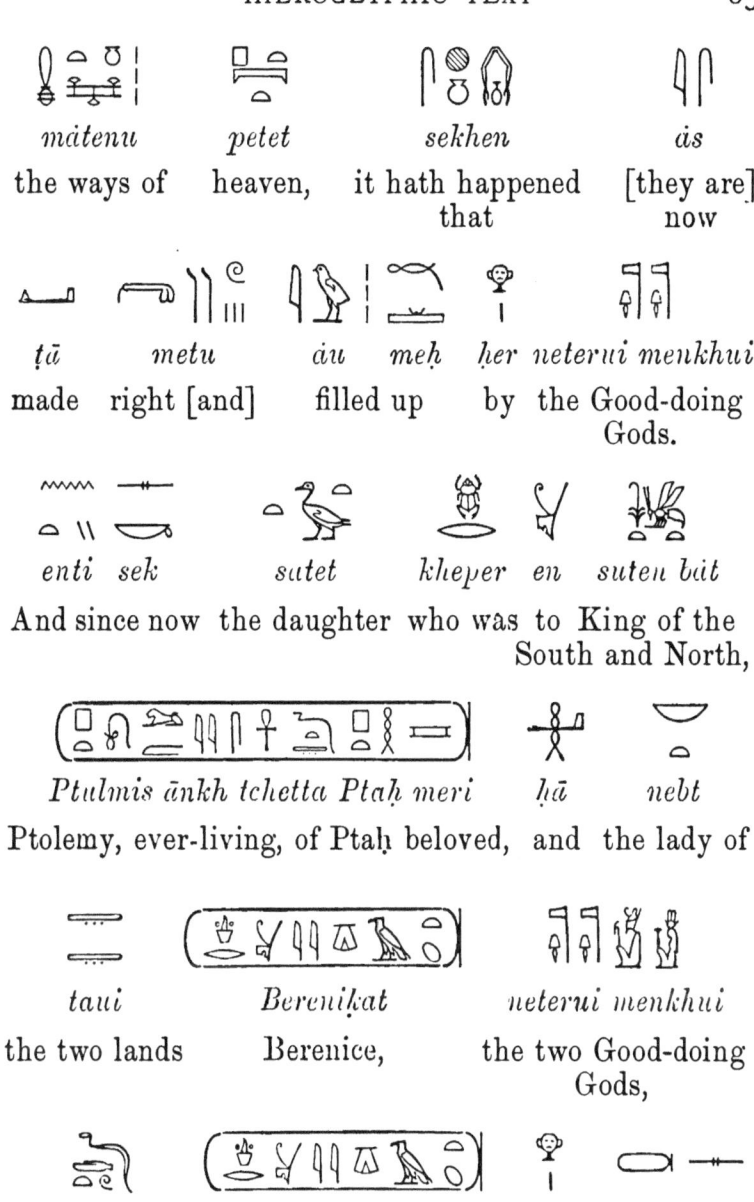

tcheṭtu Bereniḳat ḥer ren-s

who was called 'Berenice by her name,

les	.... *'ȧu*	*ḥeqti*
who was appointed	straightway	Queen,

er sekhen	*ȧs*	*netert then*	*ȧu-s*
and since it hath happened	now	[that] this goddess	being

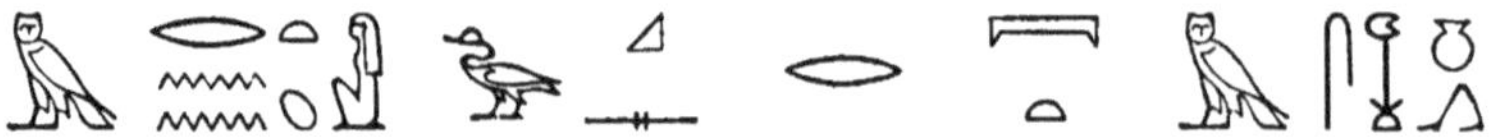

em renenet	*āq-s*	*er*	*pet*	*em sekhan*
a virgin	she entered	into	heaven	suddenly,

ȧu	*ābu*	*i*	*em*	*Ta-mert*	*kher*
were	the priests	who came	from	Egypt	under

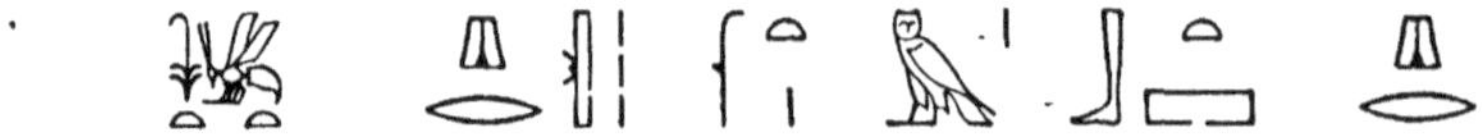

suten bȧt	*kheru*	*renpit*	*em*	*bet*	*kher*
the King of the South and North	every	year	in	the house	with

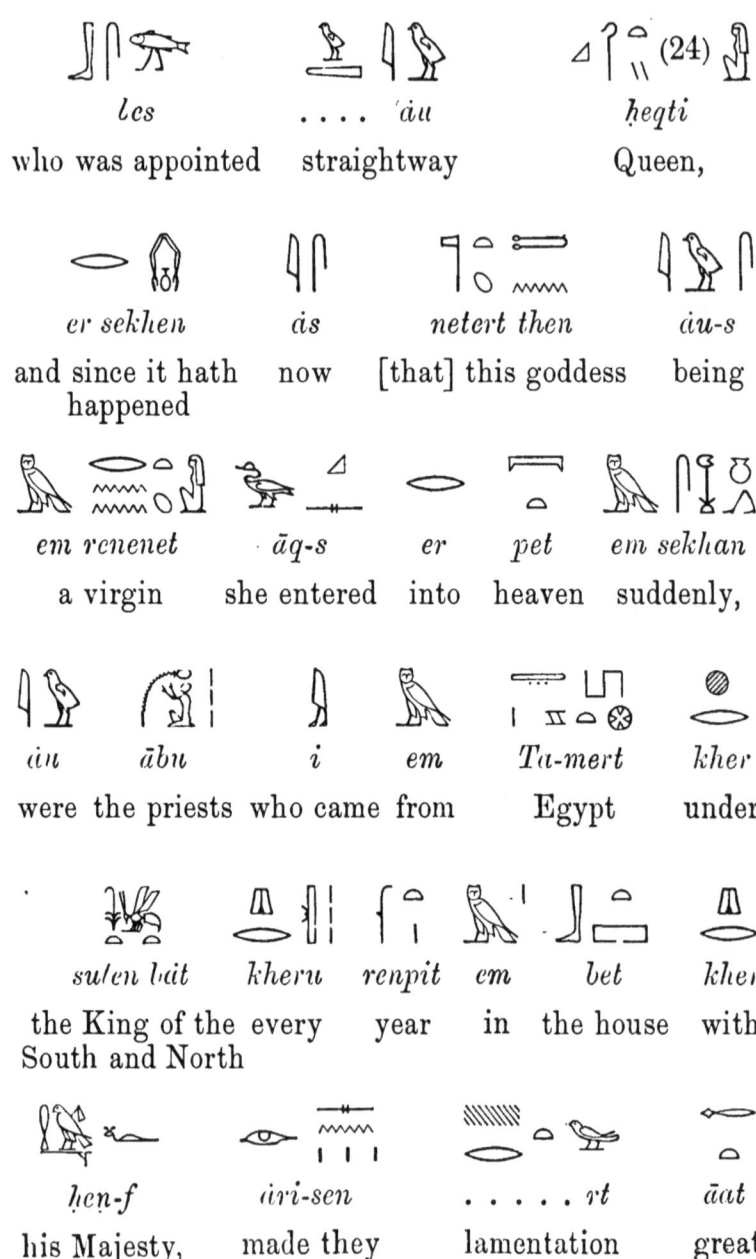

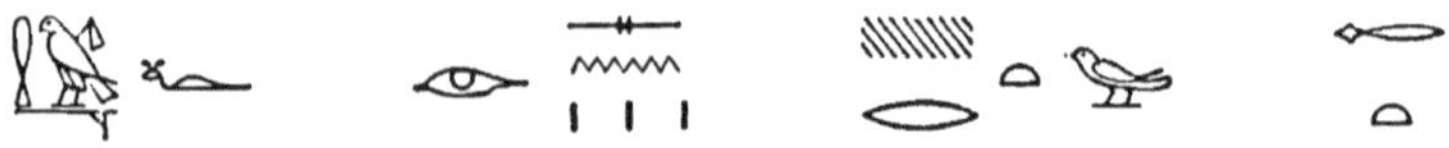

ḥen-f	*ȧri-sen*	. . . . . *rt*	*āat*
his Majesty,	made they	lamentation	great

ḥer ā ḥer sekhen kheper àu-sen

straightway because of the event which had happened. They

ḥer neḥu em-baḥ suten ḥā ḥeqet

made entreaty before the king and queen

 (25) 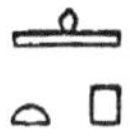

ḥer ṭāṭ em àb-sen er erṭā ḥetep

putting it in their heart[s] to make to rest

netert then ḥā Àsàr em neter ḥet en

goddess this with Osiris in the temple of

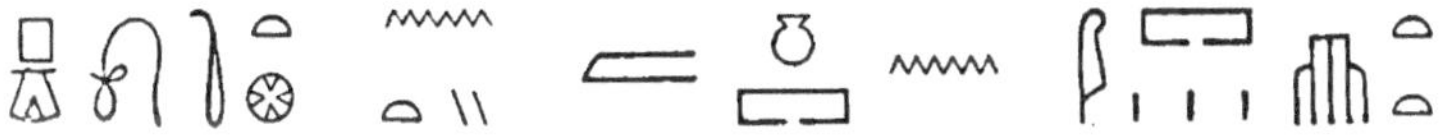

Peḳuàthet enti em khen en maāu khentet

Canopus, which is among the temples of the first rank,

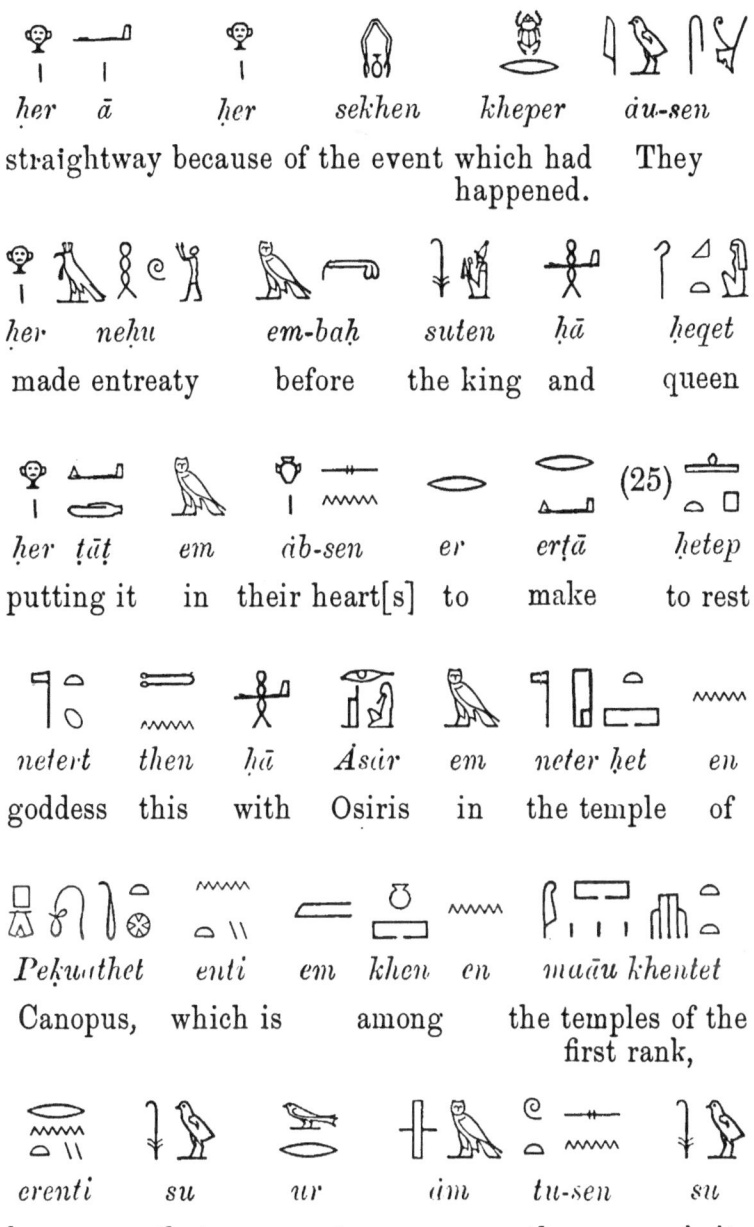

erenti su ur àm tu-sen su

because that great among them is it

em khent tcheser en suten ḥenā ānkhiu

in honour by the king and the men and women

en Ta-mert er āu-sen ȧr ȧs

of Egypt all of them, (now behold,

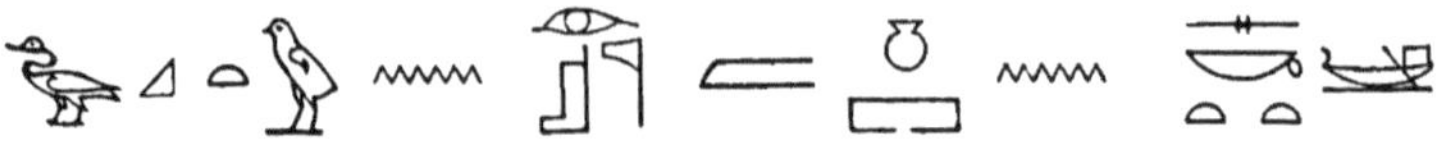

āq-tu en Ȧsȧr em-khen en Sektet

is brought in Osiris within the Sektet boat

er neter ḥet ten er . . . . en rĕnpit

to temple this at the time of the year

em neter ḥet ent Ȧḳer-bemret em

from the temple of Herakleion on

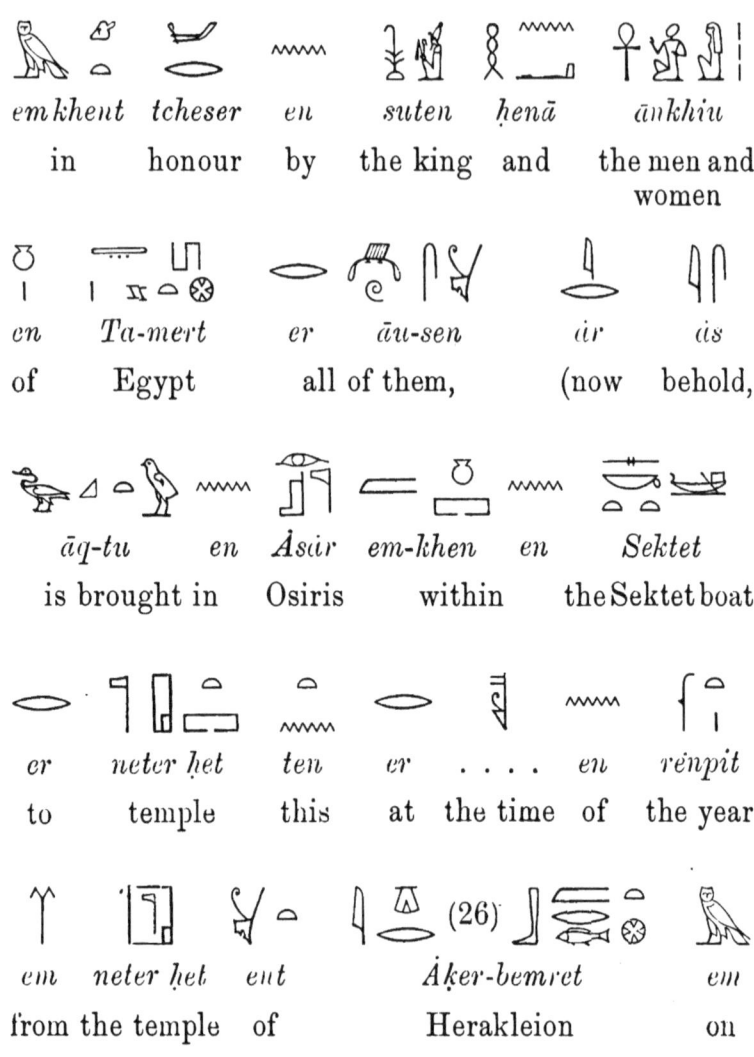

ȧbeṭ fṭu shat sesu tchaut pest ȧu ȧmmu

month four of Shat, day 29, [and] those who are in

maāu khentet er āu-sen ḥer ȧri qerer

the temples of the first class, all of them, make offerings by fire

ḥer khauti en maāu khentet ḥer

upon the altars of the temples of the first class on

unami semeḥi em kheft en neter ḥet then

the right and left of the front of temple this),

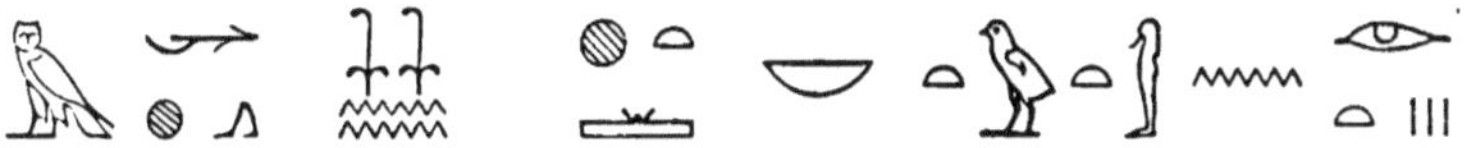

em-khet enen khet neb tut en ȧrit

after these things thing every which it was right to do

tcher ȧri-nes netert ḥer se-āb

to the end of making her a deity and the purification of

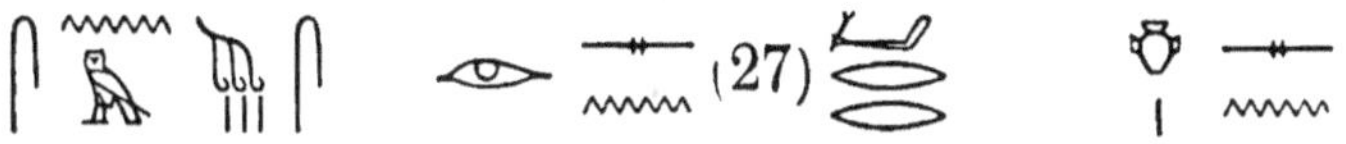

senem-s ȧri-sen serer ȧb-sen

the mourning for her they did, willing being their hearts

em seref mȧ sent en ȧri ḥer Ḥāp

with warm care, as it is customary to do for Apis

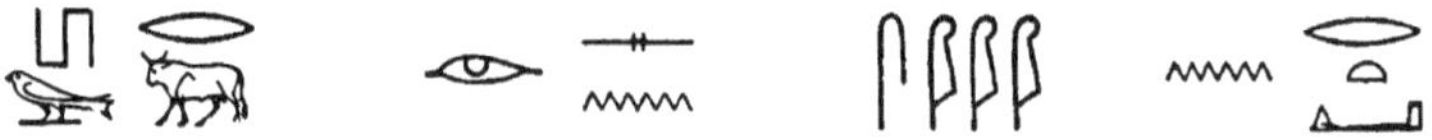

Mer-ur ȧri-sen semaāu en erṭāt

[and] Mnevis ; and they made a resolution to make

kheper meṭ peḥpeḥt en tchetta en ḥeqet

to be the word of renown for ever of Queen

Bereniḳat satet en neterui menkhui

Berenice, the daughter of the two Good-doing Gods,

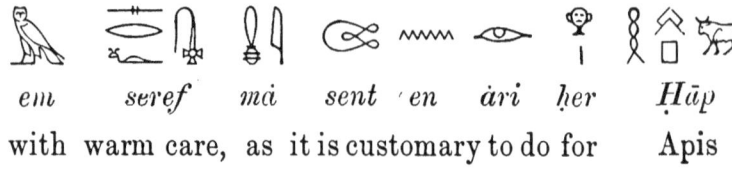

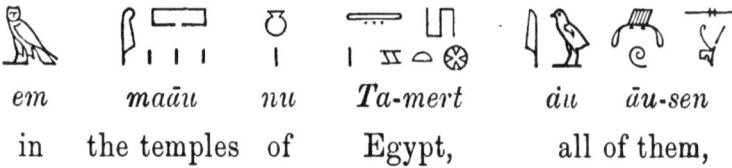

em maāu nu Ta-mert ȧu āu-sen

in the temples of Egypt, all of them,

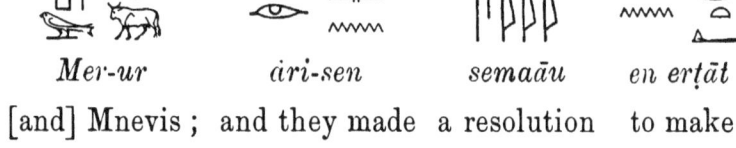

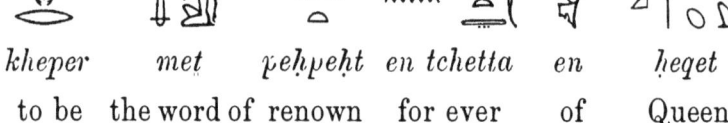

erenti khep āq-s emmā

and since it happened that she entered among

neteru em ṭep per ȧbeṭ pu

the gods in the first month of Per, the month to wit

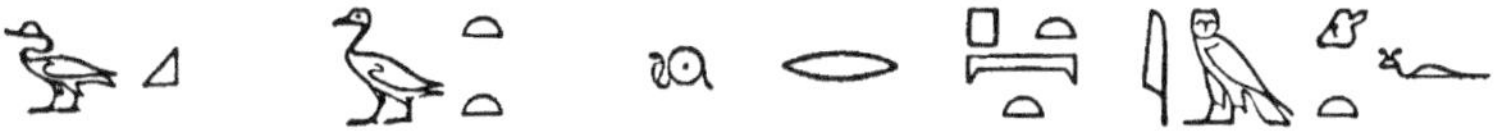

āq satet Rā er petet ȧm khent-f

entered the daughter of Rā into heaven, into it,

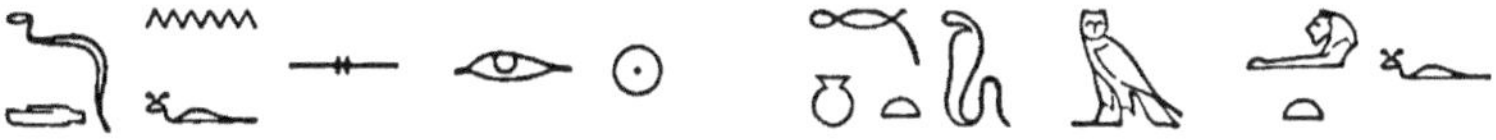

tcheṭ-nef-s maat Rā meḥenet em ḥāt-f

called he her "Eye of Rā, Meḥen crown on his brow,"

ḥer ren-s ḥer mer-nef-s ȧritu-nes

for her name, because he loved her, shall be made for her

ḥebu en khen em erpaut uru

festivals of procession in the temples great

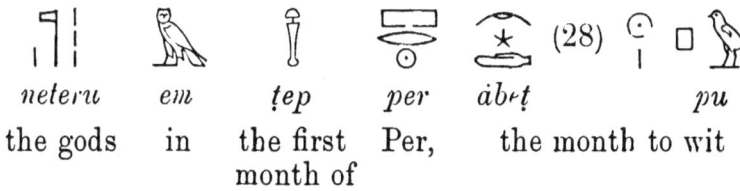

ȧmth maāu khentet em ȧbeṭ pen

among the temples of the first order in month this,

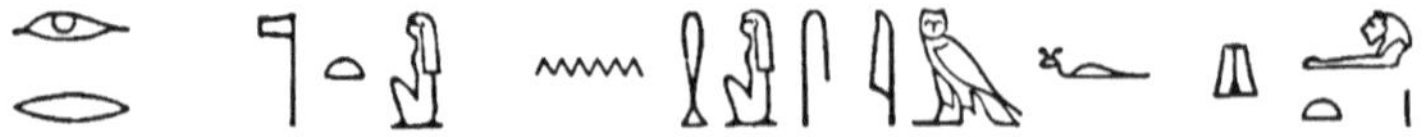

ȧri netert en ḥen-s ȧm-f kher ḥāt

was made a goddess her Majesty in it formerly;

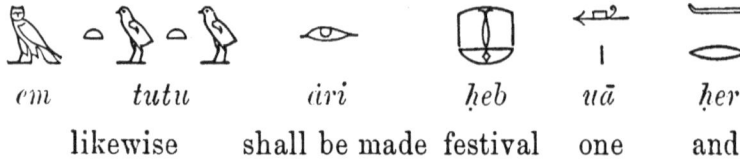

em tutu ȧri ḥeb uā ḥer

likewise shall be made festival one and

khen uā en ḥeqt Bereniḳat

procession one of the Queen Berenice,

(29)

sat-f en neterui menkhui em maāu nu

daughter of the two Good-doing Gods in the temples of

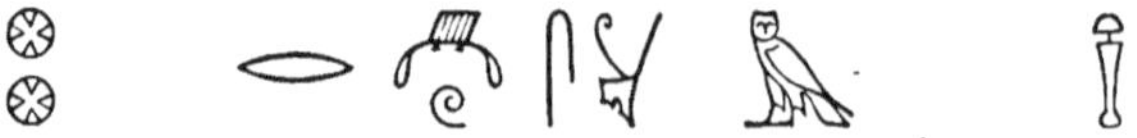

taui er āu-sen em ṭep

the North and South all of them in the first of month

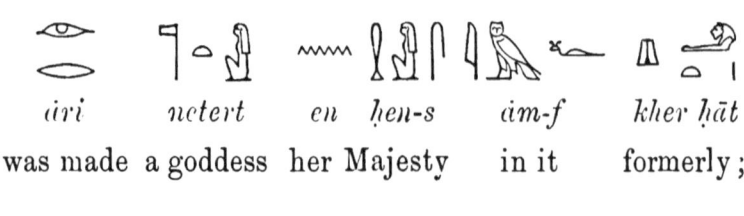

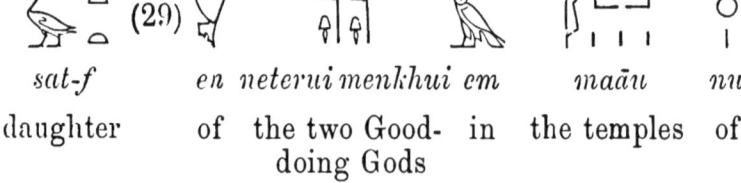

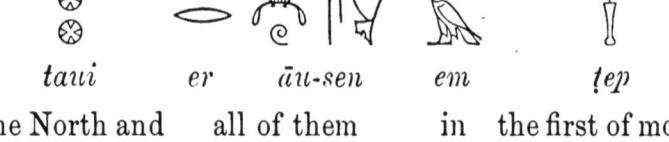

per shaā en hru x + vii ȧri

Per, beginning with day 17 [when] was made

khen-s *ḥer* *s-āb* *scnem-s*

procession her and the conclusion of her mourning

ám - f *em* *sep* *ṭep* *neferi* *er* *hru* *fṭu*

in it at time first, for days four;

emtutu *s-āḥā* *neter sesheshet* *en*

likewise shall be set up a divine statue of

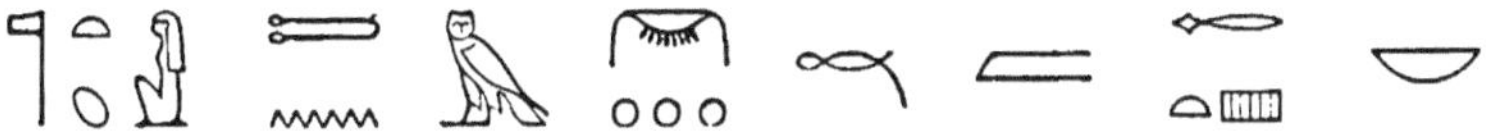

netert *then* *em* *nub* *meḥ* *em* *āat* *neb*

goddess this of gold filled with stone every

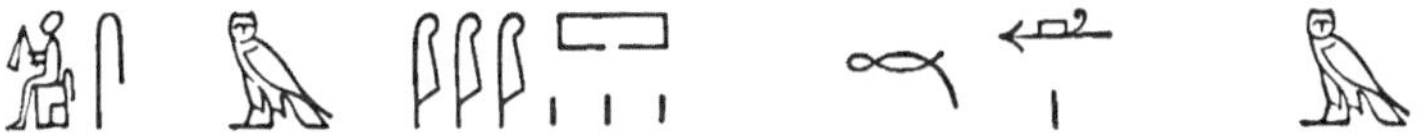

sheps *em* *maāu* *meḥ* *uā* *em*

precious in the temples of the first class, and in

mau *meḥ sen* *er* *ān-sen* *erṭā*

the temples of the second class all of them, and shall be placed

(30) 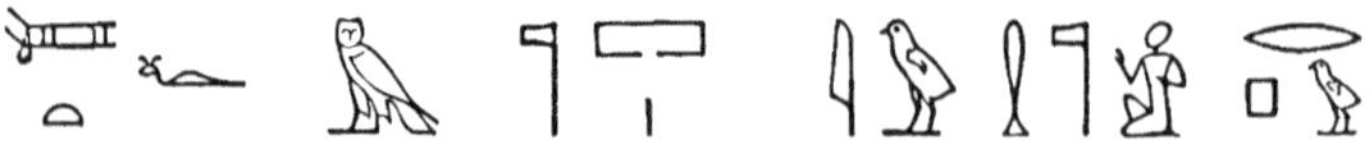

temt (?)-f em neter pa àu neter ḥen erpu

its pedestal in the temple; shall a prophet or

uā àmth ābu setep er āb

one among the priests chosen to make the libation

ur àu smār neteru em satet-sen

great and to array the gods in their ornaments

seḳāt-f ḥer ḥept-f em hru en

carry it on his arm on the day of

khāā ḥā ḥebu nu neter er āu-sen

the festival and the festivals of the god all of them,

erenti maa nebu nebt sen

so that may see people all that it is adored

em tcheser-f — *tcheṭ-tu nef* — *Berenikat*

according to its sanctity, — and it shall be called — Berenice

(31) 

ḥent renenet — *khāā* — *ȧs* — *un*

mistress of the virgins; the crown, behold, [which] shall be

ḥer — *ṭep* — *en* — *neter seshesh* — *pen* — *ȧn* — *setut*

on the head — of — divine image — this — shall not be the customary one

er — *un* — *ḥer* — *erpet* — *en* — *mut-s* — *netert*

[which] is on — the statues — of — her mother, — the goddess

Berenikat — *er* — *ȧritu-f* — *em* — *khamesu*

Berenice, — shall be made it with — ears of corn

sen — *ȧu* — *ārāt* — *ȧmth-sen* — *ȧu*

two, — shall be — an uraeus — between them, — shall be

uatch en ḥai em qa-s ḥa

a sceptre of papyrus plants in its height behind

ārāt then mȧ un em āāui

uraeus this, like [that which] is in the hands of

netert ȧu seṭ en ārāt ten

the goddesses, shall be the tail of uraeus this

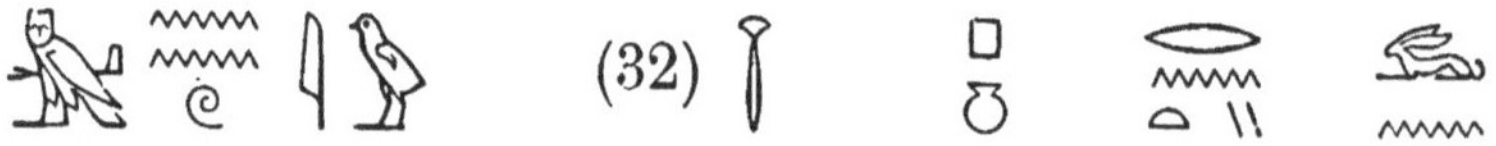

mānen ȧu (32) *uatch pen erenti un*

wound round sceptre this, so that shall

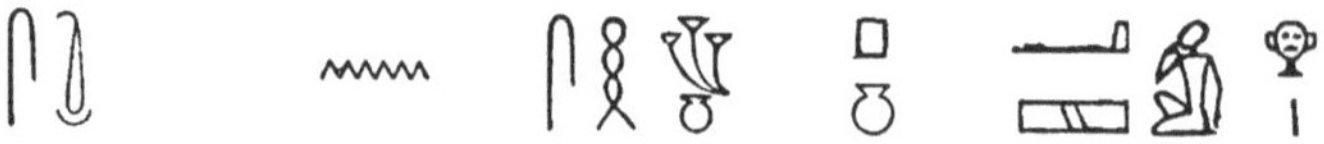

smen en seḥen pen āsh ḥer

the construction of crown this proclaim

ren en Berenikat ḥer net-f

the name of Berenice according to its symbols

em āнu nu pa-ānkh àu ḳert

in the writing of the House of Life. And moreover,

khā em hru nu Ḳaàubekh

at the festival in the days of Ḳaàubekh,

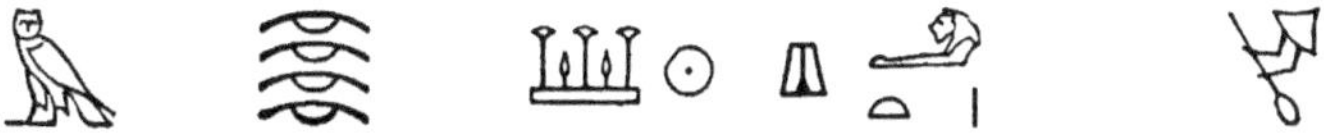

em àbeṭ fṭu Shat kher ḥāt khen

in month four of Shat, preceding the procession of

Àsàr erṭāt àn renenet ḥemt nu

Osiris, shall give the virgins [and] wives of

ābu ketut en erpet en

the priests another image of

Bereniḳat ḥent renenet àritu-nes

Berenice, mistress of virgins, shall be made to it

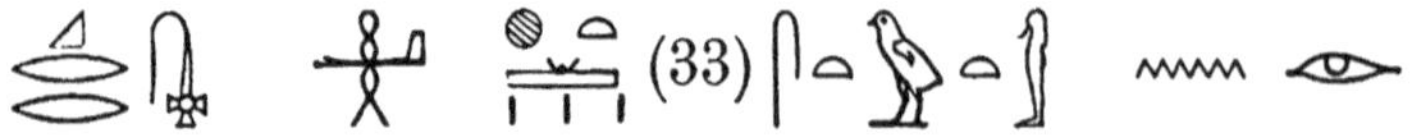

qerer ḥā khet setut en ȧri

burnt offerings and things which it is right to do

em hru nu ḥeb pen erenti un ȧs

on the days of festival this, so that, it may be, behold,

mā ketekh renenet ȧri em setut

with the other virgins to do what is right

enen en netert ten er mer-nes

in this matter to goddess this as they will.

ṭua-tu netert then ȧs ȧn qemāt

Shall be praised goddess this, behold, by the sacred women

setep er shems neteru khāā em khāāu

chosen for the service of the gods, to place the crowns

nu *neteru* *un-sen* *em* *ābut-sen*

of the gods, are they [therefore] their priestesses;

ȧr *ȧs* *qurt* *em* *ḥāt* *ȧru*

now, behold, [when there are] firstfruits thereupon

fa *khamesu* *ȧn* *qemāt*

shall be carried the ears of corn by the sacred women

ȧu *khentet* *ṭā* *en* *neter seshesh*

into the sanctuary and given to the divine image

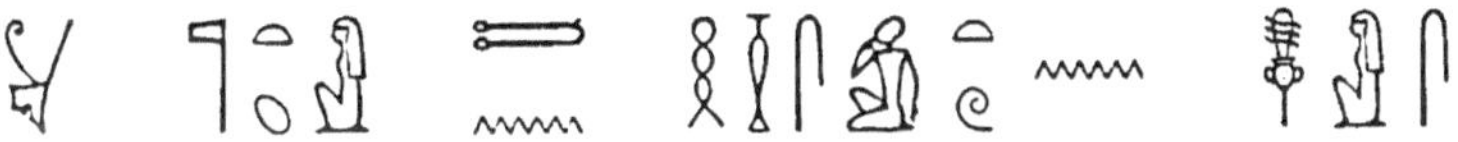

en *netert* *then* *ḥes-tu* *en* *seshesh-s*

of goddess this, shall be sung to her image

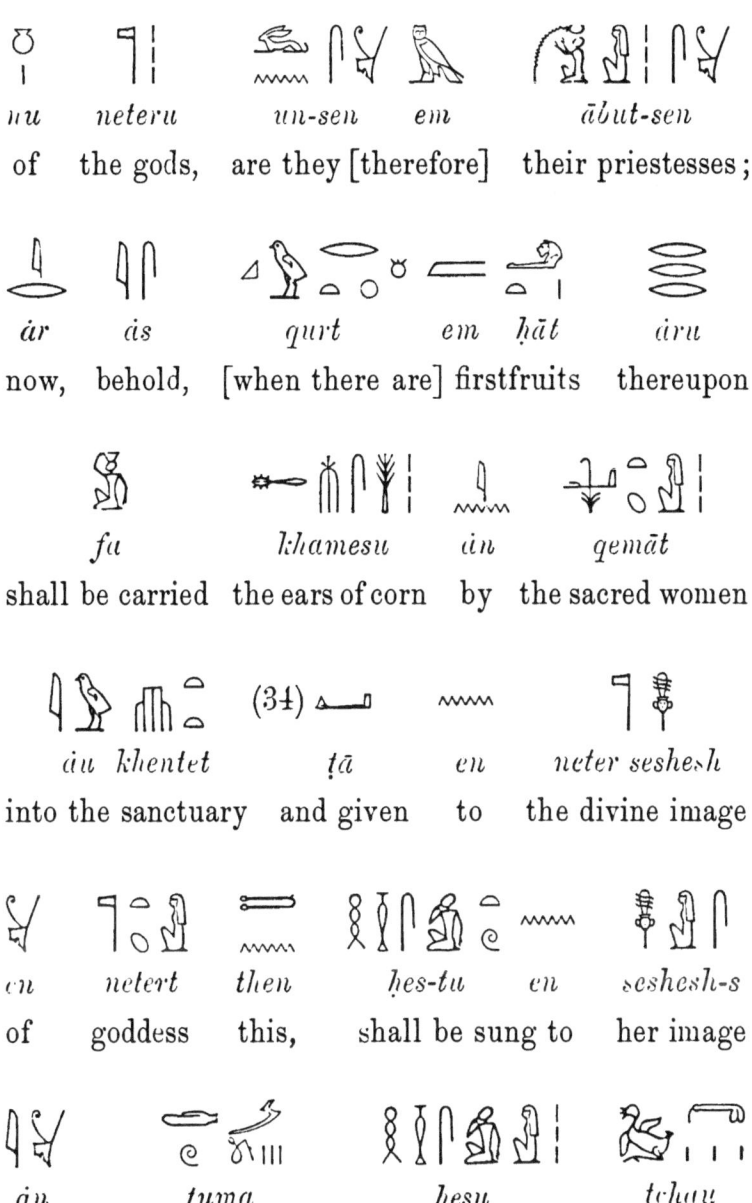

ȧn *ṭuma* *ḥesu* *tehau*

by the companies of singing women, and men

ḥemt	*em*	*khāā*	*ḥā*	*ḥebu*	*nu*	*neteru*
and women	at	feasts	and	processions	of	the gods

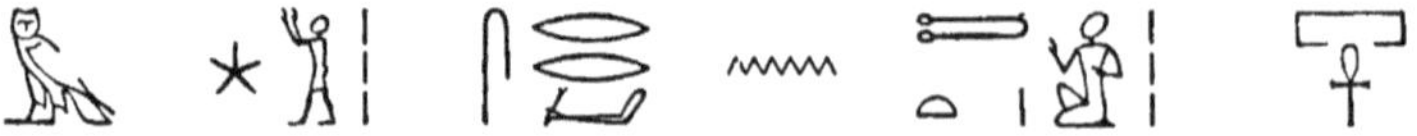

em	*ṭuau*	*serer*	*en*	*thet*	*pa ānkh*
with	hymns of praise	written	by	the learned men of	the House of Life,

ṭā	*en*	*ṭemseb*	*nu*	*ḥesu*
[and] given	to	the choir	of	singers,

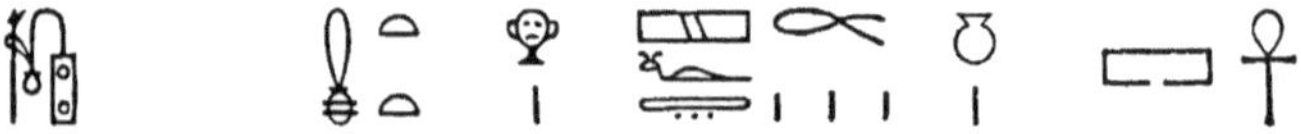

ān	*mȧtet*	*ḥer*	*shefta*	*nu*	*pa ānkh*
[and] inscribed	a copy	in	the books	of	the House of Life;

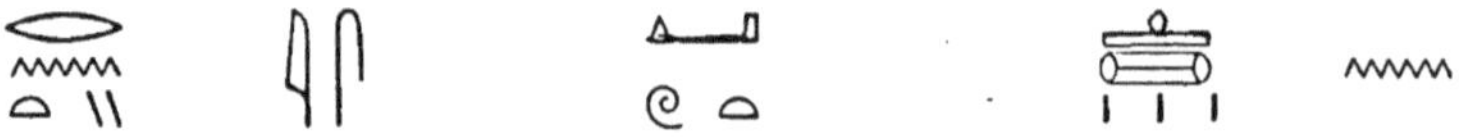

erenti	*ȧs*	*ṭātu*	*ḥetepu*	*en*
so that,	behold,	[when] shall be given	the offerings	of

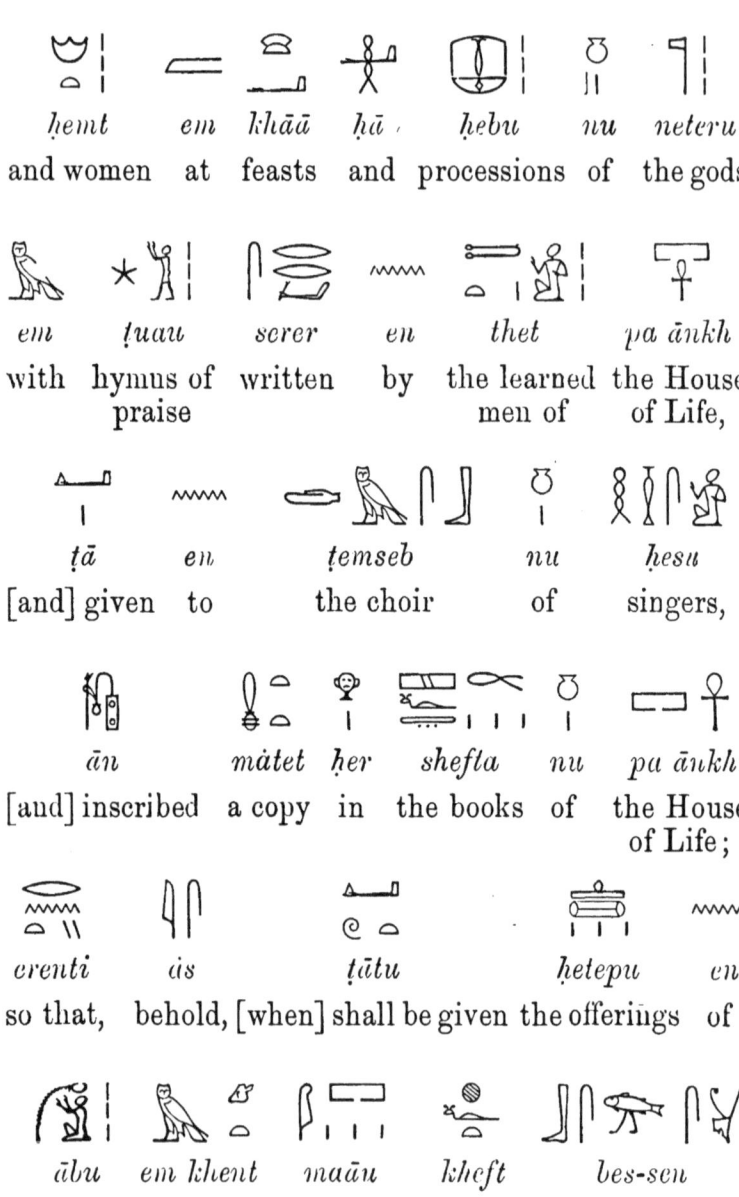

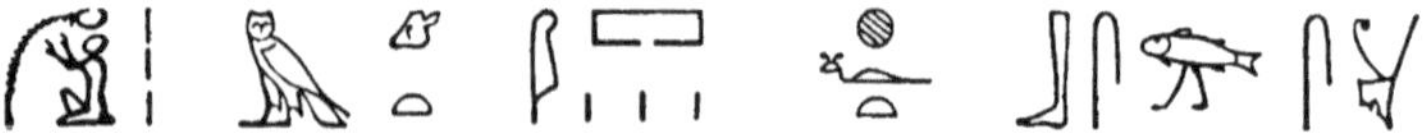

ābu	*em khent*	*maāu*	*kheft*	*bes-sen*
the priests	in	the temples,	when	they are made to enter in

(35) 

ȧn suten ȧu neter ḥet ȧu māi ṭāṭu

by the king in the temple, let there be given

kheru en mesu ḥemt nu ābu

food to the children female of the priests,

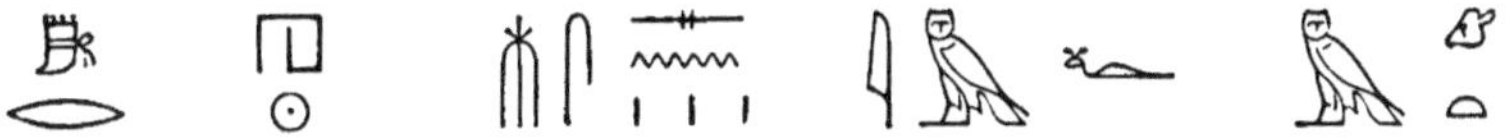

tcher hru mes-sen ȧm - f em khent

from the day were born they on it, from

neteru ḥetepu nu neteru em kheru

the divine offerings of the gods, the amount of food

ȧptu ȧn ābu netch-khet em

to be determined by the priests councillors in

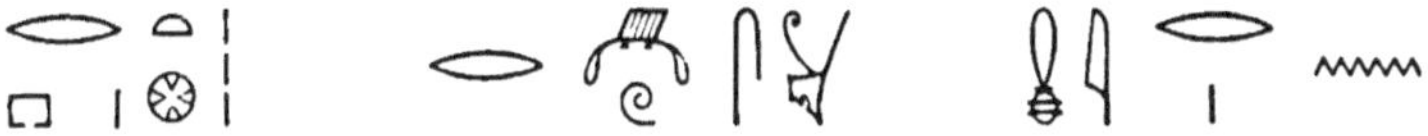

erpaut er āu-sen mā re en

the temples, the whole of them, in proportion to

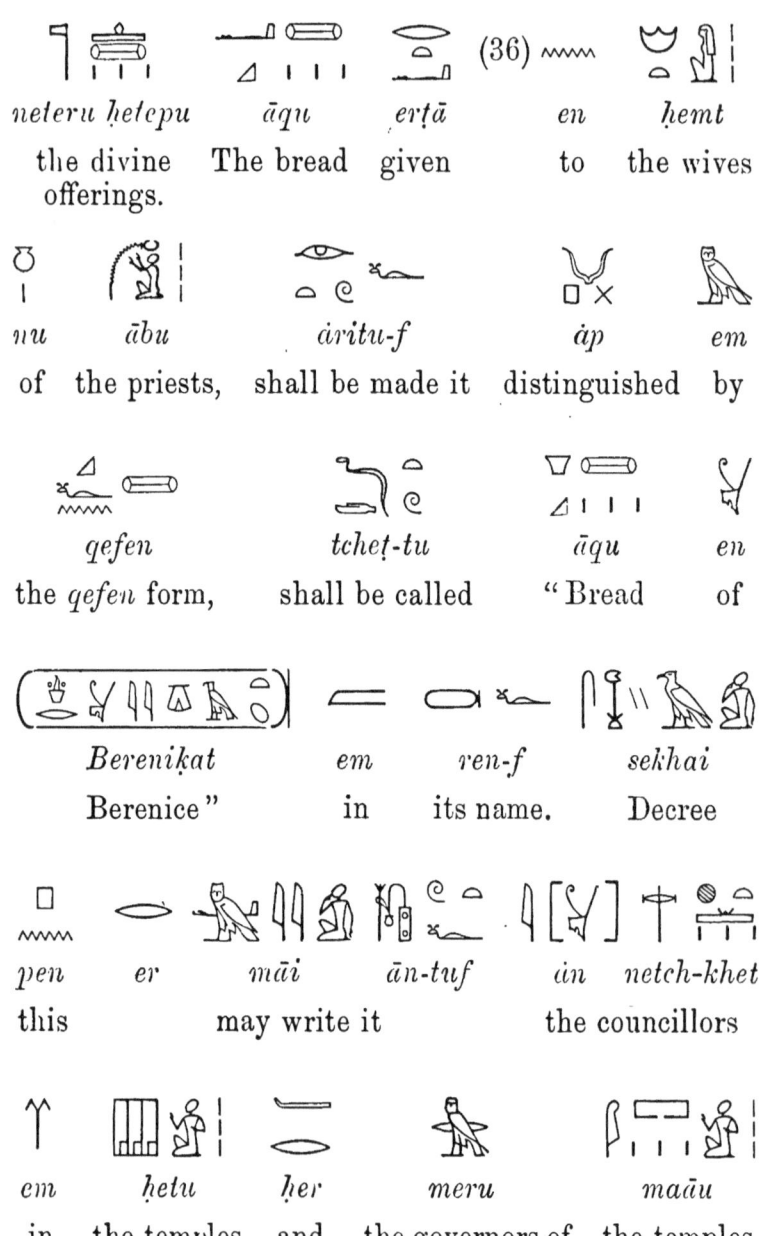

(36)

neteru ḥetepu	*āqu*	*erṭā*	*en*	*ḥemt*
the divine offerings.	The bread	given	to	the wives

nu	*ābu*	*àritu-f*	*àp*	*em*
of	the priests,	shall be made it	distinguished	by

qefen	*tchet-tu*	*āqu*	*en*
the *qefen* form,	shall be called	"Bread	of

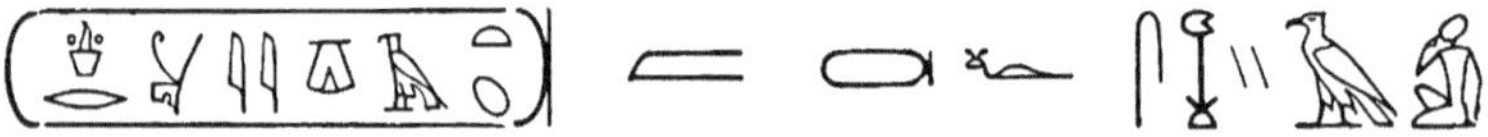

Bereniḳat	*em*	*ren-f*	*sekhai*
Berenice"	in	its name.	Decree

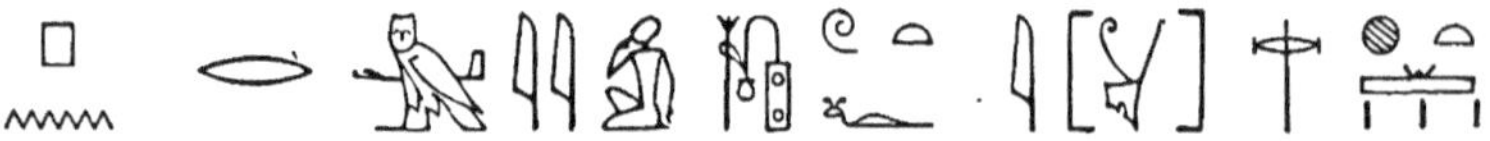

pen	*er*	*māi*	*ān-tuf*	*àn*	*netch-khet*
this		may write it			the councillors

em	*ḥetu*	*ḥer*	*meru*	*maāu*
in	the temples,	and	the governors of	the temples,

ḥā ānu nu neter ḥet khet ḥer

and the scribes of the temple [and] cut [it] on

(37)

utith en āner erpu ḥemt em khent

a stele of stone or bronze in

ān nu pa ānkh ān en

the writing of the House of Life, the writing of

shetet ān en Ḥa nebu

the books, the writing of the North-lords,

ertā āḥā-f em usekht rut

[and] make to stand it in the hall of the people

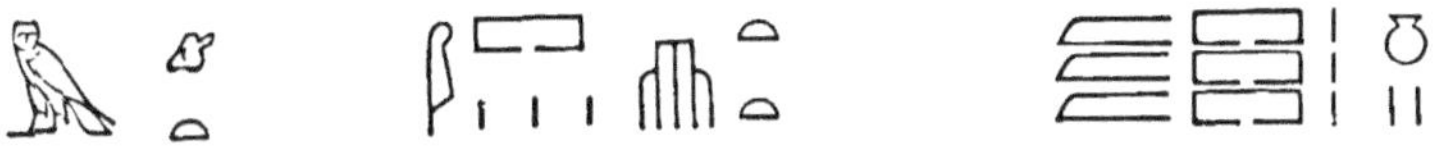

em khent maāu khentet maāu sen

in the temples of the first order, the temples of the second order,

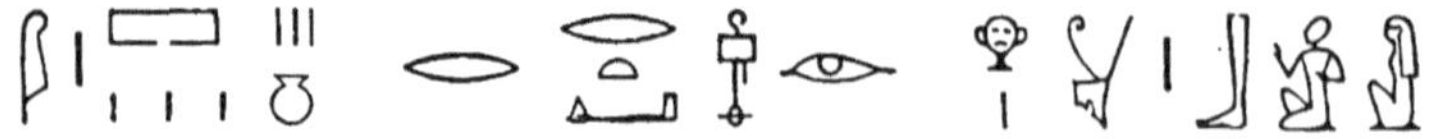

maāu khemet | *er* | *ertāt* | *ḥem* | *ḥrȧu-nebu*

the temples of the third order, | to make to know | persons

nebt | *em tcheser* | *ȧri* | *en* | *ābu* | *nu*

all | the honour | done | by | the priests | of

maāu | *Baqet* | *en* | *neterui menkhui* | *ḥā*

the temples of | Egypt | to | the two Good-doing Gods | and

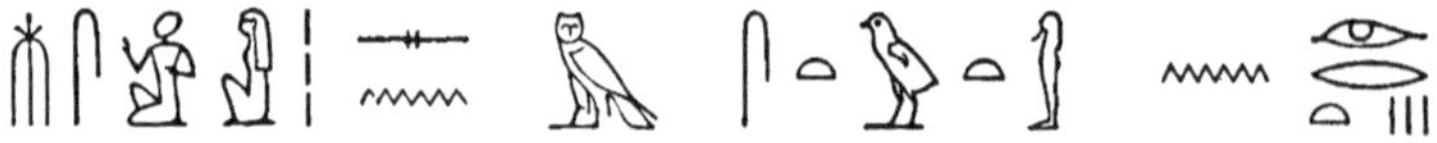

mesu sen | *em* | *setut* | *en* | *ȧritu*

their children | as | it is proper | to do [to them].

CHAPTER III.

GERMAN AND FRENCH TRANSLATIONS OF THE HIEROGLYPHIC TEXT OF THE DECREE OF CANOPUS.

I.—German Translation by Dr. R. Lepsius, Published in 1866.

(1) Jahr ix., Apellaeus Tag vii., Tybi Tag xvii. der Bewohner des Landes, unter der Regierung des Königs Ptolemaeus des unsterblichen, den Ptah liebenden, des Sohnes des Ptolemaeus (und der) Arsinoë der Götter Adelphen; Priester seiend des Alexander des gerechtfertigten und der Götter Adelphen und der Götter Euergeten Apollonides (2) Sohn des Moschion, seiend Menekrateia, die Tochter des Philammon, Trägerin des Korbes vor der Arsinoë Philadelphos; an diesem Tage (erfolgte) das Dekret: Seiend die Vorsteher der Tempel, die Propheten, die lustrirenden Priester beauftragt zu (3) bekleiden die Götter mit ihrem Schmucke, die Hierogrammaten, die Gelehrten, die heiligen Väter, (und) die Priester ihres Gleichen gekommen aus den Tempeln des obern und untern Landes auf den Dios Tag v., an welchem gefeiert wird das Geburtsfest seiner Majestät (an ihm), und Tag xxv. dieses Monats, an welchem übernahm seine Majestät

seine (4) hohe Wurde an Stelle seines Vaters (an ihm), versammelten sie sich in dem Tempel der Götter Euergeten, welcher ist in Kanopus, sprechend; dieweil sind der König Ptolemaeus, der unsterbliche, den Ptah liebende, der Sohn des Ptolemaeus und der Arsinoë, der Götter Adelphen, und die Fürstin Berenike, seine Schwester (und) Gemahlin, die Götter Euergeten, erzeigend (5) Wohlthaten, viele, grosse, den Tempeln des Landes zu aller Zeit, (und) erhebend Worte des Ruhms den Göttern immer mehr, sie sind aber auch, Sorge tragend zu jeder Zeit fur die Dinge des Apis (und) des Mneuis nebst den Thieren den heiligen allen beruhmt im Reiche, (und) geben grosse Dinge, aufwendend vieles (6) zur Herstellung ihrer Versorgung; (und) die gottlichen Bilder (betreffend), geraubt von den Barbaren von Persien aus dem Reiche, zog aus seine Majestat nach den beiden Ländern von Asien, rettete sie, brachte sie in die Heimath (und) gab sie ihrem Standorte in den Tempeln in (denen) sie standen ursprunglich; (und) er hielt in Frieden Aegypten zum (7) Vortheil kämpfend ausserhalb desselben in Thälern (und) Ebenen und vielen fremden Landern mit ihren Fursten (welche) sie beherrschen; (und) sie sind begluckend alle Menschen des Landes und aller Volker unter der Herrschaft ihrer Majestat; ferner auch als eintrat ein Jahr schwachen Nils in (8) ihrer Zeit, seiend alle Menschen des Reichs ihr Sinn niedergeschlagen uber das Geschehen, siehe, des Ereignisses, als sie sich erinnerten des Elends welches war in der

Zeit der fruheren Kŏnigs als geschah das Ereigniss eines schwachen Nils den Bewohnern des Landes in ihrer Zeit, waren seine Majestät selbst und seine Schwester (9) fursorgend in ihrem Herzen sehr fur die Bewohner der Tempel und die Bewohner des Reichs in seiner Ausdehnung; (und) sie waren uberlegend viel und viel (und) ihren Rucken kehrend vielen Angaben im Wunsche zu beleben die Menschen; (und) sie waren gestattend die Zufuhr von Getreide nach Aegypten aus dem östlichen Reten (Syrien), aus dem Lande Kaft (Phonizien) (und) aus der Insel Nebinai (Kypros) welche ist inmitten des (10) Meeres und vielen (andern) Ländern, gebend viel Geld zu seiner Bezahlung gestiegen (?) . . . ., rettend die Menschen die im heiligen Lande wohnen, (und) hinterlassend ihre Erinnerung ihrer Wohlthätigkeit fur ewige Zeit und ihrer vielen Tugenden angesichts der Gegenwartigen und der nach ihnen Kommenden—und es haben gewahrt die Gotter die Festigung ihrer Wurden in der Herrschaft uber Ober- und Unter-ägypten (11) fur dieses und werden belohnen mit Gutern allen Art fur ewige Zeit—Gluck und Heil—so sei beschlossen worden in ihrem Herzen von den Priestern des Landes, zu vergrössern die Ehre in vielen Dingen des Konigs Ptolemaeus, des unsterblichen den Ptah liebenden und der Furstin Berenike der Götter Euergeten in den Tempeln, und was geschah fur die Gotter Adelphen ihre Aeltern und was (12) geschah fur die Götter Soteren ihre Voraltern vergrössernd dieses, (dass) die

Priester nämlich, wohnend in allen Tempeln des ganzen Reichs, genannt werden Priester der Götter Euergeten mit ihrem Namen ausser mit dem Namen der Würden ihres Prophetenthums, (und) schreiben ihren Namen in allen Urkunden (und) eingraben die Würde eines Propheten der Götter Euergeten auf dem Ringe (welchen) fuhrt ihre Hand, (und dass) sie bilden eine andre (13) Phyle aus den Priestern welche sind in allen Tempeln, ausser den 4 Phylen existirend am heutigen Tage, welche genannt wird 5 Phyle der Götter Euergeten, weil geschah das glückliche Ereigniss, mit Gluck (und) Heil, der Geburt des Königs Ptolemaeus des unsterblichen, Ptah liebenden des Sohnes der Götter Adelphen am Dios Tag v., seiend wohl dieser Tag der Anfang nämlich (14) von grossen Gütern fur alle Menschen; (und dass) genommen werden (hierzu) die Priester, (welche) uberwiesen (sind) vom Konige den Tempeln seit dem Jahre i. seiner Majestät und welche sind gleicherweise uberwiesen bis zum Jahre ix. Mesori in diese Phyle, und ihre Kinder für ewige Zeit—die Priester namlich vorhanden vor ihnen bis zum Jahre i., seiend in den Phylen in welchen (15) sie waren (in ihnen) vordem, wie hinwiederum ihre Kinder von diesem Tage an fur ewige Zeit eingeschrieben in die Phylen in welchen ist ihr Vater (in ihnen)—(und) zu setzen an die Stelle von 20 Priestern Buleuten, gewahlt fur die Zeit des Jahres aus den 4 Phylen, bestehend aus 5 Personen von ihnen auf 1 Phyle, kreirend 25 Priester zu (16) Buleuten, seiend 5 Personen gebracht hinzu aus der Phyle v. der Gotter Euergeten; (und) zu geben Antheil denen in der Phyle v. der Götter Euergeten an demjenigen Allen was ist bestimmt zum Verrichten der Sühnung im Tempel und an allen Dingen unter ihrer Besorgung in den Tempeln; (und dass) ein Phylarch (sei) als Prophet in ihr, wie es ist in den andern 4 Phylen; (und) dieweil auch gefeiert wird eine Panegyrie (17) den Gottern Euergeten in allen Tempeln im Laufe eines jeden Monats am Tage v. (und) Tage ix. (und) Tage xxv. nach dem Inhalte des Dekretes (welches) publicirt (ist) fruher, und auch gefeiert wird eine Panegyrie den grossen Göttern als Volksfest allgemein im Lande zu seiner Zeit im Jahre, gleichfalls zu feiern ein Volksfest zu seiner Zeit im Jahre dem Könige Ptolemaeus, dem unsterblichen, Ptah liebenden, (18) und der Furstin Berenike, den Göttern Euergeten, in den Tempeln der beiden Lander und im ganzen Reiche am Tage des Aufgangs der göttlichen Sothis genannt Neujahr mit seinem Namen in den heiligen Schriften,—zugleich entspricht er im Jahre ix. dem Payni i. Tag i. in welchem Monat gefeiert wird die Panegyrie des Neujahrs (und) die Panegyrie der Bubastis und das Volksfest der Bubastis (in diesem Monat), gleichwie ist die Zeit des (19) Einsammelns aller Fruchte (und) das Steigen des Nils in ihm—; aber auch wenn ist das Ereigniss, siehe, einer Wanderung des Festes der gottlichen Sothis auf einen andern Tag während 4 Jahren, dass nicht vorubergegangen werde der Tag der Feier dieser Panegyrie deshalb, (sondern) dass er gefeiert werde nach seiner Weise am Payni Tag i. an welchem gefeiert wird die Panegyrie (an ihm) ebenso im Jahre ix.; (20) (und) gefeiert werde diese Panegyrie auf 5 Tage, bekranzt ihr Kopf mit Blumen (und) mit Schleifen, durch Opfer (und) durch Spendenbringen und alle Dinge die gebräuchlich sind zu thun; damit es geschehe aber auch zu ihren Jahreszeiten indem diese ihre Schuldigkeit thun jederzeit gemäss der Ordnung auf welche ist der Himmel gegrundet (auf sie) zu dieser Zeit, (21) (und) damit nicht einmal sich ereigne der Fall, dass es gebe Panegyrien allgemein im Lande, gefeiert im Winter, zu feiern im Sommer einstmals, wegen der Wanderung des Festes der göttlichen Sothis um einen Tag während 4 Jahren, dass es gebe andre Panegyrien aber, gefeiert im Sommer in diesem Augenblick, zu feiern im Winter, zu den Zeiten welche kommen, wie sich ereignete der Fall in den fruheren Zeiten (22) (und) da es ist der Fall nun auch, wenn nun bleibt das Jahr von 360 Tagen und den 5 Tagen gewohnt hinzugefugt zu werden zu ihnen am Ende, gleichfalls hinzuzufugen 1 Tag als Panegyrie der Götter Euergeten von jetzt an wahrend je vier Jahren hinter den 5 Epagomenen vor dem Neujahr; (damit) es werde bekannt dem ganzen Volke, dass was verkürzt war ein wenig an der Ordnung (23) der Jahreszeiten und des Jahres und der Bestimmungen welche sind in den Lehren der Wissenschaft von den Wegen des Himmels, gelang nun zu berichtigen und auszufullen durch die Götter Euergeten; da nun auch war eine

Tochter, geboren dem Könige Ptolemaeus dem unsterblichem Ptah liebenden und der Königin Berenike den Göttern Euergetem, genannt Berenike mit ihrem Namen, bestimmt sogleich zur Furstin, (24) da es sich ereignete nun (dass) diese Gottin, welche war Jungfrau, ging zum Himmel plötzlich, seiend die Priester, welche kommen aus dem Lande zum König alljahrlich, im Hause mit seiner Majestät, so machten sie eine grosse Trauer sogleich uber das Ereigniss welches geschehen, (und) waren beantragend vor dem Könige und der Fürstin (und) überredend sie, zu (25) vereinigen diese Göttin mit Osiris in dem Tempel von Kanopus, als welcher ist unter den Tempeln erster Ordnung (und) weil er (ist) gross unter (denen welche) sich auszeichnen in der Verehrung des Königs und der Menschen des ganzen Landes;—wenn aber (ist) die Ausfahrt des Osiris in dem heiligen Schiffe nach diesem Tempel zu seiner Zeit im Jahre aus dem Tempel vom (26) Herakleum am Choiak xxix., so sind die Bewohner aller Tempel erster Ordnung darbringend Brandopfer auf den Altären der Tempel Ister Ordnung rechts und links vom Dromos dieses Tempels; nachher (aber), alle Dinge gebrauchlich zu thun in Bezug auf ihre Vergötterung und die Suhnung ihrer Trauer, verrichtend sie (27) freigebig in ihren Herzen (und) mit Sorgfalt, wie es Sitte ist zu thun fur den Apis (und) den Mneuis, fassten sie den Beschluss zu gewahren dass geschehe die Verkundung des Ruhms fur immer der Fürstin Berenike Tochter der Götter Euergeten in den Tempeln des ganzen Landes; (und) da geschah ihr Gang zum Orte der Götter im Tybi, (28) das ist der Monat in welchem ging die Tochter des Ra zum Himmel (in ihm), welche er genannt hat (sie) Auge des Ra (und) Schlangendiadem an seiner Stirn mit ihrem Namen, da er sie liebte, (und) gefeiert wird ihr eine Panegyrie nebst einem Periplus in den grossen Tempeln unter den Tempeln 1. Ordnung in diesem Monat, in welchem war die Vergötterung ihrer Majestät (in ihm) vordem, gleichfalls zu feiern eine Panegyrie nebst einem Periplus der Fürstin Berenike Tochter (29) der Götter Euergeten in den Tempeln der beiden Länder sämmtlich, im Tybi vom Tage xvii. an welchem geschieht ihr Periplus und die Sühnung ihrer Trauer (an ihm) zum erstenmale, bis zu 4 Tagen, des gleichen aufzustellen ein göttliches Bild dieser Göttin aus Gold, verziert mit allerhand kostbaren Edelsteinen in den Tempeln 1. Ordnung (und) in den Tempeln 2. Ordnung sämmtlich (und) zu geben (30) seinen Platz im Heiligthume—es ist der Prophet oder einer von den Priestern, erwählt zur grossen Lustration und beauftragt zur Bekleidung der Götter mit ihren Schmuck, herumfuhrend es (das Bild) auf seinem Arm am Tage der Feste und Panegyrien der Götter sammtlich, damit es sei, gesehen vom ganzen Volke, angebetet nach seiner Ehre, welches genannt wird Berenike (31) Furstin der Jungfrauen—die Krone aber, seiend auf dem Haupte dieses Götterbildes nicht (wie es) gewöhnlich (ist) zu sein auf den Bildern ihrer Mutter der Königin Berenike, dass sie gemacht sei aus Aehren zwei, seiend eine Uräusschlange zwischen ihnen, seiend ein Szepter in Papyrusform in ihrer Höhe hinter dieser Schlange, wie es ist in den Handen der Göttinnen, seiend der Schwanz dieser Schlange gewunden (32) um dieses Szepter, damit sei die Anordnung dieses Kranzes gedeutet auf den Namen der Berenike nach seiner Regel in den heiligen Schriften; und das . . . . in den Tagen der Kikellien . . . . . im Choiak vor dem Periplus der Osiris besorgt werde von den Jungfrauen (und) Frauen der Priester eine andre Statue nach dem Bildniss (?) der Berenike Fürstin der Jungfrauen, (und) gemacht werde ihr ein Brandopfer und die Dinge, (33) welche hergebracht sind zu thun in den Tagen dieser Panegyrie; damit seien nun im Stande die andern Jungfrauen zu thun nach Gewohnheit hierbei dieser Göttin, wenn sie wollen; (und dass) besungen werde diese Göttin nun von den heiligen Jungfrauen erwahlt zum Dienste der Götter, anlegend die Diademe der Götter von denen sie sind (ihre) Priesterinnen; wenn ist aber die Fruhsaat bevorstehend, (dass) wiederum gebracht werden die Aehren von den heiligen Jungfrauen in das Heiligthum (und) (34) gegeben dem heiligen Bilde dieser Göttin; (und dass) gesungen werde ihrem Bilde (?) von den Chören (?) der Sänger Männern (und) Frauen an den Festen und Panegyrien der Götter mit Lobgesängen, aufgeschrieben von den Hierogrammaten (und) ubergeben den Gesanglehrern, (und) abgeschrieben in die heiligen Bucher; da aber gegeben wird der Unterhalt der Priestern in den Tempeln, sobald sie uberwiesen sind (35) vom König in den Tempel, dass möge gegeben werden der Unterhalt den weiblichen Kindern der Priester, seit dem Tage an welchem sie geboren sind (an ihm), aus den heiligen Einkünften der Götter, als Unterhalt zugebilligt von den Priestern Buleuten in allen Tempeln je nach der Proportion der heiligen Einkünfte; (und) das Brod, gegeben den (36) Frauen der Priester, bestempelt werden als Kefn, genannt das Brod der Berenike mit seinem Namen; dieses Dekret dass es möge geschrieben werden von den Buleuten der Tempel und den Tempelvorstehern und den Schreibern der Tempel, eingeschnitten auf eine (37) Stele von Stein oder Erz in heiliger Schrift, Schrift der Bucher (und) Schrift der Griechen, (und) aufgestellt werden im Versammlungssaale in den Tempeln 1. Ordnung, den Tempeln 2. Ordnung (und) den Tempeln 3. Ordnung, um zu geben Kenntniss dem ganzem Volke von der Ehre erwiesen von den Priestern der Tempel des Reichs den Göttern Euergeten und ihren Kindern, wie es recht ist zu thun.

II.—German Translation by S. Leo Reinisch and E. R. Roesler, Published in 1866.[1]

(1). Im Jahre ix. am 7. Apellaios, am 17. Tybi der Aegypter unter dem Könige Ober- und Unterägyptens

[1] *Die Zweisprachige Inschrift von Tanis zum ersten Male herausgegeben und uebersetzt*, Vienna, 1866.

Ptolemaos dem Ewiglebenden von Ptah Geliebten, Sohne des Ptolemaos und der Arsinoe, der Geschwister-Götter, da Priester des Königs Alexander, des Seligen, der Geschwister-Götter und der Wolthatigen Götter Appolloni- (2). des war, der Sohn des Moschion, und Menekrateia, die Tochter Philimmons Korbtragerin war vor der Königin Arsinoe, der Bruderliebenden, an diesem Tage erfolgte der Beschluss: Es sind die Tempelvorstände, die Propheten, die Priester, welche eintreten (3). ins Heiligtum der Götter zu deren Bekleidung, die Tempelschreiber, kundig der Dinge die göttlichen Vater und die (ubrigen) Priester nach ihrem Range zusammengekommen aus Ober- und Unter-agypten zum 5. Dios an welchem gefeiert wird das Geburtsfest Seiner Majestat, und zum 25. Tag desselben Monats, an welchem ubernommen hat Seine Majestat (4). das Königtum von seinem Vater: sie traten in das Gotteshaus der Wolthätigen Götter, welches sich befindet in Phagotha (Kanopus), um anzuordnen: "Da der König Ptolemaos der Ewiglebende von Ptah Geliebte, Sohn des Ptolemaos und der Arsinoe, der Geschwister-Götter und die Königin Berenike, seine Schwester und Gemahlin, die Wolthatigen Götter, zugewendet haben Wolthaten (5). viele und grosse den Tempeln Aegyptens fur alle Zeit; da sie angeordnet haben wirksame Gebete zu dem Göttern in überaus grosser Zahl; da sie Sorge getragen haben immerdar fur den Unterhalt des Apis, des Mnevis und aller Tempelthiere, welche Schutz geniessen in

Aegypten, denen sie anwiesen Gaben in Menge und von sorgfaltiger Auswahl; (6). da sie zugeführt haben ihrer Verehrung die Gotterstatuen, welche geraubt wurden von den Barbaren des Landes Persien aus den Tempeln Aegyptens, indem Seine Majestät auf seinem Feldzuge gegen Asien dieselben zurückerbeutete, nach Aegypten brachte und sie auf ihrem Platze in den Tempeln aufstellte, wo sie vorher gestanden hatten; da er Aegypten erhalten hat in Frieden, (7). indem er Krieg fuhrte für dessen Wol im Auslande, und zu Felde zog gegen viele Völker und deren Häupter, und gesetzliche Zustände gegeben hat denen, welche leben in Unterthänigkeit, sowol allen Bewohnern Aegyptens, als auch aller Länder, welche unterthan sind Ihren Majestaten; da ferner das Wasser des steigenden Nil hinter seiner jahrlichen Linie einst zurückblieb wahrend (8). Ihrer Regierungszeit, und allen Bewohnern Aegyptens ihr Herz schwach wurde uber dieses Ereignis, - denn siehe, durch die Erinnerung trat vor ihre Gedanken das Sterben, welches einst gekommen war in der Zeit der ersten Könige in Folge von Eintreten einer nur unzulanglichen Nilflut uber die Bewohner Aegyptens—, da nun damals Seine Majestät selbst, als auch seine Schwester (9). und Gemahlin Sorge getragen haben in ihren Herzen, welche brannten für die Bewohner der Tempel und für die Bewohner Aegyptens in seiner ganzen Weite, die in grosser Drangsal des Herzens waren, indem sie gewährten ihrerseits Nachsicht auf beträchtliche Steuern in der

Absicht, zu retten das Leben der Menschen, als auch Sorge trugen für Getreideeinfuhr nach Aegypten aus dem östlichen Rutunnu (Syrien), aus dem Lande Kafatha (Phönicien), aus der Insel Nabynai (Cypern), welche liegt im grossen Meere, (10). und aus vielen (andern) Landern, indem sie ausgaben viel Weissgold und zur Vergeltung dafur anordneten Einfuhr von Lebensmitteln, um zu retten das Leben der Menschen, welche wohnen im Lande Aegypten, auf dass diese erkennen möchten deren Güte fur immer und ewig und wodurch sie sich bereitet haben ein mächtiges Andenken an sie bei den Lebenden und denen, welche nach ihnen kommen und wofür ihnen verleihen werden die Götter den Bestand Ihrer Herrlichkeit und Herrschaft uber Ober- und Unterägypten zur Vergeltung (11). dafur und Ihrer Güter im Glanze in deren Wachstum bis in Ewigkeit: so haben daher mit Heil und Segen die Priester Aegyptens beschlossen zu vermehren die Ausübung wirksamer Ceremonien fur den König Ptolemäos den Ewiglebenden von Ptah Geliebten und fur die Konigin Berenike, die Wolthatigen Götter, in deren Tempeln und fur die Eltern, die Geschwister-Götter, deren Erzeuger, und fur (12). (deren) Eltern, die Rettenden Götter, und haben angeordnet eine Vermehrung der Priester derselben in allen Tempeln Aegyptens in seiner ganzen Weite, und sie sollten genannt werden Priester der Wolthatigen Götter mit ihrem Namen, da sie einen hoheren Rang behaupten durch den Namen ihres Amtes; und den Propheten derselben solle man einschreiben in alle Documente, und es solle eingeschnitten werden der Titel des Propheten der Wolthätigen Götter in den Ring, welchen sie auf ihrer Hand tragen, und sie sollen bilden eine weitere (13). Kaste der bestehenden Priester, welche leben in sämmtlichen Tempeln, und sie soll hinzugefügt werden zu den 4 Kasten, welche bestanden bis auf diesen Tag, und soll genannt werden die 5. Kaste der Wolthätigen Götter. Und da sich ereignet hat die glückliche und segensreiche Fügung der Geburt des Königs Ptolemäos des Ewiglebenden von Ptah Geliebten, Sohns der Geschwister-Götter am 5. Dios, so sei es dieser Tag, weil er wurde (14). eine Quelle schon vielen Woles für alle Menschen, von welchem an die Priester, welche eingesetzt hat der König in die Tempel von diesem ersten Jahre Seiner Majestät an, und welche eingesetzt worden sind bis zum Monat Mesore des 9. Jahres, gerechnet werden sollen zu dieser Kaste und ebenso deren Kinder fur ewig und immerdar; die Priester aber, welche bestanden vor dem Anfange Jener bis zum ersten Jahre, verbleiben in den Kasten, (15) in welchen sie vordem waren, wie auch deren Kinder von diesem Tage an bis in Ewigkeit in den Schriften einzutragen sind in diejenigen Kasten, in welchen sich befinden ihre Väter. Und es seien an Stelle der 20 Priesterräte, welche jährlich erwählt werden für die Dauer eines Jahres aus den 4 Kasten, indem 5 Mann von ihnen aus je einer Kaste genommen werden, zu ernennen 25 Priester (16) zu Räten, da 5 Männer zuzunehmen sind aus der vermehrten 5. Kaste der Wolthätigen Götter; man soll Antheil gewähren den Angehörigen der 5. Kaste der Wolthätigen Götter an allen Gaben, welche erwachsen aus der Verrichtung des Opfers im Tempel und aller Ceremonien, und ihr Vorsteher in den Reichstempeln sei Chef der Kaste und Prophet in derselben, wie dies der Fall ist bei den 4 anderen Kasten. Indem bereits gefeiert wird ein Fest (17). der Wolthätigen Götter in allen Tempeln in jedem Monat am 5., 9. und 25. Tage in Folge eines Beschlusses, welcher früher gefasst worden ist, und in gleicher Weise, wie begangen wird eine Panegyrie der grossen Götter und ein allgemeines Fest in Aegypten gefeiert wird jährlich zu seiner Zeit, auf dieselbe Weise werde ein grosses Fest veranstaltet zu seiner Zeit dem König Ptolemäos dem Ewiglebenden von Ptah Geliebten (18). und der Königin Berenike, der Wolthätigen Göttern, im Ober- und Unterlande und durch Aegypten in seiner Weite am Tage des Aufgangs der göttlichen Sothis, welcher genannt wird das Neujahr mit seinem Namen in den Tempelschriften. In der Gegenwart findet er statt in diesem 9. Jahre am 1. Tage des Payni, in welchem Monat auch begangen wird das Fest des Neujahrs, der Bast und das grosse Fest der Bast, und in welchem auch die Zeit ist für das (19). Einsammeln aller Früchte und das Steigen des Niles. Da nun aber der Fall eintreten wird, das vorschreitet der Aufgang der Sothis zu einem andern Tage nach jedem 4. Jahre, so soll nicht verlegt werden der Tag der Feier dieses Festes, sondern man feiere es in gleicher Weise am 1. Tage des Payni und es werde begangen das Fest an demselben wie im Jahre (20). neun; und man feiere dieses Fest 5 Tage lang: Kränze aus Blumen lege man auf die Opferstätte am Altare, und vollbringe die Opfer und aller Ceremonien nach Anordung von Vorschriften. Damit aber geschehe, dass diese Festtage gefeiert werden in ihren bestimmten Jahreszeiten nach Anordnung ihrer Wachter immerdar und nach dem Plane, nach welchem der Himmel eingetheilt ist heut zu Tage, (21). und damit nicht eintrete der Fall, dass Feste, welche allgemein gefeiert werden in Aegypten und jetzt begangen werden im Winter, zu einer Zeit gefeiert werden im Sommer wegen des Vorrückens des Aufganges der göttlichen Sothis um 1 Tag in Laufe von 4 Jahren, und andere Feste welche begangen werden zur Sommerszeit in diesem Lande, gefeiert werden im Winter in Zeiten, welche kommen werden, gleichwie es sich schon ereignete in Zeiten, (22). welche verflossen sind, so geschehe nun also; indem fortbestehe das Jahr mit den 360 Tagen und 5 Tagen; welche jenen hinzugefügt wurden am Schlusse, so werde jetzt 1 Tag als Fest der Wolthätigen Götter von diesem Tage an nach Ablauf von 4 Jahren und der 5 Schalttage eingefügt vor dem Neujahr, wodurch erfahren sollen alle Menschen, dass die frühere Lehre in den Büchern in Bezug auf die Jahres- (23). zeiten und das Jahr, ebenso die Meinungen, welche enthalten sind in den

Schriften der Gelehrten über die Wege des Himmels, nun behoben, da sie geprüft und verbessert worden sind durch die Wolthätigen Götter. Und nachdem eine Tochter, welche geboren wurde dem Könige Ptolemäos dem Ewiglebenden von Ptah Geliebten und der Herrin der beiden Länder Berenike, den Wolthätigen Göttern, welche gleichfalls genannt wurde Berenike mit ihrem Namen und ausgerufen wurde als Königin, (24). da also diese Göttin in noch jungfräulichen Zustande eingegangen war zum Himmel gegen Vermuten, da haben die Priester, welche gekommen waren aus dem Lande zum König und ein Jahr verweilten bei Seiner Majestät, angestellt ein grosses Trauern auf der Stelle uber dieses Ereignis und kamen mit der Bitte vor den König und die Königin, um es zu legen an ihr Herz, dass sie genehmigen möchten (25). die Beisetzung dieser Göttin bei dem Gotte Osiris in Tempel von Phagotha (Kanopus), welcher ist ein Heiligtum unter den Tempeln ersten Ranges, weil er der angesehenste unter ihnen ist und ihn in gleicher Weise ehren der König und die Bewohner Aegyptens in seiner ganzen Weite; auch findet der Einzug des Osiris auf dem heiligen Schiffe in diesen Tempel jährlich zur bestimmten Zeit statt aus dem Tempel von Agar- (26). bamara (Herakleion) aus, im Monat Choiach am 29. Tage, und die Bewohner der Tempel ersten Ranges in ihrer Gesammtzahl bringen Brandopfer dar auf den Altären der Tempel ersten Ranges zur rechten und linken Seite im Angesichte dieses Heiligtumes. Und nachdem alle Ceremonien in üblicher Weise verrichtet waren, welche sie ihr verrichtet hatten als Göttin dá reinigten sie sich von der Trauer um sie, welche sie ihr veranstaltet hatten, (27). und heiligten ihre Herzen durch flammendes Feuer, gleichwie nach der Beisetzung des Apis und des Mnevis, und sie beschlossen als zu Recht, dass ausgesprochen werde eine Anbetung ewiger Dauer der Königin Berenike, der Tochter der Wolthätigen Götter, in den Tempeln von Aegypten in seiner ganzen Weite. Und da sich zugetragen hat ihre Eingang zu den Göttern im Monat Tybi, im selben Monat und (28). am selben Tage, an welchem auch einzog die Tochter des Ra in dem Himmel, wo er sie benannt "das volle Auge der Uräusschlange auf seiner Stern" mit ihrem Namen, und in seiner Liebe zu ihr anordnete, ihr Feste und eine Procession zu feiern in den Haupttempeln des Landes und in den Heiligtümern erstern Ranges in dem Monate, in welchem für die Göttin ihr Apotheose anfänglich erfolgte; also werde auch angeordnet ein Fest und eine Procession der Königin Berenike, der Tochter (29). der Wolthätigen Götter, in den Tempeln beider Länder nach deren Ausdehnung im Monat Tybi vom 17. Tage an, an welchem die Procession für sie erfolgte und die Reinigung vollzogen wurde wegen der Trauer um sie, durch 4 Tage,[1] auch soll man aufrichten ein Standbild dieser Göttin aus Gold, besetzt mit allerlei kostbaren

[1] Wörtlich: vom ersten Tage an bis zum Tage vier.

Steinen in den Tempeln der ersten und in den Heiligtümern des zweiten Ranges nach deren Gesammtzahl und es sei (30). der Standort desselben im verborgenen Heiligtum des Tempels. Und der Prophet auf dem heiligen Schiffe sammt den Priestern, welche anserkoren sind zur Verrichtung des grossen Opfers und den Priestern, welche ins Heiligtum der Götter gelangen zu deren Bekleidung, trage es auf seinen Händen am Tage der Umzüge und der Fest der Götter in ihrer Gesammtheit, auf dass alle Menschen in Anbetung auf der Erde liegend schauen seine Heiligekeit, und es werde genannt das Standbild Berenikens, (31) der Königin der Jungfrauen. Und die Krone, welche sitzen soll auf dem Haupte dieses Standbildes, sei nicht nach der Weise der Krone auf dem Haupt der Bildnisse ihrer Mutter, der Königin Berenike; sie bestehe aus zwei Aehrenstielen und die Uräusschlange reckt sich empor zwischen diesen und ein Scepter von Papyrus von deren Höhe befindet sich hinter dieser Uräusschlange, gleichwie die Scepter sind in den Händen der Göttinen, und der Schweif der Uräusschlange sei gewunden um (32). dieses Scepter, weil kund werden soll durch diese Verschlingung der Ruf des Namens Berenike aus seiner tiefen Bedeutung in der Hieroglyphenschrift. Und wann feierlich begangen werden die Tage von Gaaubach im Monat Choiach von dem Umzuge des Osiris, dann soll von den jungfräulichen Töchtern und Frauen der Priester zurechtgemacht werden ein anderes Bilduiss

Berenikens, der Königin der Jungfrauen, und sie sollen diesem Opfer bringen und es durch Ceremonien ehren, (33) wie es sich gebührt zu thun an den Tagen dieses Festes; und es werde gestattet, dass auch andere Jungfrauen bezeugen die gebührenden Ehren dieser Göttin. Und es werde besungen diese Göttin von Sängerinnen, welche auserkoren sind zum Dienste der Götter, und tragen die Kronen der Götter deren Priesterinnen sie sind. Und wenn eintritt eine Frühsaat, dann sollen auch Aehren bringen die Priesterinnen in das Heiligtum, (34). und sie sollen sie legen zum Standbilde dieser Göttin, und es werde besungen ihre göttliche Kraft von einen Chore singender Männer und Frauen, gleichwie es geschieht an den Festen und Panegyrien der Götter, in einem Hymnus, welchen die Tempelschreiber aufgeschrieben und übergeben haben werden dem Meister des Gesanges, und derselbe solle zugleich auch eingeschrieben in die heiligen Tempelschriften. Und da verabreicht werden Lebensmittel an die Priester aus dem Besitztum der Tempel, nachdem dieselben eingesetzt worden sind (35). vom König in das Tempelhaus, so sollen von nun an auch verabfolgt werden Nahrungsmittel an die Töchter der Priester von dem Tage an, an welchem sie geboren worden sind, aus den heiligen Besitztümern der Götter; und diese verabreichten Gaben werden gezählt und aufgeschrieben von den Priesterräten in den Tempeln der beiden Lander in deren Weite nach Art der Listen uber die

Tempeleinkünfte. Und das Brod, welches verabreicht werden soll (36) an die Frauen der Priester, seine Zubereitung und das Gewicht geschehe nach einer heiligen Form (*qafan*) und werde genannt das Brod Berenikens mit seinem Namen. Dieser Beschluss nun werde aufgeschrieben von den Priesterräten, welche wohnen in den Tempelhäusern, und von den Tempelvorständen und von den Tempelschreibern und werde eingeschnitten in eine Stele (37). aus Stein oder Erz in Hieroglyphenschrift, in der Bucherschrift und in der Schrift der Griechen, und die Stele werde aufgerichtet in der grossen allen Menschen zuganglichen Tempelhalle in den Tempeln ersten, zweiten und dritten Ranges, auf dass kund werde allen Menschen die Verehrung der Priester in den Tempeln Aegyptens für die Wolthatigen Götter und fur deren Kinder, wie es gebührend ist zu thun."

III.—French Translation made by P. Pierret, Published in 1881.

L'an ix. le 7 d'Apellaios, répondant au 17 du premier mois de la saison des semailles des Égyptiens, du règne de Ptolémée, fils de Ptolémée et d'Arsinoë, dieux Adelphes, Appollonides, fils de Moskion, étant prêtre d'Alexandre, des dieux frères et des dieux Evergètes, et Menekrateia, fille de Philammon étant canéphore d'Arsinoe philadelphe, ce jour là, *décret :*

Les chefs de temple, les prophètes, les initiés, les purificateurs, ceux qui enveloppent les dieux de leurs étoffes, les hiérogrammates, les savants, les divins pères, enfin tous les prêtres venus des temples du sud et du nord le 5 de Dios jour de la célébration de la fête de Sa Majesté, et le 25 du même mois, jour auquel Sa Majesté reçut de son père le pouvoir suprême,—se réunirent dans le temple des dieux Evergètes qui est à Pakot pour dire :

Attendu que le roi Ptolémée, fils de Ptolémée et d'Arsinoë, ainsi que la reine Bêrênice, sa femme, dieux Evergètes, comblent perpétuellement de leurs bienfaits les temples de l'Égypte, prodiguent les plus grands honneurs aux dieux, sont constamment pleins de sollicitude pour le culte d'Apis, de Mnêvis et de tous les animaux vénérés dans tous les temples de l'Égypte et font beaucoup de dons pour leur entretien et leur approvisionnement ;

Attendu que les Perses ayant emporté hors de l'Égypte les images des dieux, Sa Majesté s'en est allée en Asie, les a délivrées, les a rapportées en Égypte et les a remises dans les temples aux lieux d'où elles avaient été déplacées ;

Attendu que Sa Majesté a sauvé le pays des perturbations en guerroyant au dehors dans des contrées lointaines, contre des peuples nombreux et leurs chefs ;

Attendu que le roi et la reine sont équitables pour tous les habitants de l'Égypte et des pays placés sous leur dépendance ;

Attendu qu'en une année d'inondation insuffisante, sous leur règne, le coeur des habitants étant três affligé de cet événement à cause des désastres survenus au temps des premiers rois par le fait d'un Nil insuffisant, le roi en personne et sa soeur furent pleins de sollicitude et de zèle pour les habitants des temples et tous les Égyptiens, s'en préoccupèrent extrêmement, firent l'abandon de nombreux impôts pour laisser vivre les hommes, firent importer en Égypte des grains du Routen oriental, de la Phénicie, de l'ile de Chypre située au sein de la mer, ainsi que de nombreuses régions, ce qui leur coûta beaucoup d'argent en raison du prix élevé des transports, cela pour sauver les habitants du pays; attendu qu'ils ont ainsi fait connaître pour toujours leurs bienfaits et leurs nombreuses vertus aux contemporains et à la postérité,

Qu'en échange les dieux ont affermi leur pouvoir et les récompensent par un bonheur complet et éternel,

SALUT ET FORCE!

Les prêtres décident :

Qu'on augmentera les honneurs à rendre dans les temples au roi Ptolémée et à la reine Bérénice, dieux Evergètes, ainsi qu'à leurs pêre et mère, les dieux Adelphes et aux dieux Soters, père et mêre de leurs pêre et mère ;

Que pour augmenter ces honneurs, les prêtres de tous les temples seront nommés prêtres des dieux Evergètes sur le cachet qu'ils ont au doigt.

On instituera dans tous les temples une nouvelle classe de prêtres, ajoutée aux 4 classes existant dêjà et qui sera nommée la cinquième classe des dieux Evergètes.

En raison de l'heureux événement de la naissance du roi Ptolémée, fils des dieux Adelphes, le 5e jour de Dios, et ce jour étant le principe d'un grand bonheur pour tous les hommes, les prêtres que le roi a fait entrer dans les temples depuis l'an i. de Sa Majesté, ainsi que ceux qu'on a fait entrer jusqu'au 4e mois de la saison de la moisson de l'an ix. seront compris dans cette classe, ainsi que leurs enfants pour toujours. Quant aux prêtres antérieurs à l'an i. ils resteront dans les classes où ils sont; dorénavant leurs enfants seront inscrits dans la classe de leur père.

Au lieu de vingt prêtres délibérants à choisir annuellement dans les 4 classes, 5 par chaque, il y en aura 25 dont les cinq derniers seront tirés de la classe cinquième des dieux Evergètes. Les prêtres de la 5me classe des dieux Evergètes prendront part a tous les rites de lustration dans les temples et à toutes les cérémonies qui en dépendent. Cette classe aura un phylarque avec qualité de prophête, comme cela est pour les quatre autres.

Attendu que dans tous les temples de ces régions on célèbre la fête des dieux Evergètes le 5, le 9 et le 25 de chaque mois, d'après un décret antérieur, et qu'en ontre on célèbre une fête aux grands dieux avec grand exode circulant dans l'Égypte, de même on fera un grand exode pour le roi Ptolémée et la reine Berenice dans les temples du sud et du nord et dans toute l'Égypte, le jour de l'apparition de Sothis que hiérogrammates appellent la fête du commencement de l'année ; on fera cet exode, pour l'an ix. le 1er jour du 2e mois de la moisson afin que la fête du nouvel an, la fête de Bast et le grand exode de Bast soient célébrés en ce même mois parce qu'il est l'époque de la cueillette des fruits et de la crue du Nil.

Mais comme il arrive que le lever de Sothis se reporte à un autre jour tous les 4 ans, pour que le jour de cette panégyrie ne soit pas déplacé, pour qu'elle ne cesse pas d'être faite le premier jour du 2e mois de l'été, pour que désormais elle soit célébrée ce jour-là comme en l'an ix., on célébrera cette fête en 5 journées pendant lesquelles les têtes seront couronnées de fleurs, pendant lesquelles on fera des sacrifices, des libations et toutes les cérémonies prescrites. Afin que ces choses arrivent en leur temps, afin de leur garder leur place conforme à la disposition actuelle du ciel, pour que les fêtes de circulation en Égypte qui sont célébrées en hiver ne viennent pas à être célébrées en été par le déplacement du lever de Sothis tous les 4 ans, et que d'autres fêtes dont la célébration est en été ne soient pas célébrées désormais en hiver comme cela est arrivé aux époques anciennes ; attendu que l'année est de 360 jours plus 5 jours supplémentaires, à partir d'aujourd'hui on ajoutera tous les 4 ans un jour comme panégyrie des dieux Evergètes, en plus des jours supplémentaires, et avant le nouvel an, afin que tout le monde sache que la petite irrégularité qui existait dans l'ordre des saisons et de l'année a été rectifiée et que les lois de la marche du ciel ont été complétées par les dieux Evergètes.

Attendu qu'une fille était née au roi Ptolémée et à la reine Bêrênice, dieux Evergètes, qui se nommait Bérénice et qui avait était promue reine, que cette déesse, encore vierge, est entrée au ciel subitement, que les prêtres qui viennent de l'Égypte annuellement prés du roi se trouvant alors chez sa majesté firent un grand deuil sur cet événement et supplièrent le roi et la reine de permettre qu'on fit reposer cette déesse auprès d'Osiris dans le temple de Canope qui est un sanctuaire parmi les temples, grand parmi eux, sanctuaire vénéré par le roi ainsi que par les habitants de tonte l'Égypte.

Lorsqu' Osiris entre dans la barque Sekti en ce temple, à son arrivée du temple d'Akerbumer, le 29 du 4e mois de la saison de l'inondation, la population des temples de sanctuaire fait des sacrifices sur les autels des temples du sanctuaire, à droite et à ganche du Dromos; après avoir accompli toutes ces cérémonies pour la déification (de la princesse) et la clôture du deuil, ils ont prodigué leur coeur avec chaleur selon la coutume de faire pour Apis et Mnèvis;

Ils ont décrété des honneurs éternels dans tous les temples de l'Égypte à la reine Bérénice, fille des dieux Evergètes. Attendu qu'elle est arrivée parmi les dieux le premier mois de la saison des semailles, qui est le mois où est entrée au ciel la fille du Soleil que ce dien dans son amour pour elle appelait son *oeil* et la *vipère de son front*, et qu'on célêbre à cette déesse une fête et périple dans les temples de sanctuaire en ce même mois où elle a été déifiée, de même on célébrera une fête et un périple à la reine Bêrênice, fille des dieux Evergètes, dans tous les temples du pays, le 17 du 1er mois de la saison des semailles, jour où pour la première fois ont été célébrés son périple et son denil, jusqu'à écoulement de 4 jours.

On érigera à cette déesse une statue en or ornée de pierres précieuses dans tous les temples de 1er, 2e et 3e ordre;

Elle reposera dans le sanctuaire;

Un prophète ou l'un des prêtres choisis pour les grandes purifications et l'habillement des dieux la soutiendra dans ses bras aux jours d'exode et de fête de tous les dieux afin qu'elle soit vue de tout le peuple qui l'adorera avec ferveur;

Elle sera nommée "Bêrênice, reine des vierges";

La couronne qui sera sur la tête de cette statue ne sera pas pareille à celle des images de sa mêre, la reine régnante, Bérénice; elle sera formée de deux épis avec un uraeus au milieu et une tige de papyrus de sa hauteur, semblable à celle que tiennent les déesses, la queue de l'uraeus étant enroulée au papyrus, de manière que cette couronne représente le nom de Bérénice selon les règles de l'écriture sacrée.

Au jour des Kikellies, le 4e mois de l'inondation,

avant le promenade d'Osiris, les vierges et les femmes des prêtres offriront une autre statue à la statue de Bêrênice, reine des vierges, et accompliront pour elle les sacrifices qu'il est prescrit de faire aux jours de cette panégyrie. Or il sera loisible aux antres vierges de s'associer au culte de la déesse qui sera adorée par des vierges sacrées, choisies pour le service des dieux, couronnées des couronnes des dieux dont elles sont les prêtresses.

Si la germination est en avance, les vierges sacrées apporteront des épis dans le sanctuaire pour les offrir à la statue de la déesse.

Une fois par jour et aux panégyries et exodes des dieux, on fera chanter en l'honneur de sa double plume par des choeurs d'hommes et de femmes des hymnes rédigés par les hiérogrammates, qui les remettront au maitre de chant, et il en sera gardé copie dans les archives du collège des hiérogrammates.

Attendu qu'il est donné des pains aux prêtres lorsque le roi les fait entrer dans les temples, qu'il en est accordé aux filles des prêtres à partir du jour de leur naissance, le tout pris proportionnellement sur les approvisionnements sacrés, en qualité d'alimentation dont la distribution dépend des prêtres délibérants de tous les temples, des pains seront remis aux femmes des prêtres et la répartition en sera faite à titre d'alimentation dite *Pains de Bérénice.*

Ce décret sera rédigé par les délibérants des temples, les chefs de temple et les scribes de temple ; il sera gravé sur une stêle de pierre ou de métal en écriture sacrée, en écriture des livres et en écriture grecque. On l'érigera dans le salle d'assemblée des temples de 2e et de 3e ordre, afin de rendre évidente à tous les hommes la vénération qu'ont les prêtres des temples de l'Égypte pour les dieux Evergètes et leurs enfants.

Ainsi qu'il est prescrit de faire.

CHAPTER IV.

ENGLISH RENDERING OF THE DEMOTIC TEXT.

(1) On the seventh day of the month Apellaios,[1] which correspondeth to the seventeenth day of the first month of the Season of sowing,[2] in the ninth year of Ptolemy, the son of Ptolemy (2) and of Arsinoë, the Brother-Gods, when Apollonides, the son of Moschion, was the priest of Alexander, and of the Brother-Gods, and of the Good-doing Gods, (3) and Menekratin (*sic*), a daughter of Philamon, was the bearer of (4) the silver basket before Arsinoë, the lover of her brother,

On this day (5)[3] (6) the Governors of the temples, and the Prophets, and the priests who go into the sanctuary to dress the gods, and the scribes of the house of the sacred scribes, (7) and the learned scribes, and the other scribes who had gathered themselves together from the temples of Egypt on the fifth day of the

[1] A month of the Macedonian year formed by a part of March and a part of April.

[2] I.e. Tybi.

[3] The fifth line is blank, but the narrative is not broken.

Ptolemy III. making an offering of Maāt.

month DIOS,[1] whereon they celebrated the Birthday of (8) the King, and for the 25th day of the same month whereon he had received the exalted rank [of sovereignty] from the hand of his father, having assembled in (9) the temple of the Good-doing Gods which is in the city of Pakute, spake thus:—

"Inasmuch as it hath happened that King PTOLEMY, "(10) the everliving, the son of PTOLEMY and ARSINOË, "the Brother-Gods, and Queen BERENICE, (11) his "sister and wife, the Good-doing Gods, have been wont "to bestow many benefits upon the temples of EGYPT at "all times, in the most bountiful manner, whereby the "honour (12) of the gods hath been magnified; and "inasmuch as at all times they have shown the greatest "care for all that concerneth Apis, and Mnevis, and the "other animals, which are held to be sacred in EGYPT; "and inasmuch as they have expended (13) very much "money on the statues of the gods, which the Persians "carried off from Egypt, for, having made an expedition "into foreign lands, the King captured them, and brought "them back to EGYPT, (14) and restored them to their "temples wherefrom they had been originally carried "off; and inasmuch as the King hath protected the "country, and hath waged war [on its behalf] in the "most remote places, against (15) many nations and "against those who had dominion in them; and inas-"much as he hath acted justly towards all the people "who belonged to EGYPT, and to those who were subject

[1] January-February.

"to his dominion outside that country; and inasmuch "as on one occasion (16) during their (i.e., PTOLEMY and "BERENICE'S) reign, when the waters of the NILE were "exceedingly low, and a famine was about to come upon "all those who dwelt in EGYPT, and the people were "terrified because of this, for they remembered the "calamity and misery which had come upon all the "inhabitants of Egypt (17) during the reigns of former "kings when the waters of the NILE had been insuf- "ficient, the hearts of the King and Queen were filled "with fervour and solicitude on behalf of those who "(18) belonged to the temples, and of those who dwelt "in Egypt, and they (i.e., the King and Queen) devoted "themselves to serving them in many things, and they "remitted many taxes with the intention of keeping "alive the people (19); and inasmuch as they made "arrangements for the import of grain into Egypt at a "very high price, from the country of SYRIA, and from "PHOENICIA, and from the Island of SALAMINA (Cyprus), "(20) and from many other places, whereby they were "enabled to maintain the people who were living in "Egypt; and inasmuch as they have thus left behind "them an everlasting benefit and a memorial of his (*sic*) "virtues, both to those who are alive at the present "time, and to those who shall (21) come after, as a "recompense for which the gods have granted them "sure and lasting sovereignty, may they grant them "in the future all other good things for ever, and bestow "upon them strength and health!—it hath (22) "entered into the hearts of the priests who belong to "EGYPT to bring it about that the honours which are "paid in the temples to King PTOLEMY and to Queen "BERENICE, (23) the Good-doing Gods, and those which "are paid to the Brother-Gods, who begat them, and to "the Saviour-Gods, who begat those who begat them, "shall be (24) greatly increased. The priests who "belong to each and every temple throughout Egypt "shall be called 'Priests of the Good-doing Gods,' in "addition to the other priestly titles which they bear, "and this title shall be inscribed (25) in documents of "every kind, and their title, so far as it refers to the "Good-doing Gods, shall be cut upon the seal-rings "which they carry, and it shall be engraved on the flat "surface thereof. And of (26) the priests who belong "to the temples of EGYPT another class shall be formed, "in addition to the four classes which exist at the "present time, and it shall be designated the 'Fifth "Class of [the Priests of] the Good-doing Gods,' (27) "inasmuch as it happened, with great good fortune, "and with strength and health, that the birth of King "PTOLEMY, the son of the Brother-Gods, took place on "the 5th day of the month DIOS, which day (28) was "the beginning of much happiness for every man; the "men who have become priests since the first year shall "be enrolled in this Class, and with them shall be "included those who have entered among them up to "the first day of the month MESORE, in the ninth year, "(29) and their children with them for ever. The "priests who had been priests up to the first year shall "remain in the Classes wherein they were formerly, "and similarly also, (30) from this day onwards, their "children shall be enrolled in the Class wherein their "fathers have been enrolled. Instead of the twenty "Councillor-Priests, who are elected each year from the "four (31) Classes of priests which now exist, five "priests being taken from each Class, there shall be "twenty-five Councillor-Priests, and the five additional "priests shall be chosen from the fifth Class (32) of the "priests of the Good-doing Gods; and the priests who "belong to the fifth Class [of priests] of the Good-"doing Gods shall take part in the holy ceremonies "above mentioned, and shall have their portion in all "things which are in the temples. And there (33) "shall be a governor over the [fifth] Class, even as "each of the other four Classes hath its governor.

"And moreover, inasmuch as festivals are kept in "the temples [in honour of] the Good-doing Gods "monthly, on the fifth, and ninth, and twenty-fifth days "[of the month], in accordance with (34) a decree which "had been passed some time ago, and religious pro-"cessions and great festivals are celebrated in honour "of the other gods throughout EGYPT, a great festival "shall be celebrated each year (35) in honour of King "PTOLEMY and Queen BERENICE, the Good-doing Gods, "alternately in the temples (36) throughout EGYPT, on "the day when the star of SIRIUS riseth, which is "called 'New Year' in the writings of the sacred "scribes, and which is now, in this ninth year, cele-"brated on the first day of the month PAYNI, whereon "(37) the procession of the inauguration of the goddess "BAST, and the great festival of BAST are celebrated, "which is the month wherein the fruits are gathered, "and the waters of the NILE rise to their greatest "height. (38) But though it happeneth that the "festival of SIRIUS passeth on to another day every "four years, the day whereon the above-mentioned "festival is kept shall not be changed, but it shall be "celebrated on the first day (39) of the month PAYNI, "on which day it was celebrated in the ninth year; "and the above-mentioned festival shall be celebrated "for five days, and the people shall wear crowns, and "they shall bring meat and drink offerings, and (40) "shall perform duly everything which is prescribed.

"And in order that it may happen that that which "hath been decreed to be done at each season of the "year may be done in accordance with the position "which the heavens have with reference to the things "which have to be performed at the present time, so "that occasion may not be given, and the case may not "arise, that some of the festivals which are celebrated "(41) in EGYPT in the winter should come to be "observed in the summer, in consequence of the rising "of SIRIUS advancing one day every four years (42), "and on the other hand, some of the festivals which are "at the present time celebrated in the summer should "come in the future to be celebrated in the winter,

"(43) a thing which actually happened in the times "which are past, and would happen at the present time "if the year consisted of 360 days and the five days, "according to the directions for adding the additional "days which have been observed: from this time "onwards one day, (44) a festival of the Good-doing "Gods, shall be added every four years to the five "additional days which come before the New Year, so "that it may happen that every man shall know that "the small amount [of time] which (45) was lacking in "the arrangement of the seasons, and of the year, and "in the things which passed as laws (*or*, principles) for "the knowledge of their movements, hath been cor-"rected, (46) and that it hath been supplied by the "Good-doing Gods.

"And since it happened that the daughter who was "born to King PTOLEMY and to Queen ARSINOË (47) the "Good-doing Gods, and who was called BERENICE, and "had been crowned Queen, and who whilst still a virgin "(48) had departed suddenly to heaven, while the priests "who came each year from EGYPT to the place where the "King was were still with him, the priests made great "mourning and lamentation (49) for her, and straightway "they entreated the King and Queen, and persuaded "them to establish for the goddess a system of worship "in connexion with that (50) of Osiris in the temple of "PAKUTE (CANOPUS), which is reckoned among the "temples of the first rank . . . . "which the King and all EGYPT (51) have held in the "highest honour, and moreover, OSIRIS, in his SEKTI "BOAT of gold maketh a journey to the aforesaid temple "each year (52), on the road to the temple of the "habitation of Ȧmen of the town of KARB, on the "twenty-ninth day of the month of CHOIACH, on which "day it is customary for all the dwellers in the temples "of the first class to prepare burnt offerings for the "altars which they themselves have set up in each of "(53) the temples of the first class, on both sides of the "*dromos*, and after this they performed the prescribed "ceremonies in connexion with her deification, and with "the purification of the mourning, (54) and with hearts "hot with feeling they carried out in a free and lavish "manner everything, as it was customary to do in "respect of APIS and MNEVIS.

"And they (i.e., the priests) decreed:—That ever-"lasting honour shall be paid to Queen BERENICE, (55) "the daughter of the Good-doing Gods, in all the "temples of EGYPT. And because it happened that she "entered among the gods on the 1st day of the month "TYBI, (56) which is the month wherein originally took "place the departure of the daughter of the Sun-God Rā, "whom he called his 'Crown,' and his 'Eye,' because "of his love for her, (57) and because they celebrate a "festival and a procession by water in many of the "temples of the first class in the aforesaid month, "wherein her deification originally took place, a "general festival and a (58) procession by water [in "honour] of Queen BERENICE, the daughter of the Good-

"doing Gods, shall be celebrated in all the temples of "EGYPT in the month of TYBI, from the seventeenth day, "on which day (59) her procession by water and the "purification from her mourning originally took place, "for four days; and a golden image of the goddess, set "with precious stones, shall be set up in the temples of "the first class, [and in] (60) the temples of the second "class, in each and every temple; and it shall have its "place in the sanctuary, and the Prophet or one of the "priests who shall be chosen to dress the gods in the "sanctuary (61) shall carry it in his arms on the days "whereon the festivals and the panegyries of the other "gods shall be celebrated, so that every man may see it "and may pray to it, and pay fitting honour to it, and "may call it (62) 'Berenice, the Queen of Virgins'; "and the golden crown with which the image of the "goddess shall be adorned shall be different from that "which adorneth (63) the image of Queen BERENICE, her "mother; and it shall be formed of two ears of corn, "between which shall be an uraeus serpent, and behind "the serpent (64) shall be fastened a papyrus sceptre, "which shall resemble the papyrus sceptres which are "held in the hands of the goddesses; and the tail of the "uraeus shall wind itself round the sceptre, so that the "(65) arrangement of the aforesaid crown shall express "the name BERENICE, according to the characters of the "hieroglyphics; and when the people come to celebrate "the days (66) of the regulations (?) of the goddess ISIS "in the month of CHOIACH, before the procession by "water of Isis, the virgins who are the daughters of the "priests shall cause another image of the goddess to be "prepared for the days of the (67) aforesaid general "festival. And it shall be permitted to the other virgins "who may wish it to have another similar image, and to "perform before it everything which it is (68) customary "to perform before the image of the goddess in the "manner aforesaid. And whilst these [virgins] sing, the "singing women who have been chosen to perform holy "ministrations to the gods shall be crowned with the "golden crowns (69) of the gods whose priestesses they "are. And when the early harvest hath drawn nigh, "the singing women shall take the ears of corn so that "they may lay the same upon (70) the image of the "goddess. And the singing men and the singing women "shall sing at the festivals and at the panegyries of the "other gods (71) the hymns from the hymns of praise "which the sacred scribes have set down in writing; and "they shall give them to the singing masters, and copies "of the same shall be prepared for the books of the house "of the sacred scribes. And moreover, since it happeneth "(72) that the food of the priests is to be provided out of "the revenues of the temples, from the time when they "became priests, the food also of the daughters of the "priests shall be provided from the same, from the days "(73) wherein they were born. And the amount which "shall be set apart for them out of the sacred revenues "of the gods shall be in proportion to that which the "Councillor-priests (74) in each and every temple receive, "and it shall be allotted by these priests in proportion to "the sacred revenues [of each temple]. And as con-"cerning the bread which shall be given to the wives of "the priests, it shall be stamped with a distinguishing "mark (75) and shall be called the 'Bread of Berenice' "by name.

"[And[1] this Decree shall be inscribed by the Councillor-"priests of [each] temple, and by the governors of [each] "temple, and by the sacred scribes, upon a stele of stone "or bronze in the sacred writing, and in the writing of "the books, and in Greek writing, and [copies of the "same] shall be set up in the hall of assembly of the "people in the temples of the first, second, and third "class, so that all people may see how great is the "honour which the priests of the temples of Egypt pay "to the Good-doing Gods, and to their children, as is "most right]."

[1] The following paragraph, which is supplied from the hieroglyphic and Greek versions, is wanting in the Demotic version.

CHAPTER V.

FRENCH AND GERMAN TRANSLATIONS OF THE DEMOTIC TEXT OF THE DECREE OF CANOPUS.

I.—French Translation by M. E. Révillout (*Chrestomathie Démotique,* tom. ii., p. 125 ff., Paris, 1880).

An 9 Apellaios 7 du roi Ptolémée vivant toujours (fils) de Ptolémée et d'Arsinoé les deux frères. etant prêtre d'Alexandre et des dieux frêres des dieux évergètes Apollonidès (fils) de Moschion etant Menecratina fille de Philammon canéphore devant Arsinoé la philadelphe. Décret . . . . . Les grands prêtres les prophètes et les prêtres qui entrent dans le sanctuaire pour faire (la) vestiture des dieux et les hiérogrammates les ptèrophores et les autres prêtres qui étaient venus des temples d'Égypte en Dios 5ᵉ que ils font le jour de naissance du roi en lui et le 25 du mois nommé que il prit la puissance suprême après son père en lui étant rassemblés dans le sanctuaire des dieux évergètes qui à Canope disant : Puisque le roi Ptolémée vivant toujours (fils) de Ptolémée et d'Arsinoé les dieux frères et la

reine Bêrênice sa soeur son épouse les dieux évergètes ont accompli bienfaits grands en quantité aux temples d'Égypte en temps quelconque et ont prodigué les honneurs aux dieux extrêmement et se sont préoccupé (*sic*) en temps tout des (choses) qui pour (concernant) Apis Mnevis et le reste (du) animaux qui consacrés d'Égypte, et ont fait dépense et ont fait préparatifs en quantité pour les images divines qui prirent les hommes Perses en dehors d'Égypte que alla le roi aux contrées qui en dehors il sauva elles il amena elles en Égypte donnant elles aux temples que ils avaient prés elles au dehors d'eux primitivement. Il sauva (Il fit salut) le pays du combat en combattant au dehors dans les lieux qui éloignés contre les peuples en quantité et les hommes qui commandaient en eux et ont fait le droit à homme quelconque qui en Égypte et aux autres hommes qui sous leur puissance suprême . . . . fut une eau petite sous eux un trouble étant à homme quelconque qui en Égypte ils se lamentaient à cause de les choses advenues quand ils se reportaient aux malheurs arrivés (étant) sous . . . . les rois qui furent auparavant que il arriva à les hommes qui en Égypte (d')être disette (?) sous eux, faisant soin et chaleur de coeur à ceux qui dans les temples et les autres qui sont en Égypte faisant pensée en quantité abandonnant en leur faveur redevances en quantité pour apporter la vie aux hommes faisant amener blé en Égypte à prix élevé d'argent du pays de Syrie du pays de Phénicie de l'île de Chypre et autre bien en quantité ils ont sauvé les hommes qui sont en Égypte établissant un bienfait éternel et le mémorial grand de son élévation (d'ame) devant ceux qui sont ceux qui seront ont donné a eux les dieux l'affermissement (de) leur puissance suprême a leur place qu'ils fussent à eux les autres biens tous jusqu'a jamais. Avec le salut et la prosperité! Il est venu dans le coeur des prêtres qui en Égypte que (les) hommes qui du roi Ptolémée et de la reine Bérénice les dieux évergètes dans les temples et ceux qui de les dieux frêres qui firent être eux et des dieux sauveurs qui firent être ceux qui firent être eux qu'on fasse grands. Les prêtres des temples d'Égypte temple chaque que l'on dise à eux les prêtres des dieux évergètes (comme) nom montre de leur autre nom de prêtre; qu'ils l'écrivent sur l'ordonnance (le protocole) des contrats de chose quelconque qu'on fasse la puissance sacerdotale des dieux évergètes sur les anneaux que ils portent qu'ils la gravent sur eux. Qu'ils fassent être à eux autre tribu dans les prêtres qui dans les temples d'Égypte en outre des 4 tribus qui sont en eux : qu'on dise à eux tribu 5e des dieux Évergètes. Puisque avec la fortune (l'aventure) bonne et le salut et le bonheur on célèbre (on fait) la naissance du roi Ptolémée de les dieux frères en Dios 5e que etant pour nommé celui qui fit commencement de biens en quantité à homme quelconque qu'on fasse les prêtres que l'on a fait à l'être de prêtre depuis année 1re dans cette tribu avec ceux que ils feront jusqu'à année de Mésoré avec leurs enfants jusqu'à jamais. Les prêtres qui étaient jusqu'à année 1^{le} qu'ils soient dans leurs tribus que ils étaient en elles primitivement de même aussi leurs enfants depuis le jour que plus haut qu'on les écrive (dans) leurs tribus que étant leurs pères en elles à la place des 20 prêtres qui accomplissant parole que l'on choisit par an dans les 4 tribus qui existaient que étaient près les 5 parmi eux par chaque tribu que 25 prêtres accomplissant parole soient qu'on prenne 5 qui étant ajoutés de tribu 5e des dieux évergètes que part soit à ceux qui dans tribu 5e de les dieux évergètes dans les *αγνεια* et autre (le reste des) choses toutes qui dans les temples. Que un (?) phylarque soit à elle comme ce qui est aux 4 tribus. Puisque on fait fêtes de les dieux évergètes dans les temples par mois le 5 le 9 le 25 selon le décret qui écrit précédemment les autres dieux grands on fait (aussi) à eux fêtes fêtes grandes solemnelles en Égypte par an qu'on fasse (de plus) une fête grande par an du roi Ptolémée et de la reine Bérénice les dieux évergètes (fête) solemnelle dans les temples et l'Égypte entière le jour que . . . . . la divine étoile d'Isis resplendit (se lève) en lui qui (pour qui) est nommé nouvel an comme nom par les hierogrammates que on fait (on célèbre) lui en an 9 Payni 1er que on fait la fête (le panégyrie) dans l'édifice (?) de Bast et la grande exode de Bast en lui qui est celui que l'on rassemble les fruits et que l'eau (la fleuve) s'emplit en lui aussi. Il arriverait transfert complet (?) des levers de l'étoile d'Isis à autre jour par an 4 (tous ces 4 ans) qu'on ne transporte pas le jour de faire la fête (panégyrie) nommée à cause de cela (?) qu'on la fasse de même en Payni 1er on fit elle en lui d'abord en année 9e qu'ils fassent la fête nommée jusqu'à jour 5 prenant couronne faisant sa sacrifice libation et autre (le reste de) chose convenable à faire. Pour que soit aussi l'ordre (??) celui qui (est) établi de saison toute comme la manière que est le ciel établi sur elles (ces saisons) aujourd'hui pour qu'il n'arrive pas être quelques-unes des fêtes solennelles d'Égypte que quand on les fait en hiver qu'on les fasse en été (en) une époque par transfert de ses apparitions totales de Sothis un jour par ans quatre et que d'autres aussi (parmi) les fêtes que quand on les célèbre en été à ce moment on les fasse en hiver en les temps postérieures ce qui était d'être en les temps antérieures serait encore à l'année qui fait jours 360 jours (*sic*) et jours 5 qu'il fut de droit d'ajouter à eux à la fin que l'on ajoute un jour de fête des dieux évergètes depuis ce jour par ans 4 en plus des 5 jours que on ajoute avant le nouvel an afin que homme quelconque sache que le peu qui était en défaut dans la disposition des saisons de l'année et des choses qui sont nécessaires à connaitre dans les marches du ciel avec (par) les destinées furent rétablies étant completées par les dieux Évergètes. Puisque aussi la fille qui fut au roi Ptolemée et à la reine Bérénice les dieux évergètes nommée Bérénice de nom qu'on allait manifester (comme) reine il arriva celle ci étant vierge alla au ciel tout à coup les prêtres qui viennent d'Égypte prés du roi par an au lieu que il est en lui faisant deuil grand des lamentations sur ce qui arrivait tout à coup suppliant devant le roi la reine ils ont persuadé leur coeur d'envoyer la déesse avec Osiris dans le sanctuaire de Canope (le premier?) parmi les temples (de) 1er (ordre) . . . . . . celui qui est en lui étant parmi ceux que . . . . le roi et les hommes d'Égypte tous exaltent lorsque (?) on introduit Osiris dans la barque d'or au temple nommé par an en remontant de le sanctuaire de l'Héracleum en χοιακ 29 alors que sont ceux qui viennent des temples (du) 1er (ordre) tous faisant sacrifice sur les autels qu'ils ont faits pour les temples (du) 1er (ordre) temple chaque sur les deux cotés (*sic*) du *dromos*. Après ces choses que de droit de faire pour sa divinisation et la clôture du deuil ils dépensèrent étant prodigues de coeur dans leur chaleur comme la coutume de faire pour Apis Mnevis. Il a paru bon de faire être honneurs éternels à la reine Bérénice fille de les dieux évergètes dans les temples d'Égypte tous. Puisque elle est allée parmi les dieux en Tybi qui est le mois que fut l'apothéôse de la fille du soleil en lui primitivement que il dit à elle son diadême (*sic*) sa prunèlle (*sic*) comme nom par amour d'elle que on fait à elle panégyrie périple en temples en quantité parmi les temples (du) 1er (ordre) dans le meis nommé que fut sa divinisation en lui primitivement qu'on fasse une panégyrie et un périple à la reine Bérénice fille de les dieux évergètes dans les temples d'Égypte tous en Tybi depuis 17 (le 17) que l'on fit son périple et sa cloture (*sic*) de deuil en lui la 1re fois jusqu'à jour 4. Que l'on produise à elle (en ce nom) une image d'or pleine de pierres précieuses dans les temples (de) 1er (ordre) les temples (de) 2e (ordre) temple chaque qu'elle pénétre dans le sanctuaire. Le prophête . . . un des prêtres qui choisis . . . . pour l'habillement des dieux qu'il la produise dans ses bras . . . dans les fêtes et les panégyries des autres dieux. Que homme quelconque voie elle qu'ils adorent (?) rendant honneur à elle disant à elle Bérénice princesse des vierges. Le diadême (*sic*) d'or que ils font apparaître l'image divine avec lui qu'il soit different de celui que ils font apparaître l'image de la reine Bérénice sa mère qu'on le fasse de épis 2 ayant un uraeus en leur milieu étant un sceptre de papyrus lié derrière comme celui qui est dans les mains des déesses en sorte que la queue de cet uraeus soit enroulée à lui afin que la disposition du diadême (*sic*) d'or nommé indique ce nom de Bérénice selon les caractères des hiérogrammates. Quand on vient à les jours des kikellia en χοιακ avant le périple d'Osiris que les vierges les femmes des prêtres fassent à elles autre statue en les jours de la panégyrie nommée. Que cela soit aussi en eux étant permis les autres vierges celles qui veulent faire les choses de droit de faire à la déesse comme celles que plus haut louant aussi (comme) les *Kemai* qui choisies pour qu'elles servent les dieux couronnées d'or de les couronnes d'or des dieux que ils sont d'eux comme prêtresses. Quand la première semaille vient que les *Kemai* portent épis que plus haut qu'elles . . . à l'image de la déesse: que les chanteurs et les chanteuses chantent (??) à elle chaque jour ainsi que les fêtes les panégyries des autres dieux selon les hymnes que . . . . les hiérogrammates écrivent afin qu'ils donnent eux au maitre de chant qu'ils écrivent copie sur les livres sacrés. Puisque . . . on donne les revenus sacrés aux prêtres de les temples lorsqu'on en fait partage qu'on donne la provende aux filles femmes des prêtres depuis le jour de leur naissance celle que a été faite dans le revenu sacré des dieux selon la provende que . . . . les prêtres accomplissant parole des temples temple chaque ont fixé selon la proportion du revenu sacré. Les pains que on donne aux femmes des prêtres qu'on fasse être à lui une marque distincte qu'on dise à lui le pain de Bérénice comme nom.

[The Demotic text has no equivalent for the end of line 73, and for lines 74, 75, and 76 in the Greek.]

II.—French Translation by M. P. Pierret, Published in 1881.[1]

L'an ix. 7 d'Apellaios, du roi Ptolémée vivant toujours, fils de Ptolémée et d'Arsinoë, les dieux frères, étant prêtre d'Alexandre et des dieux frères et des dieux Évergètes, Apollonidès, fils de Moskion, étant Menekratina, fille de Philammon, canéphore devant Arsinoë la Philadelphe, *décret:*

[1] *Le Décret Trilingue de Canope*, Paris, 1881.

Les grands prêtres, les prophètes et les prêtres qui entrent dans le sanctuaire pour faire la vestiture des dieux, et les hiérogrammates, les ptérophores et autres prêtres venus des temples d'Égypte le 5 de Dios dont on fait le jour de naissance du roi et le 25 du dit mois (jour) où il prit la puissance suprême après son père, étant rassemblés dans le sanctuaire des dieux Évergètes qui est à Pakot, dirent;

Puisque le roi Ptolémée vivant toujours, fils de Ptolémée et d'Arsinoë les dieux frères, et la reine Bérénice, sa soeur et son épouse, les dieux Évergètes, ont accompli de grands bienfaits en quantité pour les temples d'Égypte en tout temps, ont prodigué les honneurs aux dieux extrêmement, se sont préoccupés en tout temps des choses concernant Apis, Mnêvis et le reste des animaux consacrés de l'Égypte et ont fait approvisionnements nombreux pour eux;

Que les images divines qu'emportèrent les hommes Perses au dehors d'Égypte, le roi alla en pays étranger pour les délivrer, les amener en Égypte et les rendre aux temples d'où elles avaient été exportées primitivement;

Qu'il sauva le pays du combat en combattant au dehors en des pays éloignés contre des peuples nombreux et (contre) les hommes qui commandaient chez eux.

Étant fait le droit à tout homme qui est en Égypte et aux autres hommes qui sont sous leur puissance suprême.

Fut une eau petite sous eux, un trouble étant à tous

les hommes qui étaient en Égypte; ils se lamentaient à cause de ces choses advenues quand ils se reportaient aux malheurs arrivés sous les rois antérieures lorsqu'il arriva que les hommes d'Égypte furent dans la séche-resse (?) sous ces rois; (le roi et la reine) eurent des soins et furent chaleureux de coeur pour ceux des temples et les autres habitants de l'Égypte, faisant pensée en quantité, abandonnant en leur faveur rede-vances nombreuses pour apporter la vie aux hommes, faisant amener du blé en Égypte à prix élevé d'argent du pays de Syrie, du pays de Phénicie, de l'Île de Chypre (Salamina) et autres lieux; ils ont sauvé les hommes qui sont en Égypte, établissant un bienfait éternel et un grand souvenir de leur élévation d'âme devant ceux qui sont et ceux qui seront;

Les dieux leur ont donné l'affermissement de leur puissance suprême, en échange, et que leur fussent donnés lors les autres biens jusqu'à toujours;

AVEC LE SALUT ET LA PROSPÉRITÉ!

Il est venu dans le coeur des prêtres qui sont en Égypte;

D'agrandir les honneurs qui sont faits au roi Ptolé-mée et à la reine Bérénice, les dieux Évergètes, dans les temples, et ceux qui sont pour les dieux frères qui firent être eux et ceux des dieux sauveurs qui firent être ceux qui firent être eux;

Les prêtres de chacun des temples de l'Égypte seront appelés prêtres des dieux Évergètes, en outre de leur autre nom de prêtres. Qu'ils l'écrivent sur les protocoles de contrats de chose quelconque. Qu'on fasse (indique) la puissance sacerdotale des dieux Évergètes sur les anneaux qu'ils portent; qu'ils l'y gravent. Qu'ils constituent une nouvelle tribu des prêtres des temples d'Égypt en plus des 4 tribus qui y sont, qu'on l'appelle tribu cinquième des dieux Évergètes.

Puisque, avec la bonne fortune, le salut et le bonheur, on célèbre la naissance du roi Ptolémée, fils des dieux frères, le 5 Dios, jour déclaré avoir été le principe de biens nombreux pour tous les hommes, ceux qu'on a fait prêtres depuis la première année qu'on les fasse prêtres de cette tribu ainsi que ceux qu'on fera prêtres jusqu'à Mesori de l'an ix. avec leurs enfants jusqu'à toujours. Les prêtres antérieurs à la premiêre année, qu'ils soient dans les tribus où ils étaient primitivement; de même aussi leurs enfants depuis le jour indiqué plus haut, qu'on les enregistre dans les tribus où étaient leurs pêres.

À la place des 20 prêtres *accomplissant parole* que l'on choisit annuellement dans les quatre tribus existantes et qui sont pris 5 dans chaque tribu, qu'il y ait 25 prêtres *accomplissant parole*, qu'on prenne ces 5 supplémentaires dans la tribu des dieux Évergètes et ceux de cette cinquième tribu des dieux Évergètes auront part aux lustrations et à tout le reste de ce qui se fait dans les temples; qu'nn phylarque soit à elle (à cette tribu) ainsi qu'aux quatre (autres) tribus.

Puisqu'on fait fêtes des dieux Évergètes dans les temples mensuellement le 5, le 9, le 25, selon le décret écrit précédemment, qu'aux autres dieux grands on fait aussi fêtes (simples) et fêtes grandes et solennelles en Égypte annuellement, qu'on fasse (en plus) une fête grande, annuelle, au roi Ptolémée et à la reine Bérénice, dieux Évergètes, fête solennelle dans les temples de l'Égypte entière le jour où la divine étoile d'Isis se lève (nommé) nouvel an par les hiérogrammates, et fêté le 1er Payni de l'an ix. lors de la fête dans l'édifice de Bast et du grand exode de Bast (et qui est aussi le jour) où l'on rassemble les fruits et où le fleuve s'emplit;

Il arriverait transfert complet des levers de l'êtoile d'Isis à un autre jour tous les 4 ans; qu'on ne transporte pas le jour de faire la dite fête à cause de cela; qu'on la fasse de même au 1er Payni comme on l'a faite d'abord en l'an ix.; qu'on fasse la dite fête jusqu'au 5e jour, prenant couronne, faisant libation et le reste des choses qu'il convient de faire; pour que soit maintenu l'ordre de toutes les saisons conformément au ciel établi sur elles, aujourdhui, pour qu'il n'arrive pas que quelques unes des fêtes solennelles d'Égypte à célébrer en hiver soient un jour célébrées en été par transfert d'un jour en 4 ans des apparitions de Sothis, ni que d'autres fêtes à célébrer en été soient célébrées plus tard en hiver, ce qui est arrivé autrefois et arriverait encore à l'année qui fait 360 jours plus les 5 jours qu'il est de droit d'ajouter à la fin, que l'on ajoute un jour de fête des dieux Évergètes dorénavant tous les 4 ans, en plus des 5 jours que l'on ajoute avant le nouvel an, afin que tout homme sache que le peu qui était en défaut dans la disposition des saisons de l'année et des choses qui sont nécessaires à connaître dans les marches du ciel par les destinées furent rétablies, complétées par les dieux Évergètes.

Puisque la fille qui fut au roi Ptolémée et à la reine Bérénice, dieux Évergètes, nommée Bérénice, qu'on allait manifester comme reine, il arriva qu'étant encore vierge elle alla au ciel tout à coup; les prêtres qui viennent d'Égypte annuellement prés du roi au lieu où il est, faisant grand deuil de lamentations sur cet événement subit, suppliant devant le roi et la reine, persuadèrent leur coeur d'envoyer la déesse avec Osiris dans le sanctuaire de Canope, le premier parmi les temples de premier ordre . . . et étant parmi ceux qui exaltent le roi et tous les hommes d'Égypte.

Lorsqu'on introduit Osiris dans la barque d'or au dit temple annuellement, en remontant du sanctuaire de l'Héracléum, au 29 Choiac, alors que sont tous ceux qui viennent des temples de premier ordre faisant sacrifice sur les autels qu'ils ont faits pour chacun des temples de premier ordre sur les deux côtés du Dromos. Après ces choses qu'il est de droit de faire pour sa divinisation et la clôture du denil, ils dépensèrent, étant prodigues de coeur dans leur chaleur, autant qu'il est coutume de faire pour Apis et Mnévis.

Il a paru bon de faire être honneur éternel à la reine Bérénice, fille des dieux Évergètes, dans tous les temples d'Égypte. Puisqu'elle est allée parmi les dieux en Tybi qui est le mois où eut lieu primitivement l'apothéose de la fille du Soleil qu'il nommait par amour d'elle *son uraeus et son oeil*, qu'on lui fait panégyrie et périple dans beaucoup des temples de premier ordre au dit mois où eut lieu sa divinisation primitivement, qu'on fasse une panégyrie et un périple à la reine Bérénice, fille des dieux Évergètes, dans tous les temples d'Égypte en Tybi, depuis le 17, jour où l'on fit pour la première fois son périple et sa clôture de denil, jusqu'à quatre jours;

Que l'on produise à elle une image d'or pleine de pierres précieuses dans chacun des temples de premier et de deuxième ordre,

Qu'elle pénétre dans le sanctuaire;

Le prophète (ou) l'un des prêtres choisis pour l'habillement des dieux, qu'il la produise dans ses bras dans les fêtes et panégyries des autres dieux (afin) que tout homme la voie, l'adore et lui rende honneur,

Disant à elle: "Bérénice, princesse des vierges";

Le diadème d'or avec lequel ils font apparaître l'image divine, qu'il soit différent de celui (avec) lequel il font apparaître l'image de la reine Bérénice, sa mère: qu'on le fasse de deux épis ayant un uraeus au milieu, étant un sceptre de papyrus lié derriere, comme celui qui est dans la main des déesses, en sorte que la queue de cet uraeus s'y enroule, afin que la disposition du dit diadème d'or indique le nom de Bérénice selon les caractères des hiérogrammates.

Quand on vient au jour des Kikellies, en Choiac,

avant le périple d'Osiris, que les vierges, les femmes de prêtres, lui fassent une autre statue aux jours de la dite panégyrie; qu'il soit aussi permis (?) en ces jours aux autres vierges, celles qui veulent faire les choses prescrites, de faire à la déesse comme celles ci-dessus, adorant comme les pallacides choisies pour servir les dieux, couronnes d'or avec les couronnes d'or des dieux dont elles sont prêtresses.

Quand la premiere semaille vient, que les pallacides portent des épis à l'image de la déesse ;

Que des chanteurs et des chanteuses chantent à elle chaque jour ainsi qu'aux fêtes et panégyries des autres dieux en manière d'hymnes que les hiérogrammates rédigeront, qu'ils donneront au maître de chant et dont on écrira copie sur les livres sacrés.

Puisqu'on distribue les revenus sacrés aux prêtres des temples, lorsqu'on en fait partage, qu'on donne la provende aux filles, femmes des prêtres depuis le jour de leur naissance, celle qui a été faite dans le revenu sacré des dieux selon la provende que . . . les prêtres *accomplissant parole* de chaque temple ont fixée d'après la proportion du revenu sacré. Le pain qu'on donne aux femmes des prêtres, qu'on lui impose une marque distincte et qu'on l'appelle *pain de Bérénice.*

[The final clause of the Greek and hieroglyphic versions, which orders that copies of the Decree shall be set up in the temples of the first, second, and third rank, is wanting in the Demotic version.]

III.—German Translation by the late Dr. H. Brugsch (*Bautexte und Inschriften*, Leipzig, 1891, p. xiv.).

(1) Im 9. Jahre, am 7. des Monats *Apelläus*, Königs Ptolemäus, des ewig lebenden, Sohnes des Ptolemäus (2) und der Arsinoë, der Götter Brüder; als Priester war des *Alexander* und der Götter Brüder (und) der Götter Wohlthäter (3) *Apollonides*, der des *Moskion*, während *Menekratin* (*sic*), eine Tochter des *Philamon* (4), den Silberkorb vor der *Arsinoë*, der Brüderliebenden, trug.

An diesem Tage (5)[1] (6) eine Beschlussfassung, nachdem die Obersten der Tempelverwaltung, die Propheten und die Priester, welche in das Sanktuarium eintreten, um die Gottheiten zu bekleiden, und die Schreiber des Hierogrammatenhaus (7) und die gelehrten Schreiber und die andern Priester aus den Tempeln Aegyptens herbeigekommen waren zum 5. des Monats *Dios*, an welchem sie den Geburtstag (8) des Königs feierten und zum Datum des 25. des genannten Monates, an welchem er die höchste Würde aus der Hand seines Vaters empfangen hatte.

Indem sie sich in (9) dem Tempel der Götter Wohlthäter, welcher in der Stadt *Pakute* gelegen ist, versammelten, sprachen sie:

"Weil es geschehen ist, dass König *Ptolemäus*, (10) der ewig lebende, der Sohn des *Ptolemäus* und der

[1] The fifth line is blank, but the narrative is not broken.

Arsinoë, der Götter Brüder, und die Königin *Berenike*, (11) seine Schwester (und) seine Frau, die Götter Wohlthäter, sehr viel Wohlthaten den Tempeln Aegyptens zu jeder Zeit reichlichst (?) zu erweisen pflegten, damit die Ehren (12) der Götter vergrössert würden, in der Weise,

dass sie zu jeder Zeit Sorge trugen für das was den Apis, den *Wermer* (Mnevis) und die übrigen Thiere, welche geheiligt in Aegypten sind, betrifft

dass sie (13) viel für die Götterbilder aufwandten, welche die Perser betrifft, aus Aegypten weggeführt hatten, nachdem der König nach den Ländern auswärts gezogen war, sie fortnahm, um sie nach Aegypten zu bringen, (14) indem er sie ihren Tempeln, aus welchen sie fruher weggeführt worden waren, zurückgab,

dass er das Land vor Krieg bewahrte, in dem er an den fernsten Orten (15) gegen viele Völker und die Leute, welche in ihnen die Herrschaft hatten, Krieg führte,

dass für alle Leute, welche zu Aegypten gehörten, und die übrigen Leute, welche sich unter seiner Oberhoheit befanden, was gesetzlich war bestand;

und weil einmal (16) ein niedrigen Wasserstand zu ihrer Zeit war (und) eine entstandene Hungersnoth für jedermann, der zu Aegypten gehörte, beängstigend wirkte, wegen dessen, was die Folge gewesen wäre, wenn man die Unglücksschläge erwog, welche unter einigen (17) Königen, die früher waren, eingetreten waren, so dass die Leute, welche zu Aegypten gehörten, sich in Noth und Elend unter ihnen (sc. den früheren

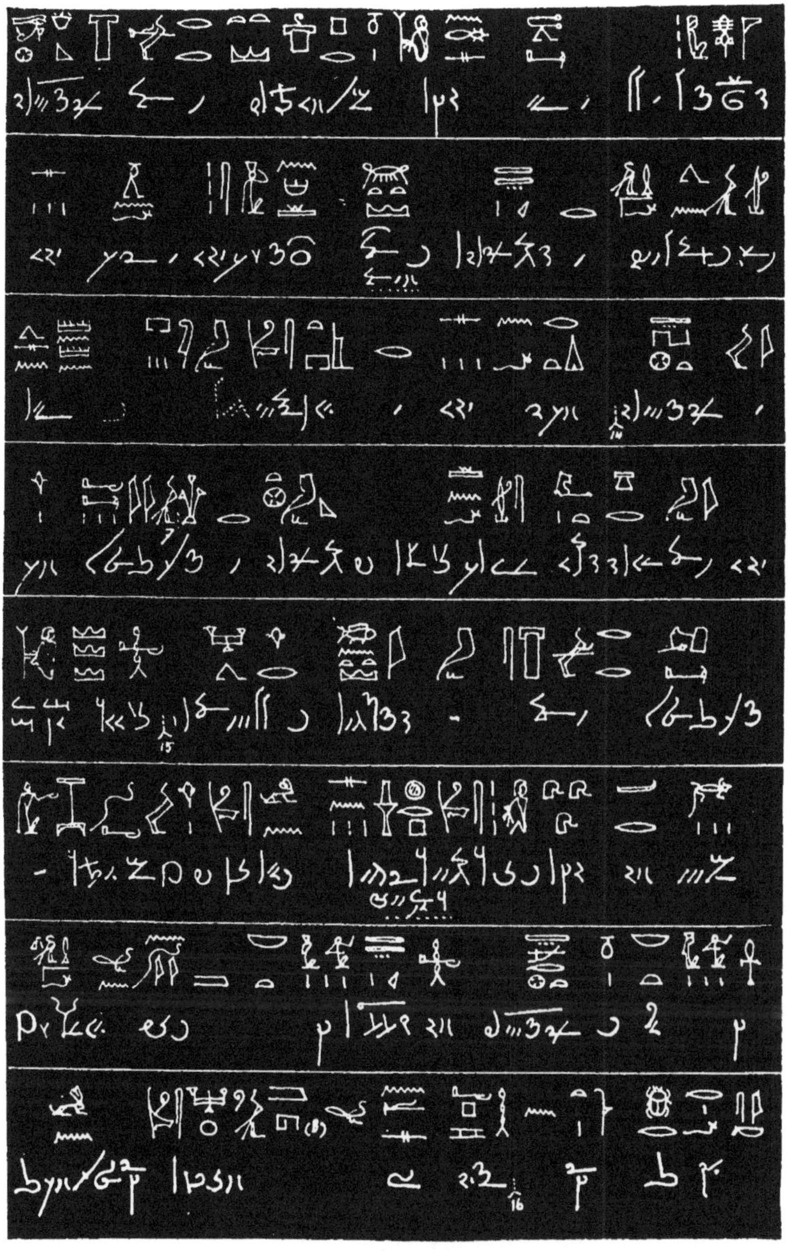

The hieroglyphic and Demotic versions of lines 13 ff. as compared by H. Brugsch.

Königen) befanden,—sie mit Herzenswärme fur diejenigen, welche zu (18) den Tempeln gehören und die Andern, welche in Aegypten weilen, Sorge trugen, indem sie viel nachdachten, wie sie die vielen Steuern zu erlassen vermöchten, in der Absicht den Leuten das Leben zu fristen, (19) (und) indem sie die Einfuhr von Getreide nach Aegypten um hohe Silberpreise, aus der provinz des *Aschur* ·(Syrien), aus der provinz der Hinterländer (*Ḫaru*, Phönizien) und der Insel *Salamina* (Cypern) (20) und aus vielen andern Orten bewerkstelligten, damit sie die Leute, welche sich in Aegypten befanden, zu erhalten vermöchten, indem sie eine ewige Wohlthat und das Mal seines (sic) Vorzuges zur Zeit derer, welche sind (21) und derer, welche sein werden, hinterliessen, wofür ihnen die Götter den Bestand ihrer Oberhoheit als Sohn gewährten—mögen sie ihnen Alles andere Gute bis in Ewigkeit hin und das Heil und die Gesundheit schenken,—(22) so hat es den Herzen der Priester, welche zu Aegypten gehören, gefallen, um zu bewirken, dass es also sei: das die Ehren, welche dem König *Ptolemäus* und der Königin *Berenike*, (23) den Göttern Wohlthätern, zu Theil werden in den Tempeln und die welche den Göttern Brüder, ihren Erzeugern, und den Göttern Retter, den Erzeugern ihrer Erzeuger, zu Theil werden, (24) vergrossert werden sollen. Die Priester, welche zu den Tempeln Aegyptens, jedem einzelnen Tempel, gehören, sie sollen mit Namen: "die Priester der Götter Wohlthäter," neben ihren andern priesterlichen

Namen heissen. Man soll ihn eintragen (25) in die Archive jeder Art. Man soll den Priestertitel, bezuglich auf die Götter Wohlthäter, auf den Siegelring, welchen sie tragen werden, einschreiben, so dass er auf seine Oberfläche eingegraben werde. Man soll für sie eine (26) andere Klasse unter den Priestern, welche zu den Tempeln Aegyptens gehören, schaffen, ausserhalb den vier Klassen, welche heutigen Tages bestehen. Man soll sie als die fünfte Klasse der Götter Wohlthäter bezeichnen. (27) Weil es geschah, in dem ein glücklicher Zufall—mit dem Heil und der Gesundheit!—eintraf, dass die Geburt des Königs *Ptolemäus*, Sohnes der Götter Brüder, am 5. Tage des Monats *Dios* stattfand, welches ist (28) der Tag, der fur jedermann der Anfang viels Guten war, so soll man diejenigen Priester, welche seit dem Jahre 1 Priester geworden waren, in diese Klasse thun, diejenigen mit eingeschlossen, welche bis zum Jahre 9, dem 1. Mesore es sein werden, (29) sammt ihren Kindern in Ewigkeit hin. Die Priester, welche es bis zum Jahre 1. waren, sie sollen verbleiben in den Klassen, in welchen sie sich früher befanden, in selbiger Weise auch (30) ihre Kinder, von dem heutigen Tage an, indem man sie in die Klassen einschreibe, in welchen ihre Väter eingeschrieben worden sind. An Stelle der 30 (*sic*) berathenden Priester, welche alljährlich gewählt werden aus den vier (31) Klassen, welche bestehen (und) aus welchen je funf genommen werden für jede Klasse, sollen 25 berathende Priester vorhanden sein, indem man die 5, welche man dazufügen wird, aus der fünften Klasse (32) der Götter Wohlthäter wählt.

Es sollen Antheil haben diejenigen, welche zur fünften Klasse der Götter Wohlthäter gehören, und der vorgeschrieben heiligen Handlungen und an allen übrigen Dingen, welche in den Tempeln (des Brauches) sind. Es soll (33) ein Klassenvorsteher für sie vorhanden sein, gleichwie der, welcher für die 4 Klassen vorhanden ist. Weil es geschieht wiederum, dass man das Fest der Götter Wohlthäter in den Tempeln allmonatlich am 5. 9. und 25 Tage feiert entsprechend (34) dem Beschlusse, welcher früher niedergeschrieben wurde, den andern Göttern (aber) Panegyrien und grosse Feste abwechselnd in Aegypten feiert, so soll man ein grosses Fest alljährlich dem (35) König *Ptolemäus* und der Königin *Berenike*, dem Göttern Wohlthäter, abwechselnd in den Tempeln, welche zu (36) ganz Aegypten gehören, feiern an dem Tage an welchem der Siriusstern aufgeht welcher mit Namen "Jahresanfang" in den Schriften der Hierogrammaten genannt wird, welchen sie im Jahre 9 am 1. des Monats Payni feiern, (37) in welchem die Panegyrie der Eröffnung der Göttin *Baste* und das grosse Fest der *Baste* gefeiert wird, welches der (Monat) ist, an welchem die Früchte eingesammelt werden, nachdem auch das volle Wasser an ihn eingetreten ist. (38)

Da est aber der Fall ist, dass die Feste des Sirius auf einen andern Tag in jedem vierten Jahre, übergehen, damit man nicht den Tag des genannten Festes deswegen verschiebe, so sei gefeiert was zu feiern ist (39) in gleicher Weise am 1. Payni, an welchem sie es vorher im Jahre 9 gefeiert hatten. Man soll die genannte Panegyrie bis zum 5. Tage feiern, indem man sich bekränzen werde, Brand und Trankopfer und alles Uebrige ausführen, (40) was zu thun vorgeschrieben ist. Damit es auch geschehe, dass man thun das, was vorgeschrieben zu jeder Jahreszeit nach dem Stande in welchem der Himmel seine Stellung hat in Bezug auf das, was am heutigen Tage ausgefuhrt wird (und) um nicht Veranlassung zu geben, das der Fall eintrete, das einige von den Panegyrien, (41) welche in Aegypten abwechselnd stattfinden (und) deren Feier man im Winter ausfuhrt, einstmal im Sommer ausgefuhrt wurden, in Folge des Vorwärtsschreitens aller Aufgänge des Sirius um einen Tag in jeden (42) vierten Jahre, andere wiederum von den Panegyrien, welche man in jetziger Stunde im Sommer zu feiern pflegt, in kommender Zeit im Winter gefeiert würden, das was (43) der Fall gewesen war in den früheren Zeiten (und) was wiederum geschehen würde bei dem Jahre, welches aus 360 Tagen und den 5. Tagen besteht, nach den Vorschriften für die Hinzufügung, welche am Schlusse geschah: so soll ein (44) Tag als Panegyric der Götter Wohlthäter von dem heutigen Tage an in jedem vierten Jahre als Ueberschuss zu den 5. Tagen hinzugefugt werden, welche man dem Jahresanfang einschalten soll, damit es geschehe, dass jedermann es wisse, warum die Kleinigkeit, welche (45) fehlte an der Anordnung der

Jahreszeiten und des Jahres und der Dinge, welche als Gesetze fur die Kenntnisse der Bewegungen galten, eben berichtigt worden sei (46) indem sie von den Göttern Wohlthäter ausgefüllt wurde. Darum weil es auch geschah, dass die Tochter, welche dem Könige *Ptolemäus* und der Königin *Arsinoë*, (47) den Göttern Wohlthäter erstanden war (und) welche man mit Namen *Berenike* hiess, welche man als Königin gekrönt hatte, dass diese, eine Jungfrau seiend, zufällig in (48) den Himmel plötzlich einging und die Priester, welche aus Aegypten zum König alljährlich kamen nach dem Platze, woselbst er sich befindet, eine grosse Trauer als Klage (49) um dieselbe anstellten (und) plötzlich der Fall eintrat, dass vor dem Könige und der Königin sie es sich erbaten und sie verlanlassten, es sich angelegen sein zu lassen, ihr, der Göttin, einen Kultus zu stiften (gemeinschaftlich) mit (50) dem des Osiris vom Gotteshause von *Pakute* (Kanopus), welches zu den Tempeln ersten Ranges gezählt (?) wird . . . . einzig allein der . . . . . der, welcher in ihm ist, in dem er zu denjenigen gehört, welchen die Könige (51) und alle Aegypter hoch ehren, wobei es geschieht, dass man den Osiris in dem goldenen *Sekti*-Schiff nach dem genannten Tempel alljährlich ziehen lässt (52) in der Richtung nach dem Gotteshause der Amonswohnung der Stadt *Karb*, am 29. des Monats Choiak, (und) wobei es zu geschehen pflegt, dass alle Insassen der Tempel ersten Ranges Brandopfer fur die Altäre bereiten, welche sie aufrichten in (53) den Tempeln ersten Ranges, in einem jeden einzelnen

Tempel, auf den beiden Seiten des Dromos, nach diesem die Vorschriften für die Handlungen bei ihrer Gottwerdung und bei der Reinigung der Trauer ausfuhrten (54) indem sie mit einem Herzen [voll] Wärme freigebigst verfuhren gleichwie das gewohnheitsmässig vom *Apis* und *Wermer* (Mnevis) geschieht,—so haben sie beschlossen, dass ewige Ehren gestiftet werden der Königin *Berenike* (55), der Tochter der Götter Wohlthäter, in allen Tempeln Aegyptens. Darum weil es geschehen ist, dass sie zu den Göttern einging am 1. des Tybi (56) welches der Monat ist, an welchem früher stattfand das Abscheiden der Tochter des Sonnengottes *Re*, welche er seine Krone und sein Auge mit Namen hiess, aus Liebe zu ihr, (und) welcher man (57) eine Panegyric der Wasserfahrt in vielen Tempeln unter den Tempeln ersten Ranges in dem genannten Monat feiert, in welchem fruher ihr Gottwerden stattfand: So soll man eine Panegyrie und eine (58) Wasserfahrt der Königin *Berenike*, der Tochter der Götter Wohlthäter, stiften in allen Tempeln Aegyptens im Monat Tybi vom 17. Tage an, an welchem man ihre (59) Wasserfahrt und ihre Reinigung der Trauer zum ersten Male vollzog, bis zum vierten Tage hin; man soll ihre ein goldenes mit Edelsteinen ausgelegtes Gottesbild aufrichten in den Tempeln ersten (und in) (60) den Tempeln zweiten Ranges, in jedem einzelnen Tempel; es soll seinen Platz finden in dem Sanktuarium des Propheten oder eines von den Priestern, welcher auserwählt ist für das Sanktuarium zur Bekleidung der Götter (61) und welcher es auf seinem Arme trägt an dem Tage, an welchem die Feste und die Panegyrien der andern Götter stattfinden, damit jedermann es schaue, dass man es anbetet, indem man ihm die Ehren erweist (62) (und) es als *Berenike*, die Fürstin der Jungfrauen bezeichnet; das goldene Diadem, mit welchem man das Götterbild schmückt, soll unterschieden sein von dem, welches (63) die Statue der Königin *Berenike*, ihrer Mutter, schmückte. Es sei aus zwei Kornhären gebildet, in deren Mitte sich eine Uräusschlange befindet, mit einem (64) Papyrusstengel, der hinterwärts befestigt ist, wie sich ein solches in der Hand der Göttinnen befindet. Es soll der Schwanz dieser Uräusschlange sich um dasselbe herumwinden, so das (65) die Ånordnung der genannten Krone den Namen "*Berenike*" ausspricht nach den Symbolen der heiligen Schriften. Ist man herbeigekommen und feiert man die Tage (66) der Satzung (? *Ki*,) der Göttin *Isis* im Monate *Choiak* vor der Wasserfahrt der *Isis*, so sollen die Jungfrauen der weiblichen Familie der Priester für sich eine andere Statue machen lassen für die Tage (67) der genannten Panegyrie. Es soll auch gestattet sein, dass eine solche in der Hand der übrigen Jungfrauen sei, welche es wünschen, (und) dass sie das, was als Vorschrift für jene in Bezug auf die Göttin gilt, auch verrichten (68), gleich wie es oben angegeben worden ist. Während auch sie dieselbe besingen, so sollen die Musikantinnen, welche auserwählt worden sind, damit sie den Göttern die (heiligen) Dienste verrichten, gekrönt sein mit den goldenen Kronen (69) der Götter deren Priesterinnen sie sind. Wenn die Frühsaat herangekommen ist, so sollen die Musikantinnen die Aehre emporheben, damit sie dieselbe auf (70) das Bild der Göttin legen. Es sollen die Sänger und die Sängerinnen ihr alltäglich die Hymnen singen an den Festen und an den Panegyrien der andern Götter, (71), nach der Vorschrift der Loblieder, welche die heiligen Schreiber in Schrift abzufassen hätten. Man soll sie den Meistersängern übergeben und man soll eine Abschrift davon für die Bücher des Hierogrammatenhauses anfertigen. Weil es auch geschieht (72), dass man den Unterhalt den Priestern von den Tempeln her gewährt, nachdem sie zu Priestern gemacht worden sind, so möge man die Ernährung den weiblichen Kinder der Priester von dem Tage (73) ihrer Geburt an gewähren. Das, was ihnen geboten wird von den heiligen Einkünften der Götter, entspreche der Ernährung, welche die Priester erhalten, die Berather in den Tempeln, (74) in jedem einzelnen Tempel, sind. Die Bestimmung sei nach dem Verhältniss der heiligen Einkünfte getroffen. In Bezug auf das Brot, welches man der Frauen der Priester reichen wird, so soll man dafür einen unterscheidenden Brotstempel einführen (75) in der Weise, dass man es "Brot der *Berenike*" mit Namen heisse.[1] Dieser Beschluss, er möge von den

[1] Da in dem demotischen Theile des Kanopus das Folgende fehlt, so ist die Uebersetzung des Schlusses nach Inhalt des hieroglyphischen Textes vorgelegt worden.

Berathern der Tempel und von den Vorstehern der Tempel und von den Tempelschreibern abgeschrieben werden und sie eingeschnitzt auf eine Stele von Stein oder Erz in heiliger Schrift, in Briefschrift und in jonischer Schrift. Sie werde aufgestellt in der Halle des Volkes, in den Tempeln ersten, zweiten und dritten Ranges, damit sie allen Leuten es vor Augen führe, welche Ehre die Priester der Tempel Aegyptens den Göttern Wohlthäter und ihren Kindern erwiesen haben entsprechend dem, was geschehen ist.

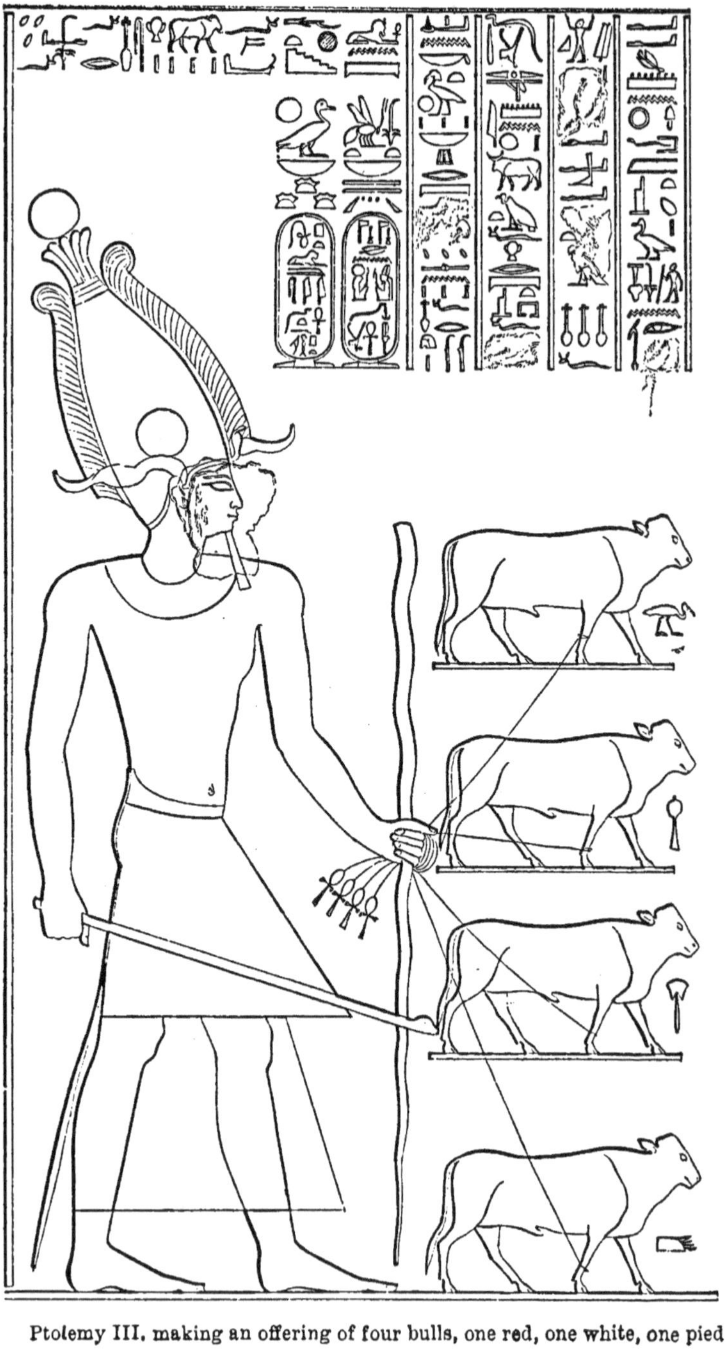

Ptolemy III. making an offering of four bulls, one red, one white, one pied

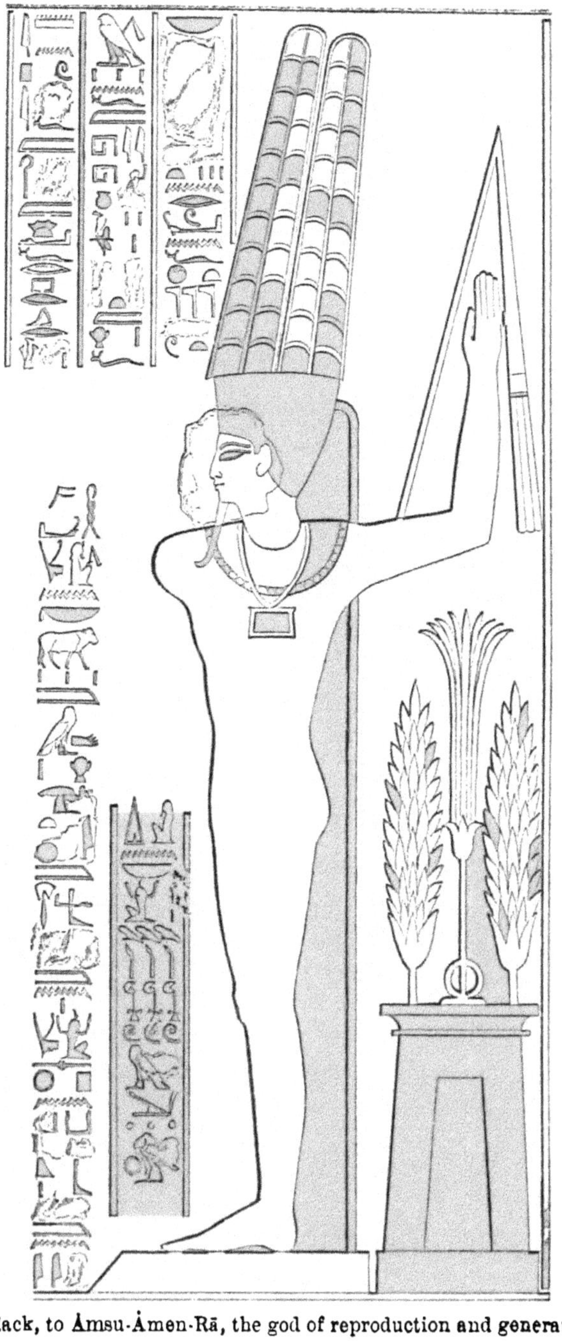

and one black, to Åmsu-Åmen-Rā, the god of reproduction and generation.

CHAPTER VI.

THE GREEK TEXT OF THE DECREE OF CANOPUS.

Transcript.

1 *Βασιλεύοντος Πτολεμαίου, τοῦ Πτολεμαίου καὶ Ἀρσινόης θεῶν Ἀδελφῶν, ἔτους ἐνάτου, ἐφ᾽ ἱερέως Ἀπολλωνίδου τοῦ*

2 *Μοσχίωνος Ἀλεξάνδρου καὶ θεῶν Ἀδελφῶν καὶ θεῶν Εὐεργετῶν, κανηφόρου Ἀρσινόης Φιλαδέλφου Μενεκρατείας*

3 *τῆς Φιλάμμονος, μηνὸς Ἀπελλαίου ἑβδομῃ, Αἰγυπτίων δὲ Τυβὶ ἑπτακαιδεκάτῃ.*

Ψήφισμα.

Οἱ ἀρχιερεῖς

4 *καὶ προφῆται καὶ οἱ εἰς τὸ ἄδυτον εἰσπορευόμενοι πρὸς τὸν στολισμὸν τῶν θεῶν κα πτεροφόραι καὶ ἱερογραμματεῖς καὶ*

CHAPTER VI.

THE GREEK TEXT OF THE DECREE OF CANOPUS.

English Rendering.

1 In the reign of Ptolemy, the son of Ptolemy and Arsinoë, the Brother Gods, the ninth year, Apollonides, the son of Moschion, being priest of Alexander,

2 and of the Brother Gods, and of the Good-doing Gods, and Menekrateia, the daughter of Philammon, being Canephoros of

3 Arsinoė Philadelphos, on the seventh day of the month Apellaios,[1] [which is] the seventeenth day of the month Tybi of the Egyptians.

Decree

The high priests,

4 and the prophets, and those who go into the holy place to array the gods in their ornamental apparel, and the bearers of feathers, and the sacred scribes,

[1] A Macedonian month answering to our December.

5 οἱ ἄλλοι ἱερεῖς οἱ συναντήσαντες ἐκ τῶν κατὰ τὴν χώραν ἱερῶν εἰς τὴν πέμπτην τοῦ Δίου, ἐν ᾗ ἄγεται τὰ γενέθλια τοῦ

6 βασιλέως, καὶ εἰς τὴν πέμπτην καὶ εἰκάδα τοῦ αὐτοῦ μηνός, ἐν ᾗ παρέλαβεν τὴν βασιλείαν παρὰ τοῦ πατρός, συνεδρεύσαντες

7 ταύτῃ τῇ ἡμέρᾳ ἐν τῷ ἐν Κανώπῳ ἱερῷ τῶν Εὐεργετῶν θεῶν εἶπαν·

Ἐπειδὴ βασιλεὺς Πτολεμαῖος Πτολεμαίου καὶ Ἀρσινοης, θεῶν Ἀδελφῶν,

8 καὶ βασίλισσα Βερενίκη ἡ ἀδελφὴ αὐτοῦ καὶ γυνή, θεοὶ Εὐεργέται, διατελοῦσιν πολλὰ καὶ μεγάλα εὐεργετοῦντες τὰ κατὰ τὴν χώραν ἱερὰ καὶ

9 τὰς τιμὰς τῶν θεῶν ἐπὶ πλέον αὔξοντες· τοῦ τε Ἄπιος καὶ τοῦ Μνηύιος καὶ τῶν λοιπῶν ἐνλογίμων ἱερῶν ζῴων τῶν ἐν τῇ χώρᾳ τὴν

10 ἐπιμέλειαν διαπαντὸς ποιοῦνται μετὰ μεγάλης δαπάνης καὶ χορηγίας· καὶ τὰ ἐξενεγχθέντα ἐκ τῆς χώρας ἱερὰ ἀγάλματα ὑπὸ

11 τῶν Περσῶν ἐξστρατεύσας ὁ βασιλεὺς ἀνέσῳσεν Αἴγυπτον καὶ ἀπέδωκεν εἰς τὰ ἱερά, ὅθεν ἕκαστον ἐξ ἀρχῆς ἐξήχθη· τήν τε

5 and the other priests who gathered themselves together from the temples throughout the country for the FIFTH day of [the month] Dios,[1] whereon are celebrated the birthday festivals of
6 the King, and for the TWENTY-FIFTH day of the same month, whereon he received the sovereignty from his father, having assembled
7 on this day in the temple of the Good-doing Gods in Canopus, spake thus:

"Inasmuch as King Ptolemy, the son of "Ptolemy and Arsinoë, the Brother Gods,
8 "and the Queen Berenice, his Sister and Wife, "the Good-doing Gods, are at all times performing "very many and great deeds of benevolence to the "temples throughout the country; and are
9 "multiplying exceedingly the honours of the gods; "and for Apis and for Mnevis, and for the other "sacred animals which are held in honour "throughout the country,
10 "they take the greatest care in every way possible, "with great expense and provisions in abundance; "and the sacred images [of the gods] which had "been carried out from the country
11 "by the Persians, the king, having carried out an "expedition, brought them back safely into Egypt, "and restored [them] to the temples wherefrom "each had been originally carried off;

[1] A Macedonian month corresponding to our October and November.

12 χώραν ἐν εἰρήνῃ διατετήρηκεν, προπολεμῶν ὑπὲρ αὐτῆς πρὸς πολλὰ ἔθνη καὶ τοὺς ἐν αὐτοῖς δυναστεύοντας· καὶ τοῖς ἐν τῇ χώρᾳ

13 πᾶσιν καὶ τοῖς ἄλλοις τοῖς ὑπὸ τὴν αὐτῶν βασίλειαν τασσομένοις τὴν εὐνομίαν παρέχουσιν, τοῦ τε ποταμοῦ ποτε ἐλλιπέστερον ἀνα-

14 βάντος καὶ πάντων τῶν ἐν τῇ χώρᾳ καταπεπληγμένων ἐπὶ τῳ συμβεβηκότι καὶ ἐνθυμουμένων τὴν γεγενημένην καταφθορὰν

15 ἐπὶ τινων τῶν πρότερον βεβασιλευκότων, ἐφ ὧν συνέβη ἀβροχίαις περιπεπτωκέναι τοὺς τὴν χώραν κατοικοῦντας, προστάντες κηδεμο-

16 νικῶς τῶν τε ἐν τοῖς ἱεροῖς καὶ τῶν ἄλλων τῶν τὴν χώραν κατοικούντων, πολλὰ μὲν προνοηθέντες, οὐκ ὀλίγας δὲ τῶν προσόδων ὑπερ-

17 ιδόντες ἕνεκα τῆς τῶν ἀνθρώπων σωτηρίας, ἔκ τε Συρίας καὶ Φοινίκης καὶ Κύπρου καὶ ἐξ ἄλλων πλειόνων τόπων σῖτον μετα-

18 πεμψάμενοι εἰς τὴν χώραν τιμῶν μειζόνων διέσῳσαν τοὺς τὴν Αἴγυπτον κατοικοῦντας, ἀθάνατον εὐεργεσίαν καὶ τῆς αὐτῶν ἀρετῆς

12 "and hath preserved the country in peace, fighting
"battles on its behalf against many peoples and
"those who were masters over them; and to all
"those who are in the country,
13 "and to [all] others who are in subjection to their[1]
"sovereignty, administers good government; and
"when on one occasion the river [NILE] did not
"rise
14 "[to its proper height], and all those who were in
"the country were terror-stricken at what had
"happened, and they recalled in their memories
"the calamities which had taken place
15 "under some of the kings who had reigned before,
"when it fell out that those who inhabited the
"country were distressed for the want of water;
"[they, i e., Ptolemy and Berenice,] aided and
"bestowed care upon
16 "those who inhabited the temples, and those who
"dwelt throughout the country, and by taking
"much forethought, and by giving up no small
"amount of their revenues
17 "in order to save men's lives, having sent into the
"country corn from SYRIA, and PHOENICIA, and
"CYPRUS, and from many other districts
18 "where prices were high, they saved those who
"lived in EGYPT, and so leave behind them a
"deathless deed of kindness, and of their own
"merit

[1] I.e., the king and queen.

19 μέγιστον ὑπόμνημα καταλείποντες τοῖς τε νῦν
οὖσιν καὶ τοῖς ἐπιγινομένοις, ἀνθ' ὧν οἱ θεοὶ
δεδώκασιν αὐτοῖς εὐσταθοῦσαν τὴν βασιλεί-
20 αν καὶ δώσουσιν τἄλλ' ἀγαθὰ πάντα εἰς τὸν
ἀεὶ χρόνον·

ἀγαθῇ τύχῃ

δεδόχθαι τοῖς κατὰ τὴν χώραν ἱερευσιν· τάς
τε προυπαρχούσας
21 τιμὰς ἐν τοῖς ἱεροῖς βασιλεῖ Πτολεμαίῳ καὶ βασι-
λισσῃ Βερενίκῃ θεοῖς Εὐεργέταις καὶ τοῖς γονε-
ῦσιν αὐτῶν θεοῖς Ἀδελφοῖς καὶ τοῖς προγόνοις
22 θεοῖς Σωτῆρσιν αὔξειν· καὶ τοὺς ἱερεῖς τοὺς
ἐν ἑκάστῳ τῶν κατὰ τὴν χώραν ἱερῶν προσ-
ονομάζεσθαι ἱερεῖς καὶ τῶν Εὐεργετῶν θεῶν.
καὶ ἐνγράφε-
23 σθαι ἐν πᾶσιν τοῖς χρηματισμοῖς, καὶ ἐν
τοῖς δακτυλίοις οἷς φοροῦσιν προςεγκολάπ-
τεσθαι καὶ τὴν ἱερωσύνην τῶν Εὐεργετῶν
θεῶν· προςαποδειχθῆ-
24 ναι δὲ πρὸς[1] ταῖς νῦν ὑπαρχούσαις τέσσαρσι
φυλαῖς τοῦ πλήθους τῶν ἱερέων τῶν ἐν ἑκάστῳ
ἱερῷ καὶ ἄλλην, ἣ προςονομασθήσεται πέμ-
25 πτη φυλὴ τῶν Εὐ[ε]ργετῶν θεῶν, ἐπεὶ καὶ[2] σὺν
τῇ ἀγαθῇ τύχῃ καὶ τὴν γένεσιν βασιλέως Πτολεμαίου τοῦ τῶν θεῶν Ἀδελφῶν συμβέβηκεν

[1] The text has προις. [2] Lepsius, [καὶ].

19 "a great memorial, both to present and future "generations, and in return wherefor the gods "have given to them firmly stablished dominion

20 "and they shall give unto them all other good "things for ever and for ever!" WITH FAVOURING FORTUNE: It hath been decreed by the priests everywhere in the country, to multiply the

21 honours which are at present [paid] in the temples to King PTOLEMY and Queen BERENICE, the Good-doing Gods, and to those who begot them, the Brother Gods, and to their ancestors,

22 the Saviour Gods; and the priests who are in each and every temple throughout the country shall, in addition [to their other titles,] be called "priests of the Good-doing Gods"; and the priesthood of the Good-doing Gods

23 shall be inscribed in all their deeds (*or*, instruments), and shall be engraved upon the rings which they wear; and there shall be established,

24 in addition to the four tribes of the company of priests which already exist in each and every temple, another tribe which shall be named the

25 Fifth Tribe of [the priests of] the Good-doing Gods, since it hath happened with favouring fortune, that the birth of King Ptolemy, the son of the Brother Gods,

26 γενέσθαι τῇ πέμπτῃ τοῦ Δίου, ἥ καὶ πολλῶν
ἀγαθῶν ἀρχὴ γέγονεν πᾶσιν ἀνθρώποις· εἰς
δὲ τὴν φυλὴν ταύτην καταλεχθῆναι τοὺς ἀπὸ
27 τοῦ πρώτου ἔτους γεγενημένους ἱερεῖς καὶ τοὺς
προςκαταταγησομένους ἕως μηνὸς Μεσορη
τοῦ ἐν τῷ ἐνάτῳ ἔτει, καὶ τοὺς τούτων ἐκγόνους εἰς τὸν ἀεὶ
28 χρόνον, τοὺς δὲ προυπάρχοντας ἱερεῖς ἕως τοῦ
πρώτου ἔτους εἶναι ὡςαύτως ἐν ταῖς αὐταῖς
φυλαῖς ἐν αἷς πρότερον ἦσαν, ὁμοίως δὲ καὶ
τοὺς
29 ἐκγόνους αὐτῶν ἀπὸ τοῦ νῦν καταχωρίζεσθαι
εἰς τὰς αὐτὰς φυλὰς ἐν αἷς οἱ πατέρες εἰσίν.
ἀντὶ δὲ τῶν εἴκοσι βουλευτῶν ἱερέων τῶν
αἱρουμένων
30 κατ' ἐνιαυτὸν ἐκ τῶν προυπαρχουσῶν τεσσάρων φυλῶν, ἐξ ὧν πέντε ἀφ' ἑκάστης φυλῆς
λαμβάνονται, εἴκοσι καὶ πέντε τοὺς βου-
λευτὰς
31 ἱερεῖς εἶναι, προσλαμβανομενων ἐκ τῆς πέμπτης φυλῆς τῶν Εὐεργετῶν θεῶν ἄλλων πέντε·
μετέχειν δὲ καὶ τοὺς ἐκ τῆς πέμπτης
32 φυλῆς τῶν Εὐεργετῶν θεῶν τῶν ἁγνειῶν καὶ
τῶν ἄλλων ἁπάντων τῶν ἐν τοῖς ἱεροῖς· καὶ
φύλαρχον αὐτῆς εἶναι, καθὰ καὶ ἐπὶ τῶν
ἄλλων τεσ-

26 took place on the fifth day of the month DIOS, which became the source of very many good things for all mankind; and among this tribe shall be

27 entered the priests who have been born since the FIRST year, and those who are to be inscribed among them, up to the month of MESORE, in the NINTH year, and those who shall be begotten by them

28 for ever; and those who were priests up to the first year shall continue in the tribes wherein they were, and similarly,

29 the children who shall be begotten by them shall be entered among the tribes wherein their fathers were; and instead of the twenty priests who formed the Council,

30 who are elected each year from the four tribes of priests which already exist, five from each tribe, the priests who form the Council shall be five and twenty [in number],

31 and the five additional priests shall be taken from the Fifth Tribe of the Good-doing Gods; and the priests of the Fifth Tribe of the

32 Good-doing Gods shall have their portion in the religious services, and also in everything which is in the temples, and there shall be a chief priest of the Tribe [Phylarch], even as there is to the other

33 σάρων φυλῶν ὑπάρχει· καὶ ἐπειδὴ καθ' ἕκαστον μῆνα ἄγονται ἐν τοῖς ἱεροῖς ἑορταί τῶν Εὐεργετῶν θεῶν κατὰ τὸ πρότερον γραφὲν ψήφισμα

34 ἥ τε πέμπτη καὶ ἡ ἐνάτη καὶ ἡ πέμπτη ἐπ' εἰκάδι, τοῖς τε ἄλλοις μεγίστοις θεοῖς κατ' ἐνιαυτὸν συντελοῦνται ἑορταὶ καὶ πανηγύρεις δημοτε-

35 λεῖς, ἄγεσθαι κατ' ἐνιαυτὸν πανήγυριν δημοτελῆ ἔν τε τοῖς ἱεροῖς καὶ καθ' ὅλην τὴν[1] χώραν βασιλεῖ Πτολεμαίῳ καὶ βασιλίσσῃ Βερενίκῃ

36 θεοῖς Εὐεργέταις τῇ ἡμέρᾳ, ἐν ᾗ ἐπιτέλλει τὸ ἄστρον τὸ τῆς Ἴσιος, ἣ νομίζεται διὰ τῶν ἱερῶν γραμμάτων νέον ἔτος εἶναι, ἄγεται δὲ νῦν ἐν τῷ

37 ἐνάτῳ ἔτει νουμηνίᾳ τοῦ Παῦνι μηνὸς, ἐν ᾧ καὶ τὰ μικρὰ βουβάστια καὶ τὰ μεγάλα Βουβάστια ἄγεται καὶ ἡ συναγωγὴ τῶν καρπῶν καὶ ἡ τοῦ

38 ποταμοῦ ἀνάβασις γίνεται· ἐὰν δὲ καὶ συμβαίνῃ τὴν ἐπιτολὴν τοῦ ἄστρου μεταβαίνειν εἰς ἑτέραν ἡμέραν διὰ τεσσάρων ἐτῶν, μὴ μετατί-

39 θεσθαι τὴν πανήγυριν, ἀλλ' ἄγεσθαι [ὁμοίως] τῇ νουμηνίᾳ τοῦ Παῦνι, ἐν ᾗ καὶ ἐξ ἀρχῆς ἤχθη ἐν τῷ ἐνατῷ ἔτει· καὶ συντελεῖν αὐτὴν ἐπὶ ἡμέρας

[1] The text actually has τηντην.

33 four tribes. And inasmuch as there are celebrated in the temples each month feasts of the Good-doing Gods, according to the Decree which was passed originally, namely on the

34 FIFTH day, and the NINTH day, and the TWENTY-FIFTH day; and since to the other great gods there are celebrated each year festivals and processions by the people generally: a general fes-

35 tival and procession shall be celebrated each year, both in the temples and by the people throughout all the country, to King PTOLEMY and Queen BERENICE,

36 the Good-doing Gods, on the day whereon the star of ISIS riseth, which, according to the holy books, is regarded as the New Year and is now kept, in

37 the NINTH year, on the first day of the month PAYNI, whereon the Greater and Lesser festivals of Bubastis are celebrated, and the garnering of the fruit and

38 the rise of the River take place; but though it shall fall out that the rising of the star shall, in the course of four years, change to another day, the festival and procession shall not be

39 changed, but they shall be celebrated on the first day of PAYNI, even as they were celebrated originally on that day in the NINTH year; and the festival shall last for

40 πέντε μετὰ στεφανηφορίας καὶ θυσιῶν καὶ σπονδῶν καὶ τῶν ἄλλων τῶν προσηκόντων· ὅπως δὲ καὶ αἱ ὧραι τὸ καθῆκον ποιῶσιν διαπαντὸς κατὰ τὴν νῦν

41 οὖσαν κατάστασιν[1] τοῦ κόσμου καὶ μὴ συμβαίνῃ τινὰς τῶν δημοτελῶν ἑορτῶν τῶν ἀγομένων ἐν τῷ χειμῶνι ἄγεσθαι ποτε ἐν τῷ θέρει, τοῦ ἄστρου

42 μεταβαίνοντος μίαν ἡμέραν διὰ τεσσάρων ἐτῶν, ἑτέρας δὲ τῶν νῦν ἀγομένων ἐν τῷ θέρει ἄγεσθαι ἐν τῷ χειμῶνι ἐν τοῖς μετὰ ταῦτα καιροῖς, καθάπερ πρό-

43 τερόν τε συμβέβηκεν γενέσθαι, καὶ[2] νῦν ἂν ἐγίνετο τῆς συντάξεως τοῦ ἐνιαυτοῦ μενούσης ἐκ τῶν τριακοσίων καὶ ἑξήκοντα ἡμερῶν καὶ τῶν ὕστερον προς-

44 νομισθεισῶν ἐπάγεσθαι πέντε ἡμερῶν, ἀπὸ τοῦ νῦν μίαν ἡμέραν ἑορτὴν τῶν Εὐεργετῶν θεῶν ἐπάγεσθαι διὰ τεσσάρων ἐτῶν ἐπὶ ταῖς πέντε ταῖς

45 ἐπαγομέναις πρὸ τοῦ νέου ἔτους, ὅπως ἅπαντες εἰδῶσιν, διότι τὸ ἐλλεῖπον πρότερον περὶ τὴν σύνταξιν τῶν ὡρῶν καὶ τοῦ ἐνιαυτοῦ καὶ τῶν νομιζο-

1 The text actually has καταστασταστασιν.

The text actually has κα.

40 five days, and crowns shall be worn, and sacrifices and libations [shall be made], and whatsoever ought to be done shall be done. And that the seasons of the year may coincide wholly with the present

41 settlement (*or*, constitution) of the world, and that it may not happen that some of the popular festivals which ought to be held in the winter come to be celebrated in the summer, [owing to] the STAR (i.e., the Sun)

42 changing one day in the course of four years, and that festivals which are now kept in the summer come to be celebrated in the winter in times to come, even as hath

43 formerly happened, and would happen at the present time if the year continued to consist of three hundred and sixty days, and the five additional days which

44 it is customary to add thereto: from this time onwards one day, a festival of the Good-doing Gods, shall be added every four years to the five additional days

45 before the New Year, so that all [men] may know that the error of deficiency which existed formerly in respect of the arrangement of the seasons, and of the year, and of the views usually believed

46 μένων περὶ τὴν ὅλην διακόσμησιν τοῦ πόλου διωρθῶσθαι καὶ ἀναπεπληρῶσθαι συμβέβηκεν διὰ τῶν Εὐεργετῶν θεῶν· καὶ ἐπειδὴ τὴν ἐγ βασιλέως Πτολεμαίου

47 καὶ βασιλίσσης Βερενίκης, θεῶν Εὐεργετῶν, γεγενημένην θυγατέρα καὶ ὀνομασθεῖσαν Βερενίκην, ἥ καὶ βασίλισσα εὐθέως ἀπεδείχθη, συνέβη ταύτην πάρθενον

48 οὖσαν ἐξαίφνης μετελθεῖν εἰς τὸν ἀέναον κόσμον, ἔπι ἐνδημούντων παρὰ τῷ βασιλεῖ τῶν ἐκ τῆς χώρας παραγινομένων πρὸς αὐτὸν κατ' ἐνιαυτὸν ἱερέων

49 οἵ μέγα [μὲν] πένθος ἐπὶ τῷ συμβεβηκότι εὐθέως συνετέλεσαν, ἀξιώσαντες δὲ τὸν βασιλέα καὶ τὴν βασίλισσαν ἔπεισαν καθιδρῦσαι τὴν θεὰν μετὰ τοῦ 'Οσίριος ἐν τῷ

50 ἐν Κανώπῳ ἱερῷ, ὅ οὐ μόνον ἐν τοῖς πρώτοις [ἱ]εροῖς ἐστιν, ἀλλὰ καὶ ὑπὸ τοῦ βασιλέως καὶ τῶν κατὰ τὴν χώραν πάντων ἐν τοῖς μάλιστα τιμωνένοις ὑπάρχει

51 καὶ ἡ ἀναγωγὴ τοῦ ἱεροῦ πλοίου τοῦ 'Οσείριος εἰς τοῦτο τὸ ἱερὸν κατ' ἐνιαυτὸν γίνεται ἐκ τοῦ ἐν τῷ 'Ηρακλείῳ ἱεροῦ τῇ ἐνάτῃ καὶ εἰκάδι τοῦ Χοῖαχ, τῶν ἐκ τῶν πρώ-

52 των ἱερῶν πάντων θυσίας συντελούντων ἐπὶ τῶν ἱδρυμένων ὑπ' αὐτῶν βωμῶν ὑπὲρ ἑκάστου

46 concerning the general ordering of the heavens hath been rectified and filled up satisfactorily by the Good-doing Gods. And since it hath happened that the daughter who was born of

47 King Ptolemy and Queen Berenice, the Good-doing Gods, and was called Berenice, who was straightway proclaimed Queen, being a virgin, departed

48 suddenly into the everlasting world, whilst there were with him the priests who were wont to gather themselves together to the King every year,

49 they made great mourning straightway because of that which had happened, and having made supplication to the King and Queen, they persuaded them to establish the Goddess (i.e., Berenice) with Osiris

50 in the temple of Canopus, which is not only among the temples of the first class, but is also held in the greatest reverence, both by the King and all the people throughout the country,

51 and the bringing up of the sacred bark of Osiris to this temple from the temple in the Herakleion taketh place each year, on the twenty-ninth day of the month Choiach, when all [the priests] from

52 the temples of the first class offer up sacrifices upon the altars which they have set up for each

ἱεροῦ τῶν πρώτων ἐξ ἀμφοτέρων τῶν μερῶν τοῦ δρόμου

53 μετὰ δὲ ταῦτα [τὰ] πρὸς τὴν ἐκθέωσιν αὐτῆς νόμιμα καὶ τὴν τοῦ πένθους ἀπόλυσιν ἀπέδωκαν μεγαλοπρεπῶς καὶ κηδεμονικῶς, καθάπερ καὶ ἐπὶ τῷ Ἄ[πει]

54 καὶ Μνηύει εἰθισμένον ἐστίν γίνεσθαι· δεδόχθαι συντελεῖν τῇ ἐκ τῶν Εὐεργετῶν θεῶν γεγενημένῃ βασιλίσσῃ Βερενίκῃ τιμὰς ἀΐδιους ἐν ἅπασι τοῖ[ς]

55 κατὰ τὴν χώραν ἱεροῖς· καὶ ἐπεὶ εἰς θεοὺς μετῆλθεν ἐν τᾷ Τῦβὶ μηνὶ, ἐν ᾧπερ καὶ ἡ τοῦ Ἡλίου θυγατὴρ ἐν ἀρχῇ μετήλλαξεν τὸν βίον, ἣν ὁ πατὴρ στέρξας ὠ[νό]-

56 μασεν ὅτε μὲν βασιλείαν ὅτε [δὲ] ὅρασιν αὐτοῦ, καὶ ἄγουσιν αὐτῇ ἑορτὴν καὶ περίπλουν ἐν πλείοσιν ἱεροῖς τῶν πρώτων ἐν τούτῳ τῷ μηνὶ, ἐν ᾧ ἡ ἀποθέωσις αὐ[τῆς]

57 ἐν ἀρχῇ ἐγενήθη, συντελεῖν καὶ βασιλίσσῃ Βερενίκῃ τῇ ἐκ τῶν Εὐεργετῶν θεῶν ἐν ἅπασι τοῖς κατὰ τὴν χώραν ἱεροῖς ἐν τῷ Τῦβι μηνὶ ἑορτὴν καὶ πε-

58 ρίπλουν ἐφ᾽ ἡμέρας τέσσαρας ἀπὸ ἑπτακαιδεκάτης,[1] ἐν ᾗ ὁ περίπλους καὶ ἡ τοῦ πένθους

[1] The text actually has επτακαιδεκατηι.

of the temples of the first class on each side of the dromos,

53 and after this they performed all the things which were connected with making her divine, and brought to an end the mourning ceremonies with all the magnificence and great care which it is wont to show [at the burials of] Apis

54 and Mnevis. It is decreed: to pay to Queen Berenice, the daughter of the Good-doing Gods, everlasting honours in all the

55 temples throughout the country; and inasmuch as she went to the gods in the month of Tybi, wherein, at the beginning, the daughter of Helios departed from life, whom her loving father

56 at one time called his "crown," and at another his "sight," and they celebrate in her honour a festival and tow round the sacred boat of Osiris in procession in the greater number of the temples of the first class in this month, wherein her apotheosis

57 took place originally; and to celebrate for Queen Berenice also, the daughter of the Good-doing Gods, in all the temples throughout the country, in the month of Tybi, a festival and

58 a procession for four days, from the seventeenth day, wherein the procession and the conclusion of

ἀπόλυσις ἐγενήθη αὐτῇ τὴν ἀρχήν· συντελέσαι δ' αὐτῆς καὶ

59 ἱερὸν ἄγαλμα χρυσοῦν διάλιθον ἐν ἑκάστῳ τῶν πρώτων καὶ δευτέρων ἱερῶν, καὶ καθιδρῦσαι ἐν τῷ ἁγίῳ ὁ δὲ[1] προφήτης ἢ τῶν εἰς τὸ ἄδυτον εἰσπορευομένων[2]

60 ἱερέων πρὸς τὸν στολισμὸν τῶν θεῶν οἴσει ἐν ταῖς ἀγκάλαις, ὅταν αἱ ἐξοδεῖαι καὶ πανηγύρεις τῶν λοιπῶν θεῶν γίντοντα[ι], ὅπως ὑπὸ πάντων ὁρώμενον

61 τιμᾶται καὶ προσκυνῆται καλούμενον, 'Βερενίκης ἀνάσσης παρθένων·' εἶναι δὲ τὴν ἐπιτιθεμένην[3] βασιλείαν τῇ εἰκόνι αὐτῆς διαφέρουσαν τῆς ἐπιτιθεμένης

62 ταῖς εἰκόσιν τῆς μητρὸς αὐτῆς βασιλίσσης Βερενίκης, ἐκ σταχύων δυῶν, ὧν ἀνὰ μέσον ἔσται ἡ ἀσπιδοειδὴς βασιλεία, ταύτης δ' ὀπίσω σύμμετρον σκῆπτρον

63 παπυροειδές, ὃ εἰώθασιν αἱ θεαὶ ἔχειν ἐν ταῖς χερσὶν, περὶ οὗ καὶ ἡ οὐρὰ τῆς βασιλείας ἔσται περιειλημμένη ὥστε καὶ ἐκ τῆς διαθέσεως τῆς βασιλείας δια-

64 σαφεῖσθαι τὸ Βερενίκης ὄνομα κατὰ τὰ ἐπί-

[1] Strack's reading is ὁ προφήτης.

[2] The text actually has ειρημενων.

[3] Strack has ἐπιτιθεμένον.

the lamentation originally took place; and to make of her

59 a sacred image of gold, set with precious stones, in each of the temples of the first and second class, and to set it up in the holy place [in each], which the prophet, or one of the [priests] who go into the sanctuary

60 for the [purpose of] dressing the gods, shall carry in his arms, when the journeyings forth [of the gods] on the festivals of the other gods are celebrated, so that being seen by all

61 it may be adored and bowed down to under the name of "Berenice, the Queen of Virgins"; and moreover, the crown which shall be placed upon the head of her image shall be different from that

62 which is placed upon the image of her mother Queen Berenice, and it shall be of two ears of corn between which shall be a serpent-shaped crown, and behind this shall be a sceptre,

63 papyrus-shaped, [similar to those] which the goddesses are wont to hold in their hands, and round this [sceptre] the tail of the serpent-crown shall be wound, so that from the arrangement of the crown

64 the name of Berenice shall be indicated according to the distinguishing signs of the hieroglyphics;

σημα τὴς ἱερᾶς γραμματικῆς καὶ ὅταν τὰ Κικήλλια ἄγηται ἐν τῷ Χοῖαχ μηνὶ πρὸ τοῦ περίπλου τοῦ 'Οσείριος, κατα-

65 σκευάσαι τὰς παρθένους τῶν ἱερέων ἄλλο ἄγαλμα Βερενίκης ἀνάσσης παρθένων, ᾧ συντελέσουσιν ὁμοίως θυσίαν καὶ τἄλλα τὰ συντελούμενα νό-

66 μιμα τῇ ἑορτῇ ταύτῃ· ἐξεῖναι δὲ κατὰ ταὐτὰ καὶ ταῖς ἄλλαις παρθένοις ταῖς βουλομέναις συντελεῖν τὰ νόμιμα τῇ θεῷ· ὑμνεῖσθαι δ' αὐτὴν καὶ ὑ-

67 πὸ τῶν ἐπιλεγομένων ἱερῶν[1] παρθένων καὶ τὰς χρείας παρεχομένων τοῖς θεοῖς, περικειμένων τὰς ἰδίας βασιλείας τῶν θεῶν, ὧν ἱέρειαι νομιζοντα[ι]

68 εἶναι·[2] καὶ, ὅταν ὁ πρώϊμος[3] σπόρος παραστῇ, ἀναφέρειν τὰς ἱερὰς παρθένους στάχυς τοὺς παρατεθησομένοως[4] τῷ ἀγάλματι τῆς θεοῦ· ᾄδειν δ' εἰς αὐτὴν

69 καθ' ἡμέραν καὶ ἐν ταῖς ἑορταῖς καὶ πανηγύρεσιν τῶν λοιπῶν θεῶν τούς τε ᾠδοὺς ἄνδρας καὶ τὰς γυναῖκας, οὓς ἂν ὕμνους οἱ ἱερογραμματεῖς γρά-

[1] The text actually has ιερειων.

[2] *Ibid.*, εικαικαι.

[3] *Ibid.*, προωριμος.

[4] *Ibid.*, παραθησομενους.

and when the Kikellia are celebrated in the month of Choiach before the procession (Periplus) of Osiris,

65 the daughters of the priests shall make ready another image of Berenice, the Queen of Virgins, whereto likewise they shall offer up sacrifices and shall perform all the other things which it is customary to perform

66 at this festival; and it shall be lawful, after the same manner, for other virgins who desire to perform the ceremonies which it is customary to perform to the goddess, so to do; and hymns shall be sung to her,

67 both by the holy virgins who are specially chosen and by those who minister unto the gods, and who shall put on their heads the crowns which are peculiar to the gods, whose priestesses they are held

68 to be; and when the early harvest is nigh, the holy virgins shall bear the ears of corn which are to be set before the image of the goddess; and both at the festivals

69 and in the panegyries of the other gods the singing men and the singing women shall sing unto her daily the songs which the sacred scribes,

70 ψαντες δῶσιν τῷ ᾠδοδιδασκάλῳ, ὧν καὶ τἀντίγραφα καταχωρισθήσεται εἰς τὰς ἱερὰς βύβλους· καὶ, ἐπειδὴ τοῖς ἱερεῦσιν δίδονται αἱ τροφαί ἐκ τῶν

71 ἱερῶν, ἐπὰν ἐπαχθῶσιν εἰς τὸ πλῆθος, δίδοσθαι ταῖς θυγατράσιν τῶν ἱερέων ἐκ τῶν ἱερῶν προσόδων, ἀφ' ἧς ἂν ἡμέρας γένωνται, τὴν συνκριθησομέ-

72 νὴν τροφὴν ὑπὸ τῶν βουλευτῶν ἱερέων τῶν ἐν ἑκάστῳ τῶν ἱερῶν κατὰ λόγον τῶν ἱερῶν προσόδων· καὶ τὸν διδόμενον ἄρτον ταῖς γυναιξὶν

73 τῶν ἱερέων ἔχειν ἴδιον τύπον καὶ καλεῖσθαι 'Βερενίκης ἄρτον.'

Ὁ δ' ἐν ἑκαστῳ τῶν ἱερῶν καθεστηκὼς ἐπιστάτης καὶ ἀρχιερεὺς καὶ οἱ τοῦ ἱεροῦ

74 γραμματεῖς ἀναγραφάτωσαν τοῦτο τὸ ψήφισμα εἰς στήλην λιθίνην ἢ χαλκὴν ἱεροῖς γράμμασιν καὶ Αἰγυπτίοις καὶ Ἑλληνικοῖς καὶ ἀναθε-

75 τωσαν ἐν τῷ ἐπιφανεστάτῳ τόπῳ τῶν τε πρώτων ἱερῶν καὶ δευτέρων καὶ τρίτων[1] ὅπως οἱ κατὰ τὴν χώραν ἱερεῖς φαίνωνται τιμῶντας (sic) τοὺς Εὐεργετὰς θεοὺς καὶ τὰ τέκνα αὐτῶν,

76 καθάπερ δίκαιόν ἐστιν.

[1] The text actually has των τε Α ιερων και Β και Γ.

70 having written them down, shall give to the singing master, whereof copies shall be inscribed in the sacred books; and when supplies of food are given to the priests out of the
71 revenues of the temples, whensoever they are brought for the whole company [of the priests], there shall be given to the daughters of the priests out of the revenues of the temples, [reckoning] from the day when they were born, the subsistence
72 which hath been calculated by the Councillor-Priests in each of the temples, according to the amount of the revenues of the temples; and the bread which shall be given to the wives of the priests shall have a special form, and shall be called the "Bread of Berenice."
73 And the governor who hath been appointed in each temple, and the high-priest, and the sacred scribes in each temple
74 shall inscribe a copy of this decree upon a stele of stone or bronze in the hieroglyphic characters, and in Egyptian and Greek characters, and shall
75 set it up in the place where it will be most seen in the temples of the first, and second, and third class, so that the priests throughout the country may show that they hold in honour the Good-doing Gods, and their children,
76 as is most right.

CHAPTER VII.

THE DECREE OF CANOPUS.

Greek Text I.

1 ΒΑΣΙΛΕΥΟΝΤΟΣΠΤΟΛΕΜΑΙΟΥΤΟΥΠΤ
ΟΛΕΜΑΙΟΥΚΑΙΑΡΣΙΝΟΗΣΘΕΩΝΑΔΕΛΦ
ΩΝΕΤΟΥΣΕΝΑΤΟΥΕΦΙΕΡΕΩΣΑΠΟΛΛΩ
ΝΙΔΟΥΤΟΥ
2 ΜΟΣΧΙΩΝΟΣΑΛΕΞΑΝΔΡΟΥΚΑΙΘΕΩΝΑ
ΔΕΛΦΩΝΚΑΙΘΕΩΝΕΥΕΡΓΕΤΩΝΚΑΝΗΦΟ
ΡΟΥΑΡΣΙΝΟΗΣΦΙΛΑΔΕΛΦΟΥΜΕΝΕΚΡΑ
ΤΕΙΑΣ
3 ΤΗΣΦΙΛΑΜΜΩΝΟΣΜΗΝΟΣΑΠΕΛΛΑΙΟΥ
ΕΒΔΟΜΗΙΑΙΓΥΠΤΙΩΝΔΕΤΥΒΙΕΠΤΑΚΑΙ
[illegible] ΔΕΚΑΤΗΙ ΨΗΦΙΣΜΑΟΙΑΡΧΙΕ
ΡΕΙΣ
4 ΚΑΙΠΡΟΦΗΤΑΙΚΑΙΟΙΕΙΣΤΟΑΔΥΤΟΝΕΙΣ
ΠΟΡΕΥΟΜΕΝΟΙΠΡΟΣΤΟΝΣΤΟΛΙΣΜΟΝ
ΤΩΝΘΕΩΝΚΑΙΠΤΕΡΟΦΟΡΑΙΚΑΙΙΕΡΟΓΡ
ΑΜΜΑΤΕΙΣΚΑΙ
5 ΟΙΑΛΛΟΙΙΕΡΕΙΣΟΙΣΥΝΑΝΤΗΣΑΝΤΕΣΕ
ΚΤΩΝΚΑΤΑΤΗΝΧΩΡΑΝΙΕΡΩΝΕΙΣΤΗΝ
ΠΕΜΠΤΗΝΤΟΥΔΙΟΥΕΝΗΙΑΓΕΤΑΙΤΑΓΕ
ΝΕΘΛΙΑΤΟΥ
6 ΒΑΣΙΛΕΩΣΚΑΙΕΙΣΤΗΝΠΕΜΠΤΗΝΚΑΙΕΙ

ΚΑΔΑΤΟΥΑΥΤΟΥΜΗΝΟΣΕΝΗΙΠΑΡΕΛΑ
ΒΕΝΤΗΝΒΑΣΙΛΕΙΑΝΠΑΡΑΤΟΥΠΑΤΡΟΣ
ΣΥΝΕΔΡΕΥΣΑΝΤΕΣ
7 ΤΑΥΤΗΙΤΗΙΗΜΕΡΑΙΕΝΤΩΙΕΝΚΑΝΩΠΩ
ΙΙΕΡΩΙΤΩΝΕΥΕΡΓΕΤΩΝΘΕΩΝΕΙΠΑΝ
ΕΠΕΙΔΗΒΑΣΙΛΕΥΣΠΤΟΛΕΜΑΙΟΣΠΤΟΛ
ΕΜΑΙΟΥΚΑΙΑΡΣΙΝΟΗΣΘΕΩΝΑΔΕΛΦΩΝ
8 ΚΑΙΒΑΣΙΛΙΣΣΑΒΕΡΕΝΙΚΗΗΑΔΕΛΦΗΑΥΤ
ΟΥΚΑΙΓΥΝΗΘΕΟΙΕΥΕΡΓΕΤΑΙΔΙΑΤΕΛΟΥ
ΣΙΝΠΟΛΛΑΚΑΙΜΕΓΑΛΑΕΥΕΡΓΕΤΟΥΝΤ
ΕΣΤΑΚΑΤΑΤΗΝΧΩΡΑΝΙΕΡΑΚΑΙ
9 ΤΑΣΤΙΜΑΣΤΩΝΘΕΩΝΕΠΙΠΛΕΟΝΑΥΞΟ
ΝΤΕΣΤΟΥΤΕΑΠΙΟΣΚΑΙΤΟΥΜΝΗΥΙΟΣ
ΚΑΙΤΩΝΛΟΙΠΩΝΕΝΛΟΓΙΜΩΝΙΕΡΩΝΖ
ΩΙΩΝΤΩΝΕΝΤΗΙΧΩΡΑΙΤΗΝ
10 ΕΠΙΜΕΛΕΙΑΝΔΙΑΠΑΝΤΟΣΠΟΙΟΥΝΤΑΙ
ΜΕΤΑΜΕΓΑΛΗΣΔΑΠΑΝΗΣΚΑΙΧΟΡΗΓΙΑ
ΣΚΑΙΤΑΕΞΕΝΕΓΧΘΕΝΤΑΕΚΤΗΣΧΩΡΑΣΙ
ΕΡΑΑΓΑΛΜΑΤΑΥΠΟ
11 ΤΩΝΠΕΡΣΩΝΕΞΣΤΡΑΤΕΥΣΑΣΟΒΑΣΙΛΕ
ΥΣΑΝΕΣΩΙΣΕΝΕΙΣΑΙΓΥΠΤΟΝΚΑΙΑΠΕΔ
ΩΚΕΝΕΗΣΤΑΙΕΡΑΟΘΕΝΕΚΑΣΤΟΝΕΞΑΡΧ
ΗΣΕΞΗΧΘΗΤΗΝΤΕ
12 ΧΩΡΑΝΕΝΕΙΡΗΝΗΙΔΙΑΤΕΤΗΡΗΚΕΝΠΡ
ΟΠΟΛΕΜΩΝΥΠΕΡΑΥΤΗΣΠΡΟΣΠΟΛΛΑ
ΕΘΝΗΚΑΙΤΟΥΣΕΝΑΥΤΟΙΣΔΥΝΑΣΤΕΥΟ
ΝΤΑΣΚΑΙΤΟΙΣΕΝΤΗΙΧΩΡΑΙ
13 ΠΑΣΙΝΚΑΙΤΟΙΣΑΛΛΟΙΣΤΟΙΣΥΠΟΤΗΝ

ΑΥΤΩΝΒΑΣΙΛΕΙΑΝΤΑΣΣΟΜΕΝΟΙΣΤΗΝ
ΕΥΝΟΜΙΑΝΠΑΡΕΧΟΥΣΙΝΤΟΥΤΕΠΟΤΑ
ΜΟΥΠΟΤΕΕΛΛΙΠΕΣΤΕΡΟΝΑΝΑ
14 ΒΑΝΤΟΣΚΑΙΠΑΝΤΩΝΤΩΝΕΝΤΗΙΧΩΡΑ
ΙΚΑΤΑΠΕΠΛΗΓΜΕΝΩΝΕΠΙΤΩΙΣΥΜΒΕΒ
ΗΚΟΤΙΚΑΙΕΝΘΥΜΟΥΜΕΝΩΝΤΗΝΓΕΓΕ
ΝΗΜΕΝΗΝΚΑΤΑΦΘΟΡΑΝ
15 ΕΠΙΤΙΝΩΝΤΩΝΠΡΟΤΕΡΟΝΒΕΒΑΣΙΛΕΥ
ΚΟΤΩΝΕΦΩΝΣΥΝΕΒΗΑΒΡΟΧΙΑΙΣΠΕΡΙ
ΠΕΠΤΩΚΕΝΑΙΤΟΥΣΤΗΝΧΩΡΑΝΚΑΤΟΙ
ΚΟΥΝΤΑΣΠΡΟΣΤΑΝΤΕΣΚΗΔΕΜΟ
16 ΝΙΚΩΣΤΩΝΤΕΕΝΤΟΙΣΙΕΡΟΙΣΚΑΙΤΩΝΑ
ΛΛΩΝΤΩΝΤΗΝΧΩΡΑΝΚΑΤΟΙΚΟΥΝΤΩ
ΝΠΟΛΛΑΜΕΝΠΡΟΝΟΗΘΕΝΤΕΣΟΥΚΟΛ
ΙΓΑΣΔΕΤΩΝΠΡΟΣΟΔΩΝΥΠΕΡ
17 ΙΔΟΝΤΕΣΕΝΕΚΑΤΗΣΤΩΝΑΝΘΡΩΠΩΝΣ
ΩΤΗΡΙΑΣΕΚΤΕΣΥΡΙΑΣΚΑΙΦΟΙΝΙΚΗΣΚΑΙ
ΚΥΠΡΟΥΚΑΙΕΞΑΛΛΩΝΠΛΕΙΟΝΩΝΤΟΠ
ΩΝΣΙΤΟΝΜΕΤΑΠΕΜ
18 ΨΑΜΕΝΟΙΕΙΣΤΗΝΧΩΡΑΝΤΙΜΩΝΜΕΙΖΟ
ΝΩΝΔΙΕΣΩΙΣΑΝΤΟΥΣΤΗΝΑΙΓΥΠΤΟΝ
ΚΑΤΟΙΚΟΥΝΤΑΣΑΘΑΝΑΤΟΝΕΥΕΡΓΕΣΙ
ΑΝΚΑΙΤΗΣΑΥΤΩΝΑΡΕΤΗΣ
19 ΜΕΓΙΣΤΟΝΥΠΟΜΝΗΜΑΚΑΤΑΛΕΙΠΟΝ
ΤΕΣΤΟΙΣΤΕΝΥΝΟΥΣΙΝΚΑΙΤΟΙΣΕΠΙΓΙΝ
ΟΜΕΝΟΙΣΑΝΘΩΝΟΙΘΕΟΙΔΕΔΩΚΑΣΙΝΑ
ΥΤΟΙΣΕΥΣΤΑΘΟΥΣΑΝΤΗΝΒΑΣΙΛΕΙ
20 ΑΝΚΑΙΔΩΣΟΥΣΙΝΤΑΛΛΑΓΑΘΑΠΑΝΤΑΕ

ΙΣΤΟΝΑΕΙΧΡΟΝΟΝ ΑΓΑΘΗΙΤΥΧΗΙΔ
ΕΔΟΧΘΑΙΤΟΙΣΚΑΤΑΤΗΝΧΩΡΑΝΙΕΡΕΥΣ
ΙΝΤΑΣΤΕΠΡΟΥΠΑΡΧΟΥΣΑΣ
21 ΤΙΜΑΣΕΝΤΟΙΣΙΕΡΟΙΣΒΑΣΙΛΕΙΠΤΟΛΕΜ
ΑΙΩΙΚΑΙΒΑΣΙΛΙΣΣΗΙΒΕΡΕΝΙΚΗΙΘΕΟΙΣΕ
ΥΕΡΓΕΤΑΙΣΚΑΙΤΟΙΣΓΟΝΕΥΣΙΝΑΥΤΩΝ
ΘΕΟΙΣΑΔΕΛΦΟΙΣΚΑΙΤΟΙΣΠΡΟΓΟΝΟΙΣ
22 ΘΕΟΙΣΣΩΤΗΡΣΙΝΑΥΞΕΙΝΚΑΙΤΟΥΣΙΕΡΕ
ΙΣΤΟΥΣΕΝΕΚΑΣΤΩΙΤΩΝΚΑΤΑΤΗΝΧΩΡ
ΑΝΙΕΡΩΝΠΡΟΣΟΝΟΜΑΖΕΣΘΑΙΙΕΡΕΙΣΚ
ΑΙΤΩΝΕΥΕΡΓΕΤΩΝΘΕΩΝΚΑΙΕΝΓΡΑΦΕ
23 ΣΘΑΙΕΝΠΑΣΙΝΤΟΙΣΧΡΗΜΑΤΙΣΜΟΙΣΚΑ
ΙΕΝΤΟΙΣΔΑΚΤΥΛΙΟΙΣΟΙΣΦΟΡΟΥΣΙΝΠΡ
ΟΣΕΓΚΟΛΑΠΤΕΣΘΑΙΚΑΙΤΗΝΙΕΡΩΣΥΝΗ
ΝΤΩΝΕΥΕΡΓΕΤΩΝΘΕΩΝΠΡΟΣΑΠΟΔΕΙ
ΧΘΗ
24 ΝΑΙΔΕΠΡΟΙΣ(*sic*)ΤΑΙΣΝΥΝΥΠΑΡΧΟΥΣΑΙ
ΣΤΕΣΣΑΡΣΙΦΥΛΑΙΣΤΟΥΠΛΗΘΟΥΣΤΩΝ
ΙΕΡΕΩΝΤΩΝΕΝΕΚΑΣΤΩΙΙΕΡΩΙΚΑΙΑΛΛΗ
ΝΗΠΡΟΣΟΝΟΜΑΣΘΕΣΕΤΑΙΠΕΜ
25 ΠΤΗΦΥΛΗΤΩΝΕΥ[Ε]ΡΓΕΤΩΝΘΕΩΝΕΠΕ
ΙΚΑΙΣΥΝΤΗΙΑΓΑΘΗΙΤΥΧΗΙΚΑΙΤΗΝΓΕΝ
ΕΣΙΝΒΑΣΙΛΕΩΣΠΤΟΛΕΜΑΙΟΥΤΟΥΤΩΝ
ΘΕΩΝΑΔΕΛΦΩΝΣΥΜΒΕΒΗΚΕΝ
26 ΓΕΝΕΣΘΑΙΤΗΙΠΕΜΠΤΗΙΤΟΥΔΙΟΥΗΚΑΙ
ΠΟΛΛΩΝΑΓΑΘΩΝΑΡΧΗΓΕΓΟΝΕΝΠΑΣΙ
ΝΑΝΘΡΩΠΟΙΣΕΙΣΔΕΤΗΝΦΥΛΗΝΤΑΥΤ
ΗΝΚΑΤΑΛΕΧΘΗΝΑΙΤΟΥΣΑΠΟ

27 ΤΟΥΠΡΩΤΟΥΕΤΟΥΣΓΕΓΕΝΗΜΕΝΟΥΣΙ
ΕΡΕΙΣΚΑΙΤΟΥΣΠΡΟΣΚΑΤΑΤΑΓΗΣΟΜΕ
ΝΟΥΣΕΩΣΜΗΝΟΣΜΕΣΟΡΗΤΟΥΕΝΤΩΙ
ΕΝΑΤΩΙΕΤΕΙΚΑΙΤΟΥΣΤΟΥΤΩΝΕΚΓΟΝ
ΟΥΣΕΙΣΤΟΝΑΕΙ
28 ΧΡΟΝΟΝΤΟΥΣΔΕΠΡΟΥΠΑΡΧΟΝΤΑΣΙΕ
ΡΕΙΣΕΩΣΤΟΥΠΡΩΤΟΥΕΤΟΥΣΕΙΝΑΙΩΣ
ΑΥΤΩΣΕΝΤΑΙΣΑΥΤΑΙΣΦΥΛΑΙΣΕΝΑΙΣΠ
ΡΟΤΕΡΟΝΗΣΑΝΟΜΟΙΩΣΔΕΚΑΙΤΟΥΣ
29 ΕΚΓΟΝΟΥΣΑΥΤΩΝΑΠΟΤΟΥΝΥΝΚΑΤΑ
ΧΩΡΙΖΕΣΘΑΙΕΙΣΤΑΣΑΥΤΑΣΦΥΛΑΣΕΝΑΙ
ΣΟΙΠΑΤΕΡΕΣΕΙΣΙΝΑΝΤΙΔΕΤΩΝΕΙΚΟΣΙ
ΒΟΥΛΕΥΤΩΝΙΕΡΕΩΝΤΩΝΑΙΡΟΥΜΕΝ
ΩΝ
30 ΚΑΤΕΝΙΑΥΤΟΝΕΚΤΩΝΠΡΟΥΠΑΡΧΟΥΣ
ΩΝΤΕΣΣΑΡΩΝΦΥΛΩΝΕΞΩΝΠΕΝΤΕΑΦΕ
ΚΑΣΤΗΣΦΥΛΗΣΛΑΜΒΑΝΟΝΤΑΙΕΙΚΟΣΙ
ΚΑΙΠΕΝΤΕΤΟΥΣΒΟΥΛΕΥΤΑΣ
31 ΙΕΡΕΙΣΕΙΝΑΙΠΡΟΣΛΑΜΒΑΝΟΜΕΝΩΝΕΚ
ΤΗΣΠΕΜΠΤΗΣΦΥΛΗΣΤΩΝΕΥΕΡΓΕΤΩΝ
ΘΕΩΝΑΛΛΩΝΠΕΝΤΕΜΕΤΕΧΕΙΝΔΕΚΑΙΤ
ΟΥΣΕΚΤΗΣΠΕΜΠΤΗΣ
32 ΦΥΛΗΣΤΩΝΕΥΕΡΓΕΤΩΝΘΕΩΝΤΩΝΑΓΝ
ΕΙΩΝΚΑΙΤΩΝΑΛΛΩΝΑΠΑΝΤΩΝΤΩΝΕΝ
ΤΟΙΣΙΕΡΟΙΣΚΑΙΦΥΛΑΡΧΟΝΑΥΤΗΣΕΙΝΑ
ΙΚΑΘΑΚΑΙΕΠΙΤΩΝΑΛΛΩΝΤΕΣ
33 ΣΑΡΩΝΦΥΛΩΝΥΠΑΡΧΕΙΚΑΙΕΠΕΙΔΗΚΑΘ
ΕΚΑΣΤΟΝΜΗΝΑΑΓΟΝΤΑΙΕΝΤΟΙΣΙΕΡΟ

ΙΣΕΟΡΤΑΙΤΩΝΕΥΕΡΓΕΤΩΝΘΕΩΝΚΑΤΑ
ΤΟΠΡΟΤΕΡΟΝΓΡΑΦΕΝΨΗΦΙΣΜΑ
34 ΗΤΕΠΕΜΠΤΗΚΑΙΗΕΝΑΤΗΚΑΙΗΠΕΜΠΤ
ΗΕΠΕΙΚΑΔΙΤΟΙΣΤΕΑΛΛΟΙΣΜΕΓΙΣΤΟΙΣ
ΘΕΟΙΣΚΑΤΕΝΙΑΥΤΟΝΣΥΝΤΕΛΟΥΝΤΑΙ
ΕΟΡΤΑΙΚΑΙΠΑΝΗΓΥΡΕΙΣΔΗΜΟΤΕ
35 ΛΕΙΣΑΓΕΣΘΑΙΚΑΤΕΝΙΑΥΤΟΝΠΑΝΗΓΥΡ
ΙΝΔΗΜΟΤΕΛΗΕΝΤΕΤΟΙΣΙΕΡΟΙΣΚΑΙΚΑ
ΘΟΛΗΝΤΗΝΧΩΡΑΝΒΑΣΙΛΕΙΠΤΟΛΕΜΑ
ΙΩΙΚΑΙΒΑΣΙΛΙΣΣΗΙΒΕΡΕΝΙΚΗΙ
36 ΘΕΟΙΣΕΥΕΡΓΕΤΑΙΣΤΗΙΗΜΕΡΑΙΕΝΗΙΕΠ
ΙΤΕΛΛΕΙΤΟΑΣΤΡΟΝΤΟΤΗΣΙΣΙΟΣΗΝΟ
ΜΙΖΕΤΑΙΔΙΑΤΩΝΙΕΡΩΝΓΡΑΜΜΑΤΩΝΝ
ΕΟΝΕΤΟΣΕΙΝΑΙΑΓΕΤΑΙΔΕΝΥΝΕΝΤΩΙ
37 ΕΝΑΤΩΙΕΤΕΙΝΟΥΜΗΝΙΑΙΤΟΥΠΑΥΝΙΜ
ΗΝΟΣΕΝΩΙΚΑΙΤΑΜΙΚΡΑΒΟΥΒΑΣΤΙΑΚΑ
ΙΤΑΜΕΓΑΛΑΒΟΥΒΑΣΤΙΑΑΓΕΤΑΙΚΑΙΗΣ
ΥΝΑΓΩΓΗΤΩΝΚΑΡΠΩΝΚΑΙΗΤΟΥ
38 ΠΟΤΑΜΟΥΑΝΑΒΑΣΙΣΓΙΝΕΤΑΙΕΑΝΔΕΚ
ΑΙΣΥΜΒΑΙΝΗΙΤΗΝΕΠΙΤΟΛΗΝΤΟΥΑΣΤ
ΡΟΥΜΕΤΑΒΑΙΝΕΙΝΕΙΣΕΤΕΡΑΝΗΜΕΡΑΝ
ΔΙΑΤΕΣΣΑΡΩΝΕΤΩΝΜΗΜΕΤΑΤΙ
39 ΘΕΣΘΑΙΤΗΝΠΑΝΗΓΥΡΙΝΑΛΛΑΓΕΣΘΑΙ
[ΟΜΟΙΩΣ]ΤΗΙΝΟΥΜΗΝΙΑΙΤΟΥΠΑΥΝΙΕ
ΝΗΙΚΑΙΕΞΑΡΧΕΣΗΧΘΗΕΝΤΩΙΕΝΑΤΩΙΕ
ΤΕΙΚΑΙΣΥΝΤΕΛΕΙΝΑΥΤΗΝΕΠΙΗΜΕΡΑΣ
40 ΠΕΝΤΕΜΕΤΑΣΤΕΦΑΝΗΦΟΡΙΑΣΚΑΙΘΥΣΙ
ΩΝΚΑΙΣΠΟΝΔΩΝΚΑΙΤΩΝΑΛΛΩΝΤΩΝ

ΠΡΟΣΗΚΟΝΤΩΝΟΠΩΣΔΕΚΑΙΑΙΩΡΑΙΤ
ΟΚΑΘΗΚΟΝΠΟΙΩΣΙΝΔΙΑΠΑΝΤΟΣΚΑΤ
ΑΤΗΝΝΥΝ

41 ΟΥΣΑΝΚΑΤΑΣΤΑΣΤΑΣΙΝ(*sic*)ΤΟΥΚΟΣΜ
ΟΥΚΑΙΜΗΣΥΜΒΑΙΝΗΙΤΙΝΑΣΤΩΝΔΗΜ
ΟΤΕΛΩΝΕΟΡΤΩΝΤΩΝΑΓΟΜΕΝΩΝΕΝΤ
ΩΙΧΕΙΜΩΝΙΑΓΕΣΘΑΙΠΟΤΕΕΝΤΩΙΘΕΡΕΙ
ΤΟΥΑΣΤΡΟΥ

42 ΜΕΤΑΒΑΙΝΟΝΤΟΣΜΙΑΝΗΜΕΡΑΝΔΙΑΤ
ΕΣΣΑΡΩΝΕΤΩΝΕΤΕΡΑΣΔΕΤΩΝΝΥΝΑΓ
ΟΜΕΝΩΝΕΝΤΩΙΘΕΡΕΙΑΓΕΣΘΑΙΕΝΤΩΙΧ
ΕΙΜΩΝΙΕΝΤΟΙΣΜΕΤΑΤΑΥΤΑΚΑΙΡΟΙΣΚ
ΑΘΑΠΕΡΠΡΟ

43 ΤΕΡΟΝΤΕΣΥΜΒΕΒΗΚΕΝΓΕΝΕΣΘΑΙΚΑ[Ι]
ΝΥΝΑΝΕΓΙΝΕΤΟΤΗΣΣΥΝΤΑΞΕΩΣΤΟΥ
ΕΝΙΑΥΤΟΥΜΕΝΟΥΣΗΣΕΚΤΩΝΤΡΙΑΚΟ
ΣΙΩΝΚΑΙΕΞΗΚΟΝΤΑΗΜΕΡΩΝΚΑΙΤΩΝΥ
ΣΤΕΡΟΝΠΡΟΣ

44 ΝΟΜΙΣΘΕΙΣΩΝΕΠΑΓΕΣΘΑΙΠΕΝΤΕΗΜΕ
ΡΩΝΑΠΟΤΟΥΝΥΝΜΙΑΝΗΜΕΡΑΝΕΟΡΤ
ΗΝΤΩΝΕΥΕΡΓΕΤΩΝΘΕΩΝΕΠΑΓΕΣΘΑΙ
ΔΙΑΤΕΣΣΑΡΩΝΕΤΩΝΕΠΙΤΑΙΣΠΕΝΤΕΤ
ΑΙΣ

45 ΕΠΑΓΟΜΕΝΑΙΣΠΡΟΤΟΥΝΕΟΥΕΤΟΥΣΟ
ΠΩΣΑΠΑΝΤΕΣΕΙΔΩΣΙΝΔΙΟΤΙΤΟΕΛΛΕΙ
ΠΟΝΠΡΟΤΕΡΟΝΠΕΡΙΤΗΝΣΥΝΤΑΞΙΝΤ
ΩΝΩΡΩΝΚΑΙΤΟΥΕΝΙΑΥΤΟΥΚΑΙΤΩΝΝ
ΟΜΙΞ(*sic*)Ο

46 ΜΕΝΩΝΠΕΡΙΤΗΝΟΛΗΝΔΙΑΚΟΣΜΗΣΙΝ
ΤΟΥΠΟΛΟΥΔΙΩΡΘΩΣΘΑΙΚΑΙΑΝΑΠΕΠ
ΛΗΡΩΣΘΑΙΣΥΜΒΕΒΗΚΕΝΔΙΑΤΩΝΕΥΕΡ
ΓΕΤΩΝΘΕΩΝΚΑΙΕΠΕΙΔΗΤΗΝΕΓΒΑΣΙΛ
ΕΩΣΠΤΟΛΕΜΑΙΟΥ
47 ΚΑΙΒΑΣΙΛΙΣΣΗΣΒΕΡΕΝΙΚΗΣΘΕΩΝΕΥΕΡ
ΓΕΤΩΝΓΕΓΕΝΗΜΕΝΗΝΘΥΓΑΤΕΡΑΚΑΙΟ
ΝΟΜΑΣΘΕΙΣΑΝΒΕΡΕΝΙΚΗΝΗΚΑΙΒΑΣΙΛ
ΙΣΣΑΕΥΘΕΩΣΑΠΕΔΕΙΧΘΗΣΥΝΕΒΗΤΑΥ
ΤΗΝΠΑΡΘΕΝΟΝ
48 ΟΥΣΑΝΕΞΑΙΦΝΗΣΜΕΤΕΛΘΕΙΝΕΙΣΤΟΝ
ΑΕΝΑΟΝΚΟΣΜΟΝΕΤΙΕΝΔΗΜΟΥΝΤΩΝ
ΠΑΡΑΤΩΙΒΑΣΙΛΕΙΤΩΝΕΚΤΗΣΧΩΡΑΣΠΑ
ΡΑΓΙΝΟΜΕΝΩΝΠΡΟΣΑΥΤΟΝΚΑΤΕΝΙΑ
ΥΤΟΝΙΕΡΕΩΝ
49 ΟΙΜΕΓΑ[ΜΕΝ]ΠΕΝΘΟΣΕΠΙΤΩΙΣΥΜΒΕΒ
ΗΚΟΤΙΕΥΘΕΩΣΣΥΝΕΤΕΛΕΣΑΝΑΞΙΩΣΑ
ΝΤΕΣΔΕΤΟΝΒΑΣΙΛΕΑΚΑΙΤΗΝΒΑΣΙΛΙΣ
ΣΑΝΕΠΕΙΣΑΝΚΑΘΙΔΡΥΣΑΙΤΗΝΘΕΑΝΜ
ΕΤΑΤΟΥΟΣΙΡΙΟΣΕΝΤΩΙ
50 ΕΝΚΑΝΩΠΩΙΙΕΡΩΙΟΟΥΜΟΝΟΝΕΝΤΟΙΣ
ΠΡΩΤΟΙΣ[Ι]ΕΡΟΙΣΕΣΤΙΝΑΛΛΑΚΑΙΥΠΟ
ΤΟΥΒΑΣΙΛΕΩΣΚΑΙΤΩΝΚΑΤΑΤΗΝΧΩΡΑ
ΝΠΑΝΤΩΝΕΝΤΟΙΣΜΑΛΙΣΤΑΤΙΜΩΜΕΝ
ΟΙΣΥΠΑΡΧΕΙ
51 ΚΑΙΗΑΝΑΓΩΓΗΤΟΥΙΕΡΟΥΠΛΟΙΟΥΤΟΥ
ΟΣΕΙΡΙΟΣΕΙΣΤΟΥΤΟΤΟΙΕΡΟΝΚΑΤΕΝΙ
ΑΥΤΟΝΓΙΝΕΤΑΙΕΚΤΟΥΕΝΤΩΙΗΡΑΚΛΕΙ

ΩΙΙΕΡΟΥΤΗΙΕΝΑΤΗΙΚΑΙΕΙΚΑΔΙΤΟΥΧΟΙ
ΑΧΤΩΝΕΚΤΩΝΠΡΩ
52 ΤΩΝΙΕΡΩΝΠΑΝΤΩΝΘΥΣΙΑΣΣΥΝΤΕΛΟ
ΥΝΤΩΝΕΠΙΤΩΝΙΔΡΥΜΕΝΩΝΥΠΑΥΤΩΝ
ΒΩΜΩΝΥΠΕΡΕΚΑΣΤΟΥΙΕΡΟΥΤΩΝΠΡΩ
ΤΩΝΕΞΑΜΦΟΤΕΡΩΝΤΩΝΜΕΡΩΝΤΟΥΔ
ΡΟΜΟΥ
53 ΜΕΤΑΔΕΤΑΥΤΑ[ΤΑ]ΠΡΟΣΤΗΝΕΚΘΕΩΣ
ΙΝΑΥΤΗΣΝΟΜΙΜΑΚΑΙΤΗΝΤΟΥΠΕΝΘΟ
ΥΣΑΠΟΛΥΣΙΝΑΠΕΔΩΚΑΝΜΕΓΑΛΟΠΡΕ
ΠΩΣΚΑΙΚΗΔΕΜΟΝΙΚΩΣΚΑΘΑΠΕΡΚΑΙΕ
ΠΙΤΩΙΑ[ΠΕΙ
54 ΚΑΙΜΝΗΥΕΙ]ΕΙΘΙΣΜΕΝΟΝΕΣΤΙΝΓΙΝΕΣ
ΘΑΙΔΕΔΟΧΘΑΙΣΥΝΤΕΛΕΙΝΤΗΙΕΚΤΩΝΕ
ΥΕΡΓΕΤΩΝΘΕΩΝΓΕΓΕΝΗΜΕΝΗΙΒΑΣΙΛΙ
ΣΣΗΙΒΕΡΕΝΙΚΗΙΤΙΜΑΣΑΙΔΙΟΥΣΕΝΑΠΑ
ΣΙΤΟΙ[Σ]
55 Τ(*sic*)ΑΤΑΤΗΝΧΩΡΑΝΙΕΡΟΙΣΚΑΙΕΠΕΙΕΙΣ
ΘΕΟΥΣΜΕΤΗΛΘΕΝΕΝΤΩΙΤΥΒΙΜΗΝΙΕΝ
ΩΙΠΕΡΚΑΙΗΤΟΥΗΛΙΟΥΘΥΓΑΤΗΡΕΝΑΡΧ
ΗΙΜΕΤΗΛΛΑΞΕΝΤΟΝΒΙΟΝΗΝΟΠΑΤΗΡ
ΣΤΕΡΞΑΣΩ[ΝΟ]
56 ΜΑΣΕΝΟΤΕΜΕΝΒΑΣΙΛΕΙΑΝΟΤΕΟΡΑΣΙ
ΝΑΥΤΟΥΚΑΙΑΓΟΥΣΙΝΑΥΤΗΙΕΟΡΤΗΝΚ
ΑΙΠΕΡΙΠΛΟΥΝΕΝΠΛΕΙΟΣΙΝΙΕΡΟΙΣΤΩ
ΝΠΡΩΤΩΝΕΝΤΟΥΤΩΙΤΩΙΜΗΝΙΕΝΩΙΗ
ΑΠΟΘΕΩΣΙΣΑΥ[ΤΗΣ]
57 ΕΝΑΡΧΗΙΕΓΕΝΗΘΗΣΥΝΤΕΛΕΙΝΚΑΙΒΑΣΙ

ΛΙΣΣΗΙΒΕΡΕΝΙΚΗΙΤΗΙΕΚΤΩΝΕΥΕΡΓΕΤΩ
ΝΘΕΩΝΕΝΑΠΑΣΙΤΟΙΣΚΑΤΑΤΗΝΧΩΡΑΝ
ΙΕΡΟΙΣΕΝΤΩΙΤΥΒΙΜΗΝΙΕΟΡΤΗΝΚΑΙΠΕ

58 ΡΙΠΛΟΥΝΕΦΗΜΕΡΑΣΤΕΣΣΑΡΑΣΑΠΟΕΠ
ΤΑΚΑΙΔΕ[...]ΚΑΤΗΙΕΝΗΙΟΠΕΡΙΠΛΟΥ
ΣΚΑΙΗΤΟΥΠΕΝΘΟΥΣΑΠΟΛΥΣΙΣΕΓΕΝΗ
ΘΗΑΥΤΗΙΤΗΝΑΡΧΗΝΣΥΝΤΕΛΕΣΑΙΔΑΥ
ΤΗΣΚΑΙ

59 ΙΕΡΟΝΑΓΑΛΜΑΧΡΥΣΟΥΝΔΙΑΛΙΘΟΝΕΝ
ΕΝ(*sic*)ΑΣΤΩΙΤΩΝΠΡΩΤΩΝΚΑΙΔΕΥΤΕΡ
ΩΝΙΕΡΩΝΚΑΙΚΑΘΙΔΡΥΣΑΙΕΝΤΩΙΑΓΙΩΟ
ΔΕΠΡΟΦΗΤΗΣΗΤΩΝ⅂(*sic*)ΣΤΟΑΔΥΤΟ
ΝΕΙΡΗ(*sic*)ΜΕΝΩΝ

60 ΙΕΡΕΩΝΠΡΟΣΤΟΝΣΤΟΛΙΣΜΟΝΤΩΝΘΕ
ΩΝΟΙΣΕΙΕΝΤΑΙΣΑΓΚΑΛΑΙΣΟΤΑΝΑΙΕΞ
ΟΔΕΙΑΙΚΑΙΠΑΝΗΓΥΡΕΙΣΤΩΝΛΟΙΠΩΝΘ
ΕΩΝΓΙΝΩΝΤΑ(*sic*)ΟΠΩΣΥΠΟΠΑΝΤΩΝ
ΟΡΩΜΕΝΟΝ

61 ΤΙΜΑΤΑΙΚΑΙΠΡΟΣΚΥΝΗΤΑΙΚΑΛΟΥΜΕ
ΝΟΝΒΕΡΕΝΙΚΗΣΑΝΑΣΣΗΣΠΑΡΘΕΝΩΝ
ΕΙΝΑΙΔΕΤΗΝΕΠΙΤΙΘΕΜΕΝΗΝΒΑΣΙΛΕΙ
ΑΝΤΗ(*sic*)ΕΙΚΟΝΙΑΥΤΗΣΔΙΑΦΕΡΟΥΣΑΝ
ΤΗΣΕΠΙΤΙΘΕΜΕΝΗΣ

62 ΤΑΙΣΕΙΚΟΣΙΝΤΗΣΜΗΤΡΟΣΑΥΤΗΣΒΑΣΙ
ΛΙΣΣΗΣΒΕΡΕΝΙΚΗΣΕΚΣΤΑΧΥΩΝΔΥΩΝ
ΩΝΑΝΑΜΕΣΟΝΕΣΤΑΙΗΑΣΠΙΔΟΕΙΔΗΣ
ΒΑΣΙΛΕΙΑΤΑΥΤΗΣΔΟΠΙΣΩΣΥΜΜΕΤΡΟ
ΝΣΚΗΠΤΡΟΝ

63 ΠΑΠΥΡΟΕΙΔΕΣΟΕΙΩΘΑΣΙΝΑΙΘΕΑΙΕΧΕΙ

ΝΕΝΤΑΙΣΧΕΡΣΙΝΠΕΡΙΟΥΚΑΙΗΟΥΡΑΤΗ
ΣΒΑΣΙΛΕΙΑΣΕΣΤΑΙΠΕΡΙΕΙΛΗΜ(*sic*)ΜΕΝΗ
ΩΣΤΕΚΑΙΕΚΤΗΣΔΙΑΘΕΣΕΩΣΤΗΣΒΑΣΙΛ
ΕΙΑΣΔΙΑ
64 ΣΑΦΕΙΣΘΑΙΤΟΒΕΡΕΝΙΚΗΣΟΝΟΜΑΚΑΤ
ΑΤΑΕΠΙΣΗΜΑΤΗΣΙΕΡΑΣΓΡΑΜΜΑΤΙΚΗ
ΣΚΑΙΟΤΑΝΤΑΚΙΚΗΛΛΙΑΑΓΗΤΑΙΕΝΤΩΙ
ΧΟΙΑΧΜΗΝΙΠΡΟΤΟΥΠΕΡΙΠΛΟΥΤΟΥΟΣ
ΕΙΡΙΟΣΚΑΤΑ
65 ΣΚΕΥΑΣΑΙΤΑΣΠΑΡΘΕΝΟΥΣΤΩΝΙΕΡΕΩΝ
ΑΛΛΟΑΓΑΛΜΑΒΕΡΕΝΙΚΗΣΑΝΑΣΣΗΣΠΑ
ΡΘΕΝΩΝΩΙΣΥΝΤΕΛΕΣΟΥΣΙΝΟΜΟΙΩΣΘ
ΥΣΙΑΝΚΑΙΤΑΛΛΑΤΑΣΥΝΤΕΛΟΥΜΕΝΑΝΟ
66 ΜΙΜΑΤΗΙΕΟΡΤΗΙΤΑΥΤΗΙΕΞΕΙΝΑΙΔΕΚΑ
ΤΑΤΑΥΤΑΚΑΙΤΑΙΣΑΛΛΑΙΣΠΑΡΘΕΝΟΙΣΤ
ΑΙΣΒΟΥΛΟΜΕΝΑΙΣΣΥΝΤΕΛΕΙΝΤΑΝΟΜΙ
ΜΑΤΗΙΘΕΩΙΥΜΝΕΙΣΘΑΙΔΑΥΤΗΝΚΑΙΥ
67 ΠΟΤΩΝΕΠΙΛΕΓΟΜΕΝΩΝΙΕΡΕΙΩΝΠΑΡΘ
ΕΝΩΝΚΑΙΤΑΣΧΡΕΙΑΣΠΑΡΕΧΟΜΕΝΩΝΤ
ΟΙΣΘΕΟΙΣΠΕΡΙΚΕΙΜΕΝΩΝΤΑΣΙΔΙΑΣΒΑ
ΣΙΛΕΙΑΣΤΩΝΘΕΩΝΩΝΙΕΡΕΙΑΙΝΟΜΙΖΟ
ΝΤΑ[Ι]
68 ΕΙΚΑΙΚΑΙΟΤΑΝΟΠΡΟΩΡΙΜΟΣΣΠΟΡΟΣ
ΠΑΡΑΣΤΗΙΑΝΑΦΕΡΕΙΝΤΑΣΙΕΡΑΣΠΑΡΘ
ΕΝΟΥΣΣΥ(*sic*)ΑΧΥΣΤΟΥΣΠΑΡΑΘΗΣΟΜΕ
ΝΟΥΣΤΩΙΑΓΑΛΜΑΤΙΤΗΣΘΕΟΥΑΙΔΕΙΝ
ΔΕΙΣΑΥΤΗΝ
69 ΚΑΘΗΜΕΡΑΝΚΑΙΕΝΤΑΙΣΕΟΡΤΑΙΣΚΑΙΠ
ΑΝΗΓΥΡΕΣΙΝΤΩΝΛΟΙΠΩΝΘΕΩΝΤΟΥΣ

ΤΕΩΙΔΟΥΣΑΝΔΡΑΣΚΑΙΤΑΣΓΥΝΑΙΚΑΣΟ
ΥΣΑΝΥΜΝΟΥΣΟΙΙΕΡΟΓΡΑΜΜΑΤΕΙΣΓΡΑ
70 ΨΑΝΤΕΣΔΩΣΙΝΤΩΙΩΙΔΟΔΙΔΑΣΚΑΛΩΙΩ
ΝΚΑΙΤΑΝΤΙΓΡΑΦΑΚΑΤΑΧΩΡΙΣΘΗΣΕΤΑΙ
ΕΙΣΤΑΣΙΕΡΑΣΒΥΒΛΟΥΣΚΑΙΕΠΕΙΔΗΤΟΙ
ΣΙΕΡΕΥΣΙΝΔΙΔΟΝΤΑΙΑΙΤΡΟΦΑΙΕΚΤΩΝ
71 ΙΕΡΩΝΕΠΑΝΕΠΑΧΘΩΣΙΝΕΙΣΤΟΠΛΗΘΟ
ΣΔΙΔΟΣΘΑΙΤΑΙΣΘΥΓΑΤΡΑΣΙΝΤΩΝΙΕΡΕ
ΩΝΕΚΤΩΝΙΕΡΩΝΠΡΟΣΟΔΩΝΑΦΗΣΑΝΗ
ΜΕΡΑΣΓΕΝΩΝΤΑΙΤΗΝΣΥΝΚΡΙΘΗΣΟΜΕ
72 ΝΗΝΤΡΟΦΗΝΥΠΟΤΩΝΒΟΥΛΕΥΤΩΝΙΕ
ΡΕΩΝΤΩΝΕΝΕΚΑΣΤΩΙΤΩΝΙΕΡΩΝΚΑΤΑ
ΛΟΓΟΝΤΩΝΙΕΡΩΝΠΡΟΣΟΔΩΝΚΑΙΤΟΝ
ΔΙΔΟΜΕΝΟΝΑΡΤΟΝΤΑΙΣΓΥΝΑΙΞΙΝ
73 ΤΩΝΙΕΡΕΩΝΕΧΕΙΝΙΔΙΟΝΤΥΠΟΝΚΑΙΚΑ
ΛΕΙΣΘΑΙΒΕΡΕΝΙΚΗΣΑΡΤΟΝΟΔΕΝΕΚΑΣ
ΤΩΙΤΩΝΙΕΡΩΝΚΑΘΕΣΤΗΚΩΣΕΠΙΣΤΑΤ
ΗΣΚΑΙΑΡΧΙΕΡΕΥΣΚΑΙΟΙΤΟΥΙΕΡΟΥ
74 ΓΡΑΜΜΑΤΕΙΣΑΝΑΓΡΑΨΑΤΩΣΑΝΤΟΥΤ
ΟΤΟΨΗΦΙΣΜΑΕΙΣΣΤΗΛΗΝΛΙΘΙΝΗΝΗΧ
ΑΛΚΗΝΙΕΡΟΙΣΓΡΑΜΜΑΣΙΝΚΑΙΑΙΓΥΠΤΙ
ΟΙΣΚΑΙΕΛΛΗΝΙΚΟΙΣΚΑΙΑΝΑΘΕ
75 ΤΩΣΑΝΕΝΤΩΙΕΠΙΦΑΝΕΣΤΑΤΩΙΤΟΠΩΙ
ΤΩΝΤΕΑΙΕΡΩΝΚΑΙΒΚΑΙΓΟΠΩΣΟΙΚΑΤΑ
ΤΗΝΧΩΡΑΝΙΕΡΕΙΣΦΑΙΝΩΝΤΑΙΤΙΜΩΝΤ
Α(*sic*)ΣΤΟΥΣΕΥΕΡΓΕΤΑΣΘΕΟΥΣΚΑΙΤΑΤ
ΕΚΝΑΑΥΤΩΝ
76 ΚΑΘΑΠΕΡΔΙΚΑΙΟΝΕΣΤΙΝ.

CHAPTER VIII.

THE GREEK TEXT OF THE DECREE OF CANOPUS.

German Translation by Dr. R. Lepsius (*Das Bilingue Dekret von* Kanopus, Berlin, 1886), p. 21.

(1) Unter der Regierung des Ptolemaeus, Sohnes des Ptolemaeus und der Arsinoë, der Götter Adelphen, im 9. Jahre; als Apollonides, Sohn des (2) Moschion, Priester des Alexander und der Götter Adelphen und der Götter Euergeten war, (und) Menekrateia, Tochter (3) des Philammon, Kanephore der Arsinoë Philadelphus; am 7. des Monats Apellaeus, das ist am 17. Tybi der Aegypter.

Dekret.

Die Erzpriester (4) und Propheten und die in das Sanktuarium zur Bekleidung der Götter Eintretenden, und Pterophoren und Hierogrammaten und (5) die andern Priester die zusammenkamen aus der Tempeln des Landes auf der 5. des Dios, an welchem das Geburtsfest (6) des Königs gefeiert wird, und auf den 25. desselben Monats, an welchem er die königliche

Würde von seinem Vater übernahm, als sie versammelt waren (7) an diesem Tage in dem Tempel der Götter Euergeten zu Kanopus, SPRACHEN AUS:

Da der König Ptolemaeus, Sohn des Ptolemaeus und der Arsinoë der Götter Adelphen, (8) und die Königin Berenike, seine Schwester und Gemahlin, die Götter Euergeten, fortwährend den Tempeln im Lande viele und grosse Wohlthaten erzeigen und (9) die Ehren der Götter immerzu vermehren;

und für den Apis und den Mneuis und die übrigen angesehenen heiligen Thiere im Lande (10) durchgängig Sorge tragen mit grossen Kosten und Ausstattungen;

und der König die aus dem Lande von (11) den Persern geraubten heiligen Bilder von seinem Feldzuge glücklich nach Aegypten zurückbrachte, und den Tempeln, aus denen jedes ursprünglich weggeführt war, wiedergab;

und (12) das Land in Frieden erhielt, indem er für dasselbe gegen viele Völker und ihre Gewalthaber Krieg führte;

und sie (13) Allen die im Lande sind und den Andern die unter ihre Herrschaft gestellt sind, Gesetz und Ordnung gewähren;

und, als der Fluss einmal unvollkommen (14) stieg und Jedermann im Lande erschreckt war über das Ereigniss und mit Sorge sich des Verderbens erinnerte, welches (15) unter einigen der fruheren Regenten eingetreten war, unter denen es geschah dass die

Bewohner des Landes in die Plage einer Dürre geriethen, sie, indem sie (16) sowohl für die in den Tempeln wie auch für die andern Einwohner des Landes eifrig sorgten sowohl durch viele Vorkehrungen für die Zukunft als durch den Nachlass nicht weniger Einkünfte (17) zum Besten des Volkes, und indem sie aus Syrien und Phönizien und Cypern und mehreren andern Orten Getreide in das Land kommen (18) liessen für hohe Preise, die Bewohner Aegyptens aus aller Noth retteten, und so eine unvergängliche Wohlthat und eine (19) mächtige Erinnerung an ihre Tugend sowohl fur die Zeitgenossen als für die Nachkommen hinterliessen, wofur ihnen die Götter eine festbeständige Herrschaft (20) gewährt haben, und alles übrige Gute für ewige Zeit gewähren werden:

so hatten die Priester des Landes beschlossen:

ZU GUTEM HEIL,

dass sie die früheren (21) Ehren in den Tempeln für den König Ptolemaeus und die Königin Berenike, die Götter Euergeten, und für ihre Eltern die Götter Adelphen, und die Grosseltern (22) die Götter Soteren vermehrten:

und dass die Priester in jedem der Tempel des Landes auch "Priester der Götter Euergeten" genannt würden;

und dass auch das Priesterthum der Götter Euergeten in allen öffentlichen Urkunden eingeschrieben

(23) und· auf den Fingerringen die sie tragen eingeschnitten werde:

dass ferner (24) zu den 4 jetzt vorhandenen Phylen der Priesterschaft in jedem Tempel noch eine andre dazu gebildet werde, welche (25) "fünfte Phyle der Götter Euergeten" genannt werden soll, da es sich auch zum guten Glück traf, das auch die Geburt des Königs Ptolemaeus, des Sohnes der Adelphen, sich am (26) 5 des Dins ereignete, welcher Tag auch der Anfang vieler Güter fur alle Menschen wurde:

dass in diese Phyle aber die Priester eingeschrieben werden sollen, welche es vom (27) 1. Jahre (des Ptolemaeus) an geworden sind so wie die welche bis zum Monat Mesore des 9. Jahres hinzugefügt sein werden und ihre Nachkommen für alle (28) Zeit; dass aber die früheren Priester bis zum 1. Jahre ebenso in denselben Phylen seien, in denen sie früher waren; gleicherweise aber auch die (29) Nachkommen derselben von jetzt an in dieselben Phylen eingetragen werden, in welchen ihre Väter sind:

dass ferner, statt der 20 den Rath bildenden Priester, welche (30) jährlich gewählt werden aus den fruheren 4 Phylen, aus denen 5 von jeder Phyle genommen werden, der Rath aus 25 (31) Priestern bestehe, indem 5 andere aus der "5· Phyle der Götter Euergeten" dazu genommen werden:

und dass auch die (Priester) aus der "5. (32) Phyle der Götter Euergeten" an den Sühnungen und allen andern (heiligen Handlungen) in den Tempeln Theil haben:

und dass dieselbe einen Phylarchen habe, wie dies auch bei den (33) 4 andern Phylen der Fall ist:

und dass, da jeden Monat in den Tempeln als Feste der Götter Euergeten nach dem früher abgefassten Dekrete (34) der 5. und der 9. und der 25. (Tag) gefeiert werden, den höchsten Göttern aber jährlich (auch) öffentliche Feste und Panegyrien (35) abgehalten werden, jährlich eine öffentliche Panegyrie sowohl in den Tempeln als im ganzen Lande dem Könige Ptolemaeus und der Königin Berenike, (36) den Göttern Euergeten, gefeiert werde an dem Tage, an welchem der Stern der Isis aufgeht, welcher in den heiligen Schriften als Neujahr angesehen, jetzt aber im (37) 9. Jahre am 1. des Monats Payni gefeiert wird, in welchem auch die kleinen Bubastia und die grossen Bubastia gefeiert werden und die Einbringung der Früchte und das (38) Steigen des Flusses geschieht:

dass aber, auch wenn der Aufgang des Sterns auf einen andern (Kalender-) Tag im Verlauf von 4 Jahren übergehen würde, (dennoch) die Panegyrie nicht (39) verlegt, sondern am 1. Payni gefeiert werde, an welchem sie von Anfang an im 9. Jahre gefeiert wurde:

und dass sie (40) 5 Tage lang abgehalten werde mit einen Stephanephorie und Opfern und Spenden und was sonst dazu gehört:

dass aber, damit auch die Jahreszeiten fortwährend nach der jetzigen (41) Ordnung der Welt ihre Schuldigkeit thun und es nicht vorkomme, dass einige der öffentlichen Feste welche im Winter gefeiert werden, einstmals im Sommer gefeiert werden, indem der Stern (42) um einen Tag alle 4 Jahren weiterschreitet, andere aber die im Sommer gefeiert werden, in spätern Zeiten im Winter gefeiert werden, wie dies sowohl (43) früher geschah, als auch jetzt wieder geschehen würde, wenn die Zusammensetzung des Jahres aus den 360 Tagen und den 5 Tagen, welche später (44) noch hinzuzufügen gebräuchlich wurde, so fortdauert: von jetzt an ein Tag als Fest der Götter Euergeten alle vier Jahre gefeiert werde hinter den 5 (45) Epagomenen (und) vor dem neuen Jahre, damit Jedermann wisse, dass das, was fruher in Bezug auf die Einrichtung der Jahreszeiten und des Jahres und des hinsichtlich der ganzen Himmels-Ordnung (46) Angenommenen fehlte, durch die Götter Euergeten glücklich berichtigt und ergänzt worden ist:

und, da es geschah, dass die von dem Könige Ptolemaeus (47) und der Königin Berenike, den Göttern Euergeten, entsprossene und Berenike genannte Tochter, welche sogleich auch als Königin proklamirt wurde, diese als Jungfrau (48) plötzlich hinuberging in die ewige Welt, während bei dem Könige die jährlich aus dem Lande zu ihm kommenden Priester noch verweilten, (49) welche sogleich eine grosse Trauer über das Ereigniss veranstalteten, bei dem Könige und der Königin aber beantragten und sie bewogen die Göttin aufzustellen zur Seite des Osiris in dem Tempel (50) zu Kanopus, welcher nicht nur einer von dem

Tempeln erster Ordnung ist, sondern auch zu den von dem Könige und allen Bewohnern des Landes am meisten geehrten gehört, (51)—auch geschieht die Fahrt des heiligen Schiffes des Osiris nach diesem Tempel jährlich aus dem Tempel im Herakleion am 29. Choiach, wobei alle (Priester) aus den (52) Tempeln erster Ordnung Opfer vollbringen auf den von ihnen gegründeten Altären für einen jeden der Tempel erster Ordnung auf beiden Seiten des Dromos,—(53) nachher aber das zur Vergötterung derselben Gehörige und die Ablösung der Trauer reich und sorgfaltig ausführten, wie es bei dem Apis (54) und Mneuis zu geschehen pflegt, so hätten sie beschlossen:

der von den Göttern Euergeten erzeugten Königin Berenike ewige Ehren in allen (55) Tempeln des Landes zu erweisen:

und, da sie zu den Göttern hinüberging im Monat Tybi, in welchem auch die Tochter des Helios einst aus dem Leben schied, welche der Vater aus Zuneigung (56) bald seine Krone bald seine Augenlicht nannte, und (da) man dieser ein Fest und einen Periplus in den meisten Tempeln erster Ordnung feiert in diesem Monate, in welchem die Apotheose (57) zuerst geschah: auch der Königin Berenike, der (Tochter) der Götter Euergeten in allen Tempeln des Landes im Monat Tybi ein Fest und einen (58) Periplus zu feiern 4 Tage lang vom 17. an, an welchem von Anfang an der Periplus und die Ablösung der Trauer für sie geschah:

wie auch (59) ein heiliges Bild von ihr aus Gold und mit edeln Steinen besetzt in jedem Tempel der ersten und zweiten Ordnung anzufertigen und im Sanktuarium aufzustellen—der Prophet aber oder einer von den Priestern, welche in das Sanktuarium eintreten (60) zur Bekleidung der Götter wird (es) in den Armen tragen, wenn die Auszüge und Panegyrien der übrigen Götter geschehen, damit es, für Jedermann sichtbar, (61) geehrt und angebetet werde, unter dem Namen der "Berenike der Fürstin der Jungfrauen":—

dass ferner das dem Bilde derselben aufgesetzte Diadem, verschieden von dem welches (62) den Bildern ihrer Mutter der Königin Berenike aufgesetzt ist, aus zwei Aehren bestehe, in deren Mitte das schlangenförmige Diadem sein soll, hinter diesem aber ein im richtigen Verhältniss stehendes (63) papyrusförmiges Szepter, welches die Göttinnen in den Handen zu halten pflegen, (und) um welches auch der Schwanz des (Schlangen)-Diadems herumgewunden sein soll, damit auch aus der Anordnung des Diadems (64) die Benennung der Berenike erkannt werde nach den Sinnbildern der heiligen Schriftkunde:

und dass, wenn die Kikellien gefeiert werden im Monat Choiach vor dem Periplus des Osiris, (65) die Jungfrauen der Priester ein andres Bild der "Berenike Furstin der Jungfrauen" zurichten, dem sie gleichfalls ein Opfer und das Uebrige, (66) welches an diesem Feste dargebracht zu werden pflegt, darbringen sollen:

und dass es gleicher Weise auch dem andern

Jungfrauen die es wünschen freistehe der Göttin das Herkömmliche zu erweisen:

und dass sie auch besungen werde von den (67) ausgewählten heiligen Jungfrauen, und denen welchen die Bedienung der Götter obliegt, bekränzt mit den besondern Diademen der Götter als deren Priesterinnen sie gelten:

(68) und dass, wenn die Frühsaat naht, die heiligen Jungfrauen die dem Bilde der Göttin aufzusetzenden Aehren beschaffen:

und dass (69) täglich auch bei den Festen und Panegyrien der übrigen Götter sowohl die männlichen Sänger als die Frauen ihr die Gesänge singen, welche die Hierogrammaten (70) schriftlich dem Gesangmeister übergeben und von welchen (Gesängen) auch die Abschriften in die heiligen Bücher eingetragen werden sollen:

und dass, da den Priestern, sobald sie der Körperschaft überwiesen worden, der Unterhalt aus den (71) Tempeln gegeben wird, (auch) den Töchtern der Priester aus den heiligen Einkünften von dem Tage ihrer Geburt an der ihnen (72) von den im Rathe sitzenden Priestern eines jeden Tempels je nach Verhältniss der heiligen Einkünfte zugemessene Unterhalt gegeben werde:

und dass das den Frauen (73) den Priester gegebene Brod ein besonderes Prägzeichen habe und genannt werde "das Brod der Berenike."

Der einem jeden Tempel bestellte Vorstehen und der Erzpriester und (74) die Schrieber des Tempels sollen dieses Dekret auf eine steinerne oder eherne Stele aufschreiben in heiliger und Aegyptischer und Griechischer Schrift und (75) es an dem sichtbarsten Orte in den Tempeln der 1. und 2. und 3. Ordnung aufstellen, damit die Priester des Landes sich als solche zeigen, welche die Götter Euergeten und ihre Kinder ehren, (76) wie es recht ist.

VOCABULARY.

C = Canopus text. R = Rosetta text.

 *áa*, island, C. 9.

 *Apalius*, C. 1.

 *Apulaniṭes*, Apollonides, C. 1.

 *aḥet*, field, estate, R. 14, 30.

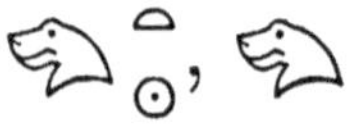 *at*, time, moment, C. 21; R. 32.

 *ateb* (?), a word of doubtful reading and meaning, R. 9.

, *áaut*, dignity, rank, honour, C. 4; R. 10, 13; , , C. 12; R. 12, 35, 45, 51.

 *áaut*, ranks, grades, honours, C. 10; , C. 12; , R. 51.

 *áu*, to be, C. 2; R. 4, 6, 7.

 *àu* =  *er*, C. 3, 5; R. 9, 11, 12.

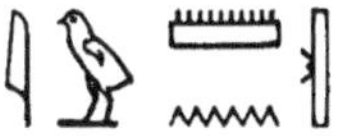 *àu-men* =  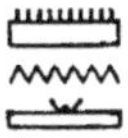 *er-men*, until, up to, C. 14.

 *àb*, heart, desire, wish, C. 8, 9, 27; R. 2, 23, 31, 36.

 *àb neter*, heart of a god, R. 11.

 *àb*, left hand, C. 26; R. 45.

 *àbt*, east, C. 9.

 *àb*, to desire, to wish, to love, R. 52.

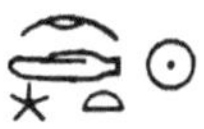, ,  *àbet*, month, C. 3, 17, 18, 28; R. 47; , R. 46; , C. 26, 32; 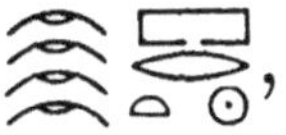, R. 1; , C. 18; , R. 46.

 *àp*, distinguished, C. 35.

 *àptu*, adjudged, decided, C. 22, 35.

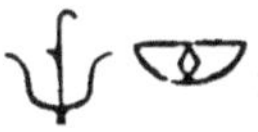, 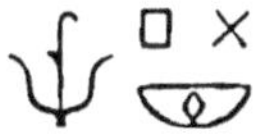 *àp renpit*, opening of the year festival, i.e., New Year's feast, C. 3, 18.

 *àp renput*, New Year festivals, R. 17.

 *àpen*, these, R. 40, 45.

 *ȧm*, in, on, thereon, C. 3, 4, 6; , C. 27.

 *ȧm*, in, on, R. 12, 16, 18, 42.

 *ȧm*, in, C. 19.

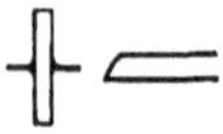 *ȧm*, in, R. 10.

 *ȧm*, in, among, C. 15, 16; R. 12.

 *ȧmmu*, those in, C. 1, 16; 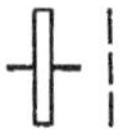, C. 9.

 *ȧmmu*, those in, R. 1.

 *ȧmmu*, those in, C. 8, 9, 12, 26; R. 23.

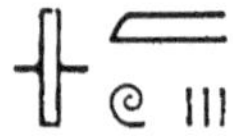 *ȧmmu*, those in, R. 53.

 *ȧmi*, let!, O let!, R. 51.

 *ȧm-tu*, among, C. 25.

 *ȧmth*, among, C. 13, 22, 28, 30.

 *ȧn*, C. 35; R. 8.

 *ȧn*, C. 33; R. 25.

 *ȧn*, to cut, to destroy, R. 12.

 *ȧn*, to bring back, C. 6.

àntu, brought back, C. 9, 16.

àn, not, C. 31.

ànebu, walls, fortifications, mounds cast up by a besieging force, R. 24.

Àneb ḥetchet, "White Wall," a name of Memphis, R. 7.

àner, stone, C. 37.

àntet, valley, C. 7.

ànetch, avenger, R. 10.

àr, emphatic particle, C. 21; R. 14, 42.

àr às, C. 25, 33; R. 42.

àref, C. 13, 19.

àri, belonging to, C. 12, 16, 20; R. 51; , R. 52.

àri, to do, R. 1, 17.

àrit, C. 6; R. 18.

àriti, R. 14.

àritu, done, performed, C. 3, 16, 17, 18, 19; , C. 21.

àrit, things done, C. 37.

àri tchet, to make speech, C. 4.

àri neter, to deify, C. 26, 28.

àru, form, rite, ceremony, R. 47.

àrp, wine, R. 31.

àlel, vine, vineyard, R. 14, 31.

àru, thereupon (see *màtet*), C. 33.

Àrsenat, Arsinoë, wife of Ptolemy III., C. 1, 4; wife of Ptolemy IV., R. 2.

Àrsenat ta-sen-s-meri, Arsinoë Philadelphus, R. 5.

Àrsenat ta-àtef-s-mer, Arsinoë Philopator, R. 6.

Àrsenat, the Canephoros, C. 2.

Àrsenat, daughter of Cadmus, R. 5.

 *Ȧlksantrs* =  *Ȧlkṣȧnṭers*, King Alexander, C. 1; R. 3.

 *Alksȧntrs-t*, city of Alexander, i.e., Alexandria, R. 17.

 *ȧs*, an enclitic conjunction, C. 19, 22, 31, 33, 34; R. 47, 52;  *ȧs-su*, R. 8, 10; , C. 5, 8, 19, 20, 22; R. 16, 17, 27; 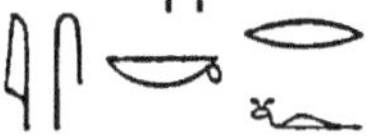, C. 7.

 *ȧsu*
 *ȧsiu*
 *ȧsiu*
} *em ȧsiu*, in return for, C. 10, 15; R. 35, 43.

 *Ȧsȧr*, Osiris, C. 25, 32; R. 10.

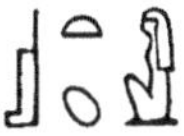 *Ȧst*, Isis, R. 1, 10.

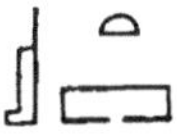 *ȧst*, seat, throne, C. 6.

 (?) *ȧsebiu*, rebels, R. 23.

 *Ȧḳerbemret*, name of a temple district, C. 26.

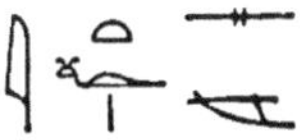 *ȧtef·s mer*, loving her father, i.e., Philopator, R. 6.

 *àterti*, the great sanctuaries of the South and North, C. 3, 18; R. 7, 36.

 *àthi*, prince, sovereign, R. 2.

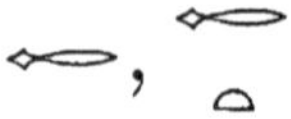 *āa*, *āat*, great, R. 18, 26;   *àu-āa-ur*, *er-āa-ur*, exceedingly, C. 5; R. 18.

 *āa-en-sa*, chief of an order of priests, Phylarch, C. 16.

 *āat*, stone, C. 29; R. 41, 54.

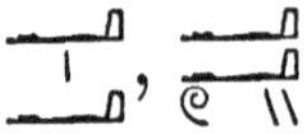 *āāui*, the two hands, C. 31; R. 16, 52.

 *āu*, totality; 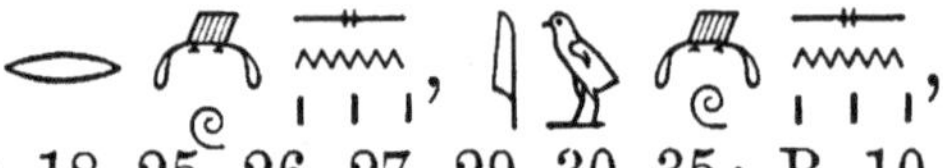 C. 9, 11, 12, 13, 18, 25, 26, 27, 29, 30, 35; R. 10, 13, 14, 35, 48.

 *āq*, middle, R. 45.

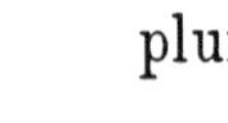 *āui*, sacred animal kept in a shrine, R. 31; plur. 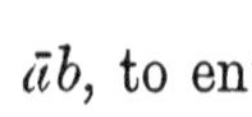 *āutu*, C. 5.

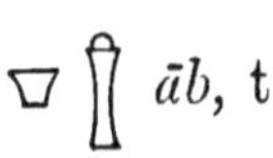 *āb*, to enter, go in, R. 8.

 *āb*, to embalm (?), R. 32.

 āb, libation, C. 16, 30.

 *āb*, priest, libationer, C. 1; R. 3.

 *ābu*, C. 12, 13, 14, 15; R. 36.

 *ābu*, R. 50.

 *ābu*, libationers, C. 3.

 *ābu*, libations, or, libationers, C. 11.

,  *ābu*, libationers, C. 2; R. 6.

 *ān*, to write, to inscribe, scribe, writing, C. 3, 12, 37; R. 54; , C. 35; , C. 15, 18, 32; , C. 36; 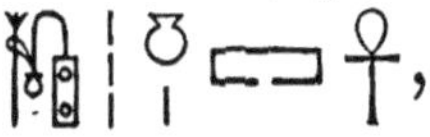, scribes of the house of life.

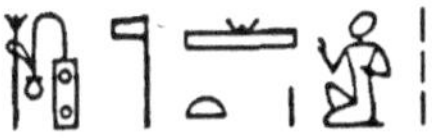 *ānu neter shāt*, scribes of divine books, C. 3; R. 7.

 *ānkh*, to live, life, R. 2.

 *ānkh tchetta*, ever-living, C. 1, 4, 11, 13, 17, 23.

 *ānkhiu*, living folk, C. 7, 8, 10, 14, 25.

 *ārāt*, uraeus, C. 31.

 *ārq*, last, end of, R. 46, 47.

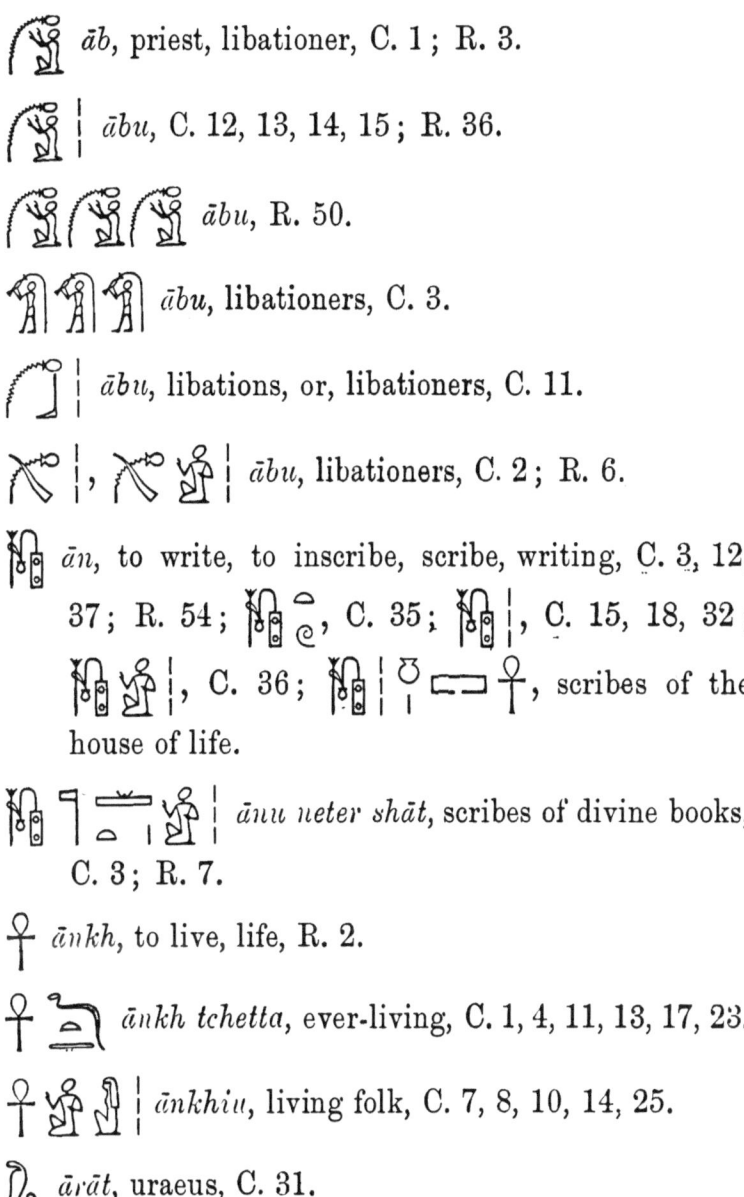

, , *āḥā*, to stand, C. 37; R. 18, 30, 54.

āḥāi, stele, tablet, R. 53.

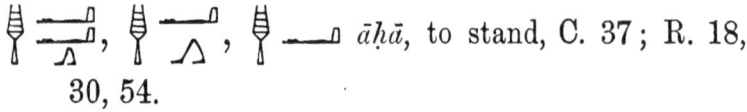

āsh, many; , howsoever many they be, R. 34, 36.

ākh, offering by fire, R. 32, 48.

āsht, many, C. 7, 10; , C. 9.

āsh, to call, proclaim, C. 32.

, *āq*, to enter, R. 6, 31, 36.

, *āqu*, bread-cakes, temple bread, C. 35, 36.

āṭ, slaughter, R. 26.

ua, to set aside, remit, R. 30.

uaḥ, to add, C. 22; R. 32, 48; *em uaḥ*, in addition, C. 16; , C. 13; , C. 12.

uatch, papyrus-sceptre, C. 31, 32.

, *uatch-ur*, "Great Green Water," i.e., the Mediterranean Sea, C. 10; R. 21.

 *uā*, one, C. 14, 15, 28.

 *uāt*, C. 15; , a festival, C. 22.

,  *un*, to be, C. 4, 5; R. 13, 14, 23, 27.

 *unen*, to be, R. 9, 10, 12, 15, 16, 18, 29.

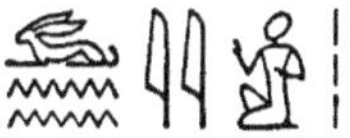 *uneniu*, those who exist, men and women, R. 12, 52.

 *unami*, right side, C. 26.

 *ur*,  *urt*, great, C. 4; R. 1, 12, 36; , R. 32; , R. 26; , C. 5;  *uru*, C. 5, 10; R. 9.

 *s-ur*, to magnify, C. 11, 12.

 *urtet*, two uraei, R. 43.

 *usekht*, hall of assembly in a temple, C. 37.

 *utu*, to order, order, command, R. 14, 16.

 *utui*, journey, R. 16.

 *utuith*, stele, C. 36.

 *uṭeb*, change, C. 19.

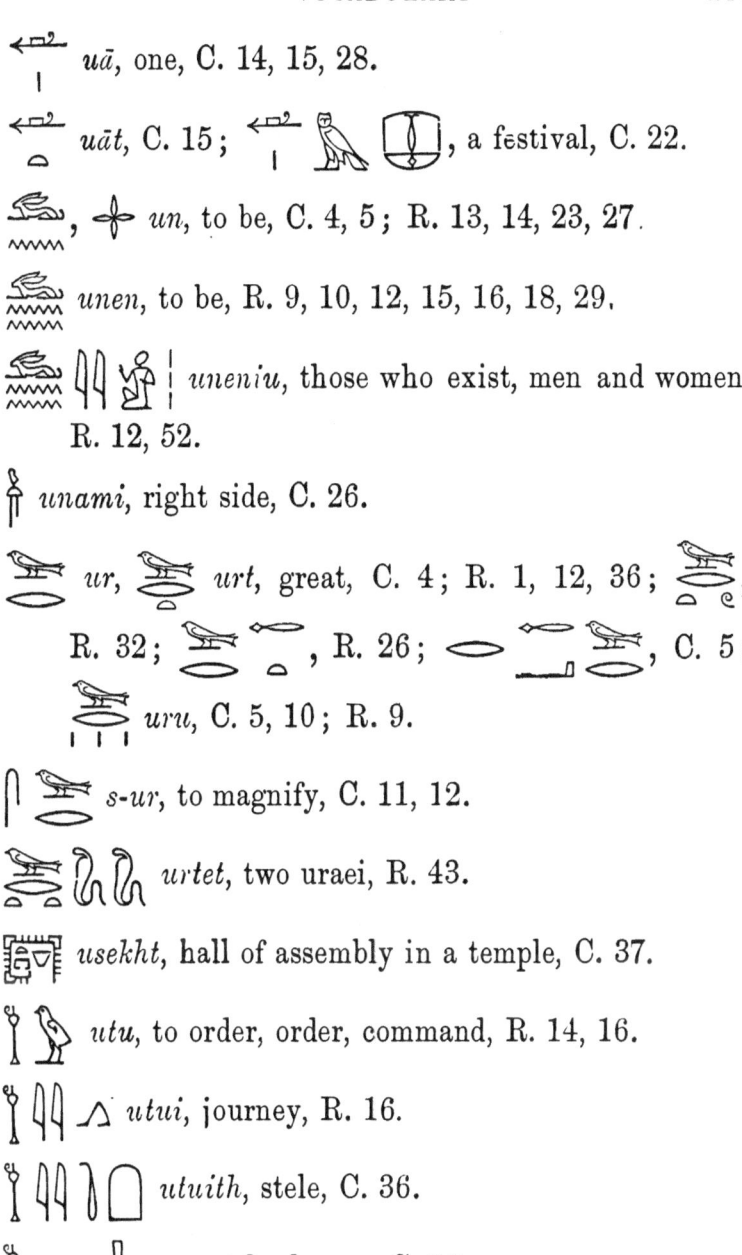

uṭen, libations and offerings, C. 20; R. 32.

utcha, strength, C. 11, 13; R. 5.

utcha, to set out, C. 6.

utchat, the country of the eye of Rā (or, Horus), i.e., Egypt, R. 39.

i, to come, C. 3, 21; R. 7; , C. 10; , R. 20.

Irenat, Irene, R. 6.

baḥ, R. 40, and see *em baḥ*.

, *Bast*, the great goddess of Bubastis, C. 18.

baq-tu, prosperous, R. 12.

, *Buqet*, the land of the olive, i.e., Egypt, C. 5, 6, 9, 12, 18, 37; R. 13, 23, 48.

bu, place, R. 6, 27, 42.

bu-nebt, everyone, all people, R. 2, 22.

bu-nefer, felicity, happiness, C. 14.

ben, not, C. 21.

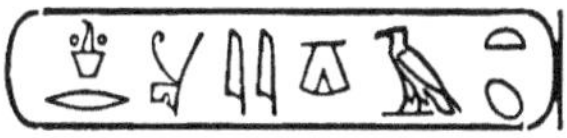 *Bereniḳat*, Berenice, wife of Ptolemy III., C. 4, 11, 18, 23.

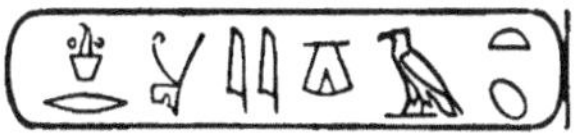 *Bereniḳat*, daughter of Ptolemy III., C. 25, 27, 28, 30, 31, 32, 36.

 *Bereniḳat ta menkhet*, Berenice Euergetes, R. 5.

 *beḥā* (?), interpretation, meaning, R. 39, 46.

 *bes*, to enter in, brought in, C. 14, 16, 34; , R. 45; , C. 14.

 *Beq*, Egypt, C. 8.

 *bet*, house, C. 24.

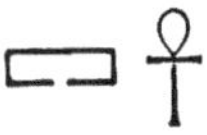 *pa ānkh*, "house of life," C. 18, 32, 34, 37.

 *paui ānkh*, "double house of life," R. 7.

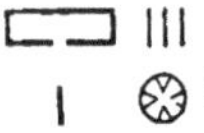,  *pau*, houses, temples, C. 9; R. 29.

 *Pailamna*, Philammon, C. 2.

 *pu*, this, C. 12, 13, 14; R. 39, 46.

, ,  *pan*, *pen*, this, C. 13, 14, 15, 18, 19, 20, 23, 28, 53; R. 6, 26, 27, 30, 45.

 *per*, to come forth, R. 42.

 *per*, appearance, or rise of a star, C. 18.

 *Per*, *Pert*, the season of Spring, C. 1, 21, 27; R. 1.

 *peru*, corn, C. 9.

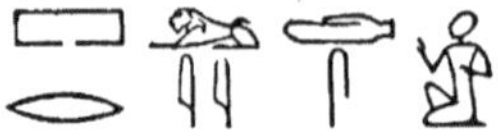 *Perriṭes*, Pyrrhides, R. 4.

 *Persatet*, Persia, C. 6.

 *peḥui*, end, C. 22.

 *peḥpeḥ*, *peḥpeḥt*, renown, fame, C. 5, 27; R. 1.

 *pest*, *paut*, nine, C. 1, 14.

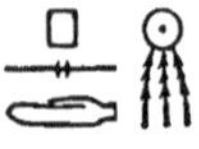 *peṣt*, to shine, R. 44.

 *peq*, byssus, R. 17, 29.

 *Peḳuthet*, C. 4, 25.

 *pet*,  *pet-et*, heaven, C. 20, 23, 28.

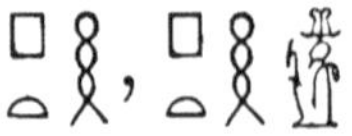 *Ptaḥ*, the great god of Memphis, C. 1, 4, 11, 17, 23; R. 2, etc.

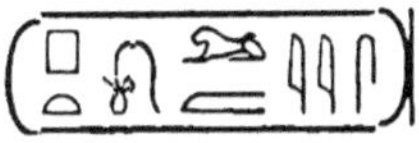 *Ptulmis*, Ptolemy II., C. 1, 4, 11, 13, 17, 23.

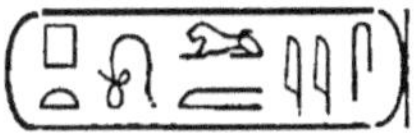 *Ptulmis*, Ptolemy IV., R. 2, 41.

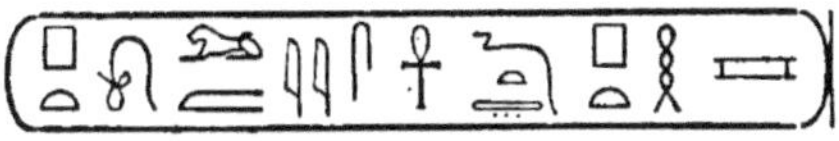 *Ptulmis ānkh tchetta Ptaḥ meri*, Ptolemy, ever-living, beloved of Ptaḥ, (Ptolemy V.), R. 2, 8, 9, 38, 41, 49, 54.

 *Ptulmis*, Ptolemy, father of Irene, R. 6.

 *Ptulmis*, Ptolemy, son of Pyrrhides, R. 4.

 *f*, he, his, its, C. 3, 4, 5.

 *f*, he, his, its, C. 4.

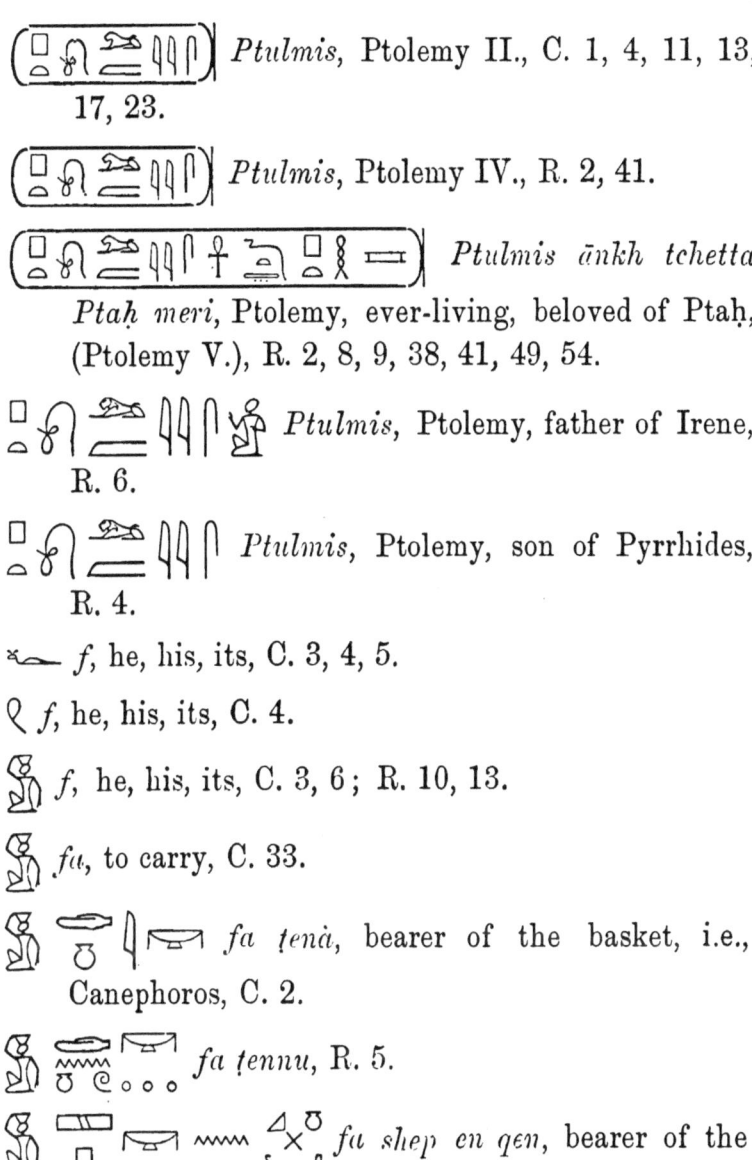

 *f*, he, his, its, C. 3, 6; R. 10, 13.

 *fa*, to carry, C. 33.

 *fa ṭenȧ*, bearer of the basket, i.e., Canephoros, C. 2.

 *fa ṭennu*, R. 5.

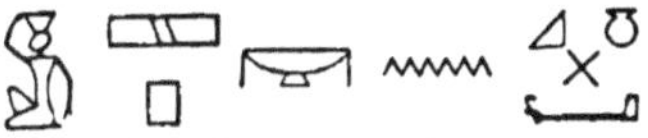 *fa shep en qen*, bearer of the basket of victory, i.e., Athlophoros, R. 4.

 *feqau*, rewards, gifts, C. 11.

fṭu, four, C. 13.

, , *em*, in, into, among, as, like, according, by means of, C. 3, 4, 5, 8, 17, 25, 35; R. 1, 6, 10, 17, 20, 29, 40.

em ȧsiu, in return for, C. 10, 15.

, *em baḥ*, before, C. 2, 24; R. 40.

em kheft ḥer, opposite, C. 26.

em khen, within, C. 25.

em khent, at the head of, C. 11, 15.

em kher hru, in course of the day, R. 40.

em khet, after, C. 26.

em sa, by the side of, R. 45.

em sekhan, suddenly, C. 24.

emtutu, likewise, moreover, R. 40, 48, 52.

emtutu, R. 38, 42, 45.

emtutu, C. 17, 18, 22, 28, 29.

ma (or, *ḳes*), place, R. 26.

maa, to see, C. 30.

maat, eye, C. 28.

maā, justice, what is right, R. 19.

maā, a legal rite or ceremony (?), R. 34, 45; , R. 31.

maā, genuine (of precious stones), R. 41.

maā kheru, one whose word is law, C. 1.

maāu, temples, C. 2, 5, 6, 11, 27, 29, 34.

maāu, R. 6, 11, 17, 40, 47, 50, 54.

maāu, C. 29; , temples of first rank, C. 25, 26, 37; , C. 28; , temples of second rank, C. 37; , temples of third rank, C. 37; , C. 29; , R. 29.

mau, to care for greatly, C. 9.

Makha-taui, the part of Egypt near Memphis which marks the division between the Upper and Lower country, R. 8.

mȧ, as, like, according to, C. 3, 10, 20, 27; R. 2.

 *mà-re*, in proportion to, C. 35.

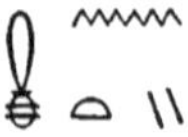 *mà enti*, like that, so that, R. 18.

 *màtet*, copy, something like something else, likewise, C. 19, 34, 52; R. 13.

 *màtet àru*, like them, likewise, C. 15; R. 18, 19, 29, 30, 46.

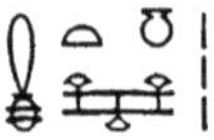 *màtenu*, ways, courses, C. 23.

 *mā*, from, C. 4, 27, 33; R. 8;  (?), R. 4.

 *Māanaqeraṭa*, Menekrateia, C. 2.

 *Māuskian*, Moschion, C. 2.

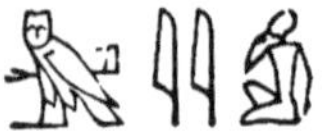 *māi*, O grant! let it be! C. 36; R. 47.

 *māi*, given, C. 35.

 *mānen*, twisted round, C. 31.

 *mākheru*, tributes, gifts, C. 6.

 *māsha* (?), soldiers (?), R. 27.

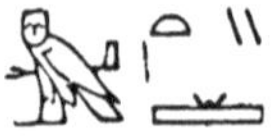 *māti*, since, R. 9.

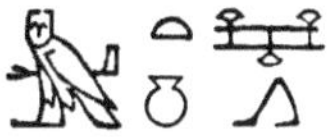 *māten*, way, road, R. 23.

 *mut*, mother, C. 31.

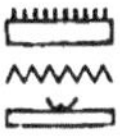 *men*, to remain, be firm, R. 16; 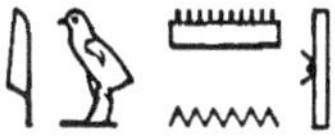 *àu-men*, until, C. 14.

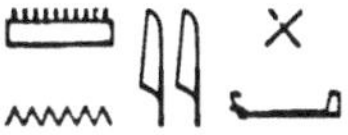 *meni*, a piece of linen cloth, R. 30.

 *menfet*, soldiers, R. 12.

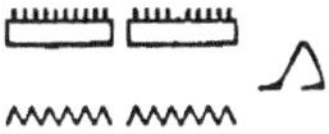 *menmen*, to stand, to remain firm, C. 6.

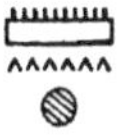 *menkh*, beneficence, good deed, C. 10.

 *menkhu*, benefits, C. 4.

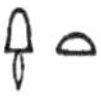 *menkhet*, good deed, something good, R. 10, 13, 34, 47; , good-hearted, R. 2, 11.

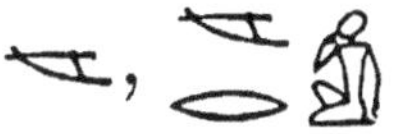 *mer*, to love, to wish, C. 2, 28, 33.

 *mer*, to love, R. 9; 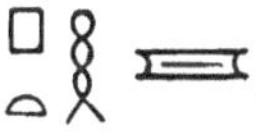, beloved of Ptaḥ, C. 1, 4, 11, 13, 17, 23.

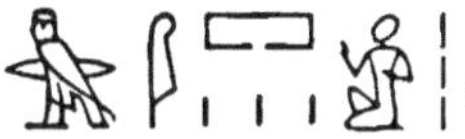, ,  *meru maāu*, governors of temples, C. 2, 36; R. 6.

 *Mer-ur*, the Bull Mnevis, C. 5, 27; R. 31.

 *meḥ*, garland, wreath of flowers, R. 50.

meḥ, to be crowned, C. 20.

meḥ, to fill, be filled, inlaid, C. 29; R. 16, 41.

meḥ, sign of an ordinal number; , C. 29; , C. 29; R. 54; , R. 54.

, , *meḥ sa*, to take care for, to provide for, C. 5, 9; R. 18, 19.

Meḥenet, the serpent on the brow of Rā, C. 28.

Meḥt, North, R. 36.

mekha, to burn, be ardent (of the heart), C. 9.

mes, to be born, C. 35; *mestu*, be born, C. 13; , birthday, R. 46.

, , *mesu*, children, C. 14, 15, 35, 37.

meses, statue, R. 40.

meṭ, word, speech, C. 27; , C. 5; , rules, laws, C. 23.

metu, order, arrangement; *ṭā metu*, to set in order, C. 23.

met, ten; , seventeen, C. 1, 29; R. 46.

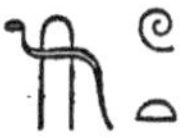 *metch-tu*, depth, R. 25.

,  *en*, of, a preposition, C. 1, 2, 4; R. 1, 2; , R. 13; , C. 2.

 *na*, the, R. 7.

 *nu*, of (used after plural), C. 5, 6; R. 13, 14, 15.

, 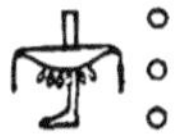 *nub*, gold, C. 29; R. 11, 14, 21, 29, 33.

 *neb*, lord, master, R. 2, 8.

 *neb*,  *nebt*, all, every, C. 5; , C. 14.

 *nebu*, everybody, i.e., people, C. 30.

 *Nebinaitet*, Cyprus (this reading is corrupt), C. 9.

 *nef*, he, his, its, C. 6; R. 12.

 *nef*, R. 11.

 *nef*, C. 13; R. 16.

 *nefer*, good, beautiful, happy, C. 13; R. 35, 36, 46.

 *neferu*, benefits, R. 8, 9, 38, 41, 51, 52, 54; , R. 9.

 *neferui*, doubly beautiful, R. 34.

neferit er, up to, until, C. 29; R. 16, 29, 50.

nema, new (of work), R. 34.

(*sic*), *enen*, this, C. 11, 26; R. 35.

enen, rest, release, R. 14.

neh-tu, shortened, C. 22.

neḥu, to entreat, to beseech, C. 24.

neḥem, to seize, to carry off, C. 6; R. 17.

nekht, strength, victory, R. 26, 35.

net, rules, ordinances, C. 32.

entāu, ordinances, C. 16.

ent, of, C. 25.

enti, who, which, C. 4, 9, 14, 25; R. 1, 24, 52.

neter, god.

neteru, gods, C. 5, 17; R. 2, 6, 14;

, gods and goddesses, R. 35.

netert, goddess, C. 24, 25; R. 10.

neteru pau, houses of the gods, i.e., temples, C. 9, 12.

neter per, "god appearing," i.e., Epiphanes, R. 4, 8, 38, 41, 42, 49, 50, 51, 52, 54.

neter meṭu, divine words, i.e., hieroglyphic writing, R. 54.

neter ḥen, priest, R. 50.

neteru ḥenu, priests, C. 2; R. 6.

neter ḥet, temple, C. 3, 25; plur. , , R. 30, 32, 34, 49.

neteru ḥet unnut (?), an order of priests, R. 15, 16.

neter ḥetepet, offerings, C. 35.

neter Septet, the star Sothis, C. 18, 19.

neter sesheshet, divine figure bearing a sistrum, C. 6, 29, 31, 34.

neter shāt, holy writing, or book, C. 3.

neteru tefu, divine fathers, i.e., priests, C. 3.

neter, god, R. 10; *netert*, goddess, C. 31.

neteru, gods, C. 3, 11, 14.

neterui ȧtui merui, the two father-loving gods, R. 2, 3, 4, 9, 41.

neterui menkhui, the two good-doing gods, C. 1, 4, 11, 12, 13, 16, 18, 22, 23, 27, 29, 37; R. 3.

neterui netchui, the two Saviour-gods, C. 12; R. 3, 38.

neterui senui, the two Brother-gods, C. 1, 4, 11, 13; R. 3.

neterui perui, the two Epiphanes-gods, R. 2, 9.

neṭes, little, small, low (of the Nile), C. 7, 8.

enth, of, C. 4.

netch, to save, to protect, R. 39.

netch khet, the guardians of temple property, councillors, C. 15, 16, 35, 36.

netchi, subjection, C. 7.

netches, little, R. 26.

er, at, by, C. 4, 6; R. 6; , C. 6; , C. 5; , C. 7.

er-men, up to, until, C. 14.

, *er-enti*, to that which, since, C. 13, 16, 22, 25, 27, 30, 33, 34.

er-enth, since, inasmuch as, C. 4.

er erṭu, outside, C. 6, 7.

er-ḥai, C. 6.

er kheper sekhen, at the happening of the event, C. 8.

er-sa, at the side of, R. 42.

er-ḳes, at the place of, R. 54

re, mouth, opening, R. 25.

mā re, in proportion to, C. 35.

rai-uat (?), remit, set aside, R. 19.

Rā, the Sun-god, C. 28; R. 2.

 *rut*, R. 54.

 *rut* (?), people, C. 37.

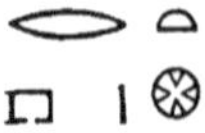 *erpat*, temple, C. 28.

 *erpau*,  *erpat*, temples, C. 16, 35; R. 40, 41, 50, 54.

 *erpu*, or, C. 30, 37.

 *erpet*, statue, image, C. 31, 32.

 *ren*, name, C. 12; R. 39, 40, 50, 54.

 *ren*, name, R. 2, 18.

 *renpit*, year, C. 1, 7, 14, 15, 25; R. 1.

 *renenet*, virgin, C. 24; plur. , C. 24, 31, 32, 33.

 *rer*, general, universal (of a festival), C. 17, 21.

 *reri*, time, season, C. 20.

 *rekh*, to know, C. 10, 22.

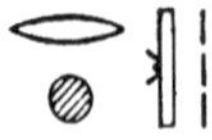 *rekh*, science, C. 23.

 *rekh khet*, knowers of things, i.e., learned men, C. 3.

rekhit, rational beings, men and women, C. 9.

Reset, South, R. 36.

rek, time, season, C. 8; R. 13, 26.

erṭāt, to give, C. 6, 9, 10, 16; R. 10, 11, 12, 13, 15, 16, 28, 32, 35, 40, 42, 45; R. 51; R. 19.

Retennutet, Syria, C. 9.

reṭ, fruit, C. 19.

reṭ (?), foot-soldiers, R. 12, 35.

ha, *hau*, time, season, C. 8.

hu, *hru*, day, C. 2, 3, 13, 15; R. 6, 43.

hebs, injury, R. 23.

hepu, laws, C. 23.

hamemet, men and women, folk, R. 2, 13.

heru, more, addition, R. 31, 51.

 *ḥa*, behind, C. 31.

 *ḥa*,  *ḥaui*, more, addition, R. 16, 28.

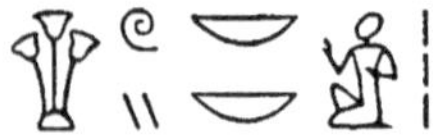 *Ḥaui-nebui*, Greeks, R. 54.

 *Ḥa-nebu*, Greeks, C. 37.

 *ḥai*, Nile flood, C. 19.

 *ḥaiā* (?), exceedingly, C. 6.

 *ḥai*, papyrus plants, C. 31.

 *ḥā*, grain, corn, R. 11, 15, 21, 29, 33.

 *ḥā*, and, C. 1, 4, 5, 6, 7, 8, 10, 11, 13, 37; R. 3, 4, 7, 10, 11, 12, 13, 14, 15, 23, 24, 26, 29, 34, 36, 41.

 *ḥāai*, and, R. 40.

 *ḥāu*, flowers, C. 20.

 *Ḥāp*, Apis Bull, C. 5, 27; R. 31, 34.

 *Ḥāp*, Nile, C. 7, 8, 19.

 *ḥāpt*, square, R. 45.

,  *ḥāt*, front of, the beginning of, C. 6, 22 R. 46; first (of fruits), C. 33; brow, C. 28.

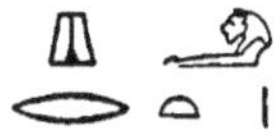 *kher ḥāt*, formerly, C. 14, 15.

 *ḥunnu*, youth, R. 1.

 *ḥeb*, festival, C. 16, 17, 18, 19; R. 2; plur. , R. 52; 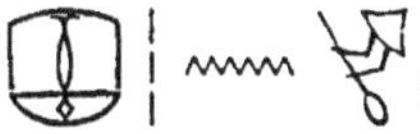, festivals of boat processions, C. 28.

 *ḥept*, breast, arm, C. 30.

 *ḥem*, to see, C. 37.

 *ḥemt*, bronze, C. 37.

 *ḥemt*, wife, C. 4, 34; plur. , C. 32; R. 35, 36.

 *ḥen*, majesty, C. 1, 3, 6, 7, 8, 14; R. 1, 8, 10, 13, 14, 22.

 *ḥen*, majesty (fem.), C. 28.

 *ḥent*, mistress, lady, C. 31, 32.

 with , see *neter ḥen*.

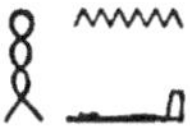 *ḥenā*, and, with, together, C. 3, 4, 9, 10, 25; R. 3, 4, 7, 9.

 *ḥer*, and, C. 7, 18, 26, 28, 29, 36; R. 10, 21, 34, 35, 43.

 *ḥer*, and, R. 15, 38, 40, 42.

 *ḥer*, plain, C. 7.

 *ḥer*, upper, R. 45.

 *ḥer*, on, over, concerning, C. 5; R. 1.

 *ḥer ȧb*, middle, C. 9; , R. 44.

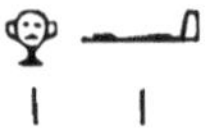 *ḥer ā*, straightway, C. 24.

 *ḥer en*, on behalf of, C. 10.

 *ḥer tep*, on top of, R. 43, 44.

 *ḥer*, with verbs, , C. 4;  *āḥa*, C. 7; 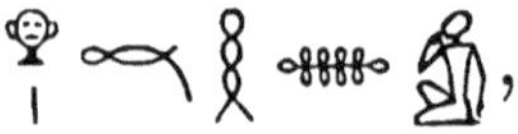, C. 5; , C. 24; , C. 5.

 *ḥeru sesheta neter*, men over the secrets of the god, C. 2; R. 6.

 *ḥrȧu nebu*, all faces, i.e., everybody, C. 37.

 *ḥert*, prison, R. 14.

 *Ḥeru*, Horus, R. 10.

Ḥeru nub, golden Horus, R. 2.

Ḥeru-Rā, Horus-Rā, R. 1.

Ḥeru taiu, Horus lands, i.e., temple estates, R. 9, 21, 23, 46.

ḥesu, singers, C. 34.

ḥes-tu, praised, C. 34.

ḥesbet, reckoning, account, R. 13.

ḥespet, nome, R. 15; plural, R. 40, 42.

ḥeq, sovereignty, to capture, C. 10; R. 26.

ḥeqt, queen, C. 4, 11.

ḥetu (?), temple men, C. 36.

Ḥet-ka-Ptaḥ, Memphis, R. 44.

ḥetep, to rest, C. 25; R. 42.

ḥetch, silver, C. 10.

ḥetrāt, revenues, C. 9.

ḥetepu, offerings, C. 34.

khau, sacred places containing altars, R. 34.

khaiu, altars, C. 20, 26; R. 50.

khamesu, ears of corn, C. 31, 33.

kharṭu, children, R. 36.

khasu, vile men, C. 6.

khā, *khāā*, to rise (of a king on his throne, or of the sun), R. 1.

khā, crown, C. 31; coronation, R. 40; crowned, C. 33.

khāu, crowns, C. 33; R. 52.

khā, feast, festival, C. 30, 34; , C. 17, 18.

khu, to be good, to do good deeds, to be held as good, C. 5; R. 14, 21, 31.

khu, blessings, C. 11.

khebkheb, to slaughter, R. 26.

khep = , to take place, to come into being, to exist, C. 8, 13, 14, 16, 21, 27.

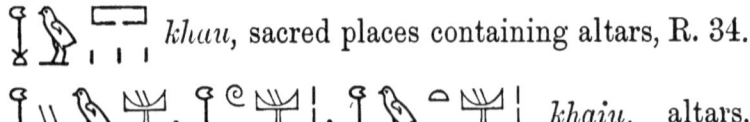

 *kheper*, to happen, to become, C. 7, 8, 11, 12.

 *kheperu*, existing men and women, C. 10.

 *kheft*, when, C. 34; R. 45.

 *kheft*,  *khefti*, in front of, opposite, C. 8, 26.

 *khemt*, three, R. 40.

 *khemt*, third, C. 37.

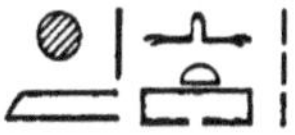 *khemt*, sanctuaries, shrines, R. 34.

 *khen*, to sail round, or about, C. 27; a boat procession, C. 28, 29, 30.

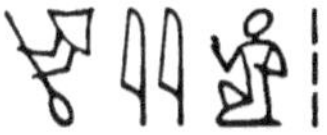 *kheni*, sailors, R. 17.

 *khent*, image, statue, R. 38, 40, 41, 54.

 *khentet*, first, in point of time or rank, C. 8, 13, 25, 26; advancement, R. 11.

 *em-khent*, in, at the head of, C. 11, 15, 16, 18, 25, 34, 37.

 *khentet*, sanctuary, C. 33.

 *kher*, under, C. 1, 14, 24; R. 1, 2, 15.

kher, under, with, R. 16, 36.

kher em, with, R. 29, 40.

kher ḥāt, formerly, originally, C. 6, 14, 15, 17, 28, 32; R. 46.

kheru, food, C. 35.

kheru renpit, belonging to the year, C. 24.

khert, what belongs to some one, property, R. 15.

kher-ā, to stablish, R. 11, 19.

kherāu (?), dues, revenues, R. 29.

kherit, calamities, disasters, C. 8.

kherp, to rule, C. 7.

khesef, to remit, send back, R. 18, 20.

khet, cut, engraved, C. 12, 36.

khet, to follow, C. 26.

khet, thing, property, R. 9; plur. , C. 3, 5; R. 14.

khetem, ring, C. 12; R. 51.

s = *senb*, health, R. 35.

, s = , , *sen*, they, them, theirs, C. 6.

sa, to know, to recognize, R. 43, 53.

sa, a tribe of priests, C. 12, 14, 15; , phylarch, C. 16; plur. , C. 14, 15; , C. 6, 13, 15; , C. 13, 16.

sa, side, back, , , C. 9; R. 18.

sa, person, C. 15, 16; R. 10, 13, 14, 48; plur. , R. 17.

, *sa*, son, C. 1, 2, 4; R. 3, 10; , son of Rā, R. 2, 9.

, *sat*, daughter, C. 2, 23; R. 4.

sat, ground, R. 30.

, *satet*, divine apparel, ornaments of the gods, C. 3, 30; R. 6.

Satet, Asia, C. 6.

s-ári, to cause to make, R. 45.

s-āb, to purify, C. 26, 29.

s-ānkh, to make to live, C. 9.

, , *s-āḥā*, to set up, C. 29; R. 38, 52.

su, it, he, C. 25; R. 52.

, *suten*, King of the South, C. 14, 24, 25; R. 1, 24.

suteniu, kings, C. 8.

suten bȧt, King of the South and North, C. 1, 4, 11, 13, 17, 23; R. 2, 8, 9, 38, 41, 49.

sutenit, sovereignty, R. 8, 28.

sutenet, royal house, treasury, or palace, R. 17.

suten khā, royal coronation, R. 47.

, , *sutchā*, *sutcha*, to make strong, do good to, C. 6, 7, 10.

seb, to rebel, rebel, R. 27.

sebȧth (?), C. 10.

, *sep*, time, season; , first time, C. 29; , twice, C. 9; , thrice, R. 40.

 *sepu*, seasons, times, phases, qualities, C. 10.

 *sept*, provision, C. 5.

 *semaāu*, to declare or do what is right, C. 27.

 *smār*, to array, to dress a statue, C. 2, 30; , R. 6.

 *smu*, metal like gold, electrum, R. 41.

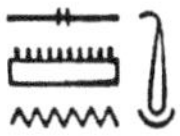,  *smen*, to make permanent, to stablish, C. 10, 20, 22, 32; R. 1.

 *semsem*, horses, R. 20.

,  *semtu*, foreign lands, C. 7, 10.

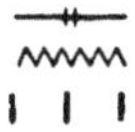, ,  *sen*, they, them, their, C. 3, 4, 5, 6; R. 6, 10, 12.

 *ṣen*, two, C. 9, etc.

 *sen*, two, C. 31.

 *sen*, brother; 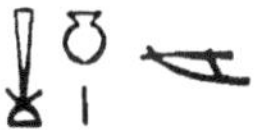 *sen-mer*, brother-loving, i.e., Philadelphus, C. 2.

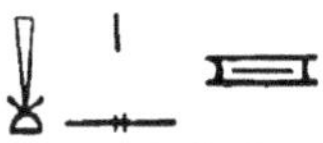 *sen-s mer*, "her brother loving" = Philadelphia, R. 5.

 *sent*, sister, C. 8.

 *sent-ḥemt*, sister-wife, C. 4.

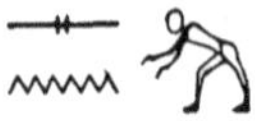 *sen*, to bow down, C. 30.

 *s-nefer*, to beautify, R. 1.

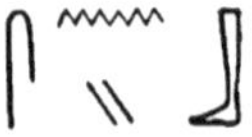 *snib*, health, C. 11, 13.

 *s̱enem*, to mourn, C. 26, 29.

 *sent*, to be settled, firm, a fixed custom, C. 27.

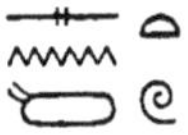 *sentu*, to move, or pass on, C. 19.

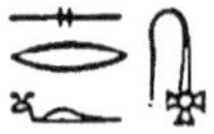 *seref*, warm care, C. 27.

 *ser*, to write, R. 51.

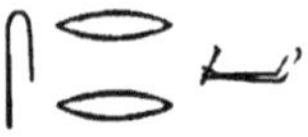 *serer*, inscribed, C. 17, 27, 34.

 *se-ḥeb*, to make or keep a feast, R. 50.

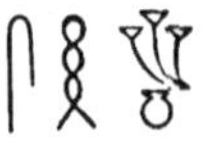 *seḥen*, crown, C. 32.

 *seḥetch*, name of a chamber in the temple, R. 8.

 *seḥetch*, to lighten, R. 46.

 *s-kh* =  (?), to create, to beget, C. 12.

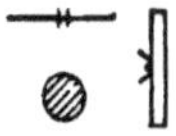 *sekh*, matter, event, R. 18.

 *sekhau*,  *sekhaiu*, 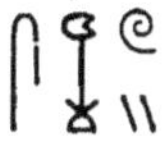 *sekhaui*, decree, C. 2, 36; R. 6, 53, 54.

 *sekhau*, memory, C. 8.

 *sekhau*, memorial service, C. 17.

 *s-khā*, to keep or make a feast, R. 34, 42.

 *s-kheper*, to make to be, C. 12, 15.

 *sekhef*, seven, C. 1.

 *sekhan*, to hasten, C. 24.

 *s-khaker*, to ornament, R. 34.

 *sekhen*, to happen, to take place, R. 8, 32, 34, 36.

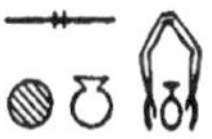 *sekhen*, to occur, to happen, an event, C. 8, 13, 19, 21, 23.

,  *sekhen*, existing, being, C. 24; R. 34.

 *sekhet*, *sekhent*, the double-crown, R. 43, 44, 45.

 *sekhent*, crowns, R. 45.

, *sekher*, offerings of different kinds, R. 32, 48.

sekherā, to put in good condition, R. 21.

sekheru, documents, ordinances, C. 12, 20.

sekhet, field, R. 14.

ses (?), C. 21.

, , , *sesu*, day, C. 1, 3, 13, 17; R. 39.

sesheshet, statues of a goddess holding a sistrum, C. 6.

sek = *āsk* (q.v.), C. 23.

Sektet, name of a sacred boat, C. 25.

seḳāt, to carry, C. 30.

sta, to carry, to compare, to confront (?), R. 30.

, *setut*, to do or make something in imitation of something, customary, C. 19, 20, 37; R. 10; *ān setut*, unusual, not customary, C. 31.

sti, wine measure, R. 30.

setep, to be elected, chosen, C. 15, 30, 33.

seṭ, tail, C. 31.

seṭem, to disturb (?), R. 27.

se-ṭeṭṭeṭ, to make stable, R. 11.

sha, hundred; , C. 22.

sha, season of growing, C. 32; R. 50.

shat, C. 26; R. 46.

shaā, to begin, beginning, C. 14, 22, 29; , R. 50.

shaās, to march, R. 22.

shāi, book, R. 54.

shāt, book, C. 3.

shep, a kind of basket or vessel, a prize of victory, R. 5.

shep, to receive, to take, C. 3; R. 7, 28.

shepiu, captured, prisoners, R. 14.

, ,  *sheps*, holy, noble, august, C. 29; R. 15, 41; 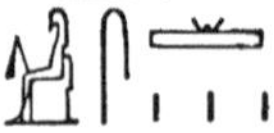, R. 11.

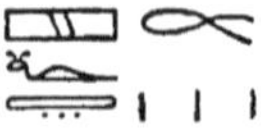 *sheft*, books, C. 34.

,  *shemu*, season of inundation, C. 14, 18, 21; R. 46.

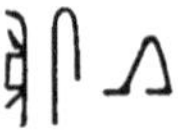,  *shems*, to follow, C. 33; R. 40.

 *sher*, little, C. 22.

 *shes*, a cord, thread of linen; 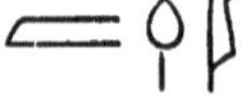 *em shes maāt*, regularly, R. 34.

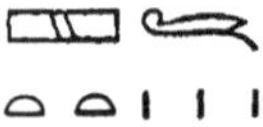 *shetet*, books, C. 37.

 *sheṭ*, levied, R. 30.

 *k(i)*, also, moreover, C. 16.

 *ka*, to call, R. 39; , R. 50; , R. 8.

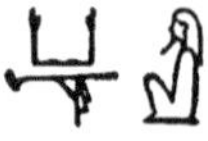 *ka*, double (of a god), R. 40.

 *kara*, shrine, 41, 42, 43, 52; plur. , R. 42, 44.

 *kat*, work, R. 34.

 *ki*, another, C. 12, 16; R. 7.

kebenu, boats, R. 20.

Keftet, Phoenicia, C. 9.

keṭut, another, C. 32.

ketekh, other, C. 33.

qa, height, C. 31.

Qāṭmus, Cadmus, R. 5.

qāf, side, R. 45.

qurt, fruit, C. 33.

qebḥet, place of libation, R. 42.

qefen, a kind of bread, C. 36.

qema, to beget, C. 11.

qemāt, singing women, C. 33.

Qemt, Egypt, C. 6, 9; R. 20.

qen, strength, victory, R. 5.

, , , *qennu*, many, C. 5, 11; R. 1, 9, 11.

 *Qerpiaiset*, the month Gorpaios, R. 1.

 *qerer*, burnt offering, C. 26, 32.

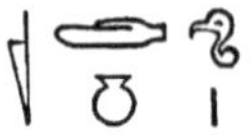 *qeṭ*, grade, rank, C. 3; , R. 12.

 *Ḳaȧubekh* . . . . (?), C. 32.

 *ḳer*, but, further, C. 17.

 *ḳert*, moreover, C. 32.

 *ḳes*, place, R. 45.

 *ḳesen*, grief, C. 8.

 *ḳesen* (?), time, C. 5, 17, 18, 25; plur. 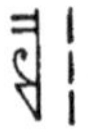, C. 21, 22.

 . . . . . ., Lord of the shrines of Nekhebet and Uatchet, R. 1, 46.

 two-thirds, R. 18.

. . . . .  . . . . . *sh*, foot-soldiers (?), R. 20.

 *ta*, the (fem. art.), R. 5.

 *ta*, land, earth, country, R. 13, 28; plur.  (*sic*) *taiu*, lands, C. 6.

taiu, land's folk, inhabitants, C. 7.

Ta-mert, "land of the Inundation," a name of Egypt, C. 1, 5, 6, 7, 8, 11, 17, 21, 24; R. 1, 11, 21, 53.

Ta-netert, "divine land," i.e., Egypt, C. 10.

taui, the two lands, i.e., Upper and Lower Egypt, C. 3, 10, 29; R. 1, 7, 46.

tut, what is usual, or customary, or right, C. 3, 14, 19, 26; R. 38, 40; , what is usually done, R. 18, 48, 50.

tef, father, C. 4, 15; R. 1; plur. *tefu*, C. 3.

tem, not, R. 16, 17.

ten, this, C. 21, 25; R. 26, 52.

ten, each, every, C. 22; R. 13.

tĕnnu, each, every, C. 19.

ter, cloth, R. 17, 30.

tra, time, season, C. 5, 15; plur. , C. 20, 23.

 *teh*, to attack, R. 23.

 *Teḥuti*, Thoth, R. 26.

 *tesh*, boundaries, R. 27.

 *ṭā*, to give, C. 5; , C. 6; , made, given, C. 14; 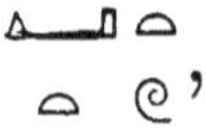, R. 18;  *ṭāṭ*, to place, C. 24.

 *ṭit*, land, R. 21.

 *Ṭiaus*, the month Dios, C. 3. 13.

 *ṭua*, five, C. 3.

 *ṭuau*, hymns, C. 34.

 *ṭua-tu*, praised, C. 33.

 *ṭuma*, choirs, C. 34.

 *ṭebu*, price, C. 10.

 *ṭep*, first, C. 1; 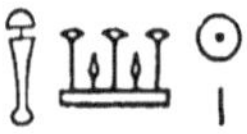, R. 50; 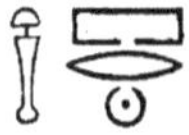, C. 27.

 *ṭep*, head, source, first, former state, C. 20, 29; R. 18, 19, 27, 47; , R. 52; , R. 15, 49, 52; 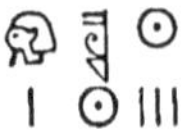, R. 40.

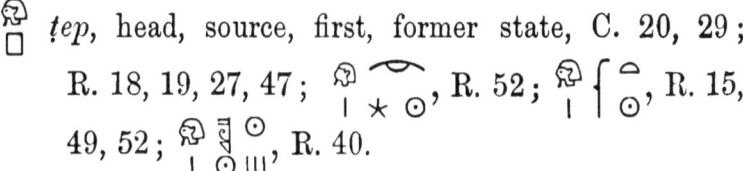

ṭepāu, ancestors, C. 8, 22; R. 31.

ṭepu, captive chiefs, C. 6.

ṭep reṭ, ordinance, regulation, R. 40.

ṭemȧit, town, village, R. 26.

ṭemseb, choir, C. 34.

ṭemt (?), pedestal, C. 30.

Ṭemeṭriat, Demetria, R. 4.

ṭenȧ, basket, C. 2.

ṭenȧ, to divide with, to share with, C. 16.

ṭennu, basket, R. 5.

ṭennut, a government building, or office, R. 16.

ṭen, drain, dig trenches, R. 24.

ṭer, piece, R. 29.

ṭet, hand, C. 12; R. 51.

then, throughout, C. 17.

thes, to arrange, C. 20.

thes, high (of price), C. 10.

thet, to carry off, C. 6; R. 32.

thet, sages, C. 34.

tchau, males, C. 34.

tet̤tet̤-th, stablished, R. 46; R. 36.

tet̤tet̤-t, things established, R. 18.

thi, learned men, R. 7.

Thălimkus, Telemachus, R. 4.

then, this, C. 24, 25; R. 43.

tchaut, twenty, C. 15; , R. 1; , C. 3, 15; R. 1; , C. 17.

tchār, to require, necessary, R. 32.

tchenf, R. 38.

tcher, from, since, to the end that, C. 15, 26, 35.

tcher enti, because, C. 18; R. 23, 44, 46.

tchesef, self, C. 8.

tcheser, to exalt, to glorify, to honour, C. 5, 11, 25, 30, 37; R. 6, 42, 53.

tcheser-tu, magnificently, R. 32.

tchet, body, R. 32.

tchetta, eternity, ever, R. 9, 36, 46; , C. 10, 11, 14, 15.

tcheṭ, to call, to say, C. 28; R. 14; , *tcheṭtu*, C. 12, 13, 18, 23.

tcheṭeb, to lead, R. 27.

END OF VOL. III.

www.ingramcontent.com/pod-product-compliance
Lightning Source LLC
Chambersburg PA
CBHW061244230426
43662CB00020B/2421
* 9 7 8 1 6 3 9 2 3 9 7 3 3 *